The Public Law Outline: The Court Companion

The Public Law Outline: The Court Companion

Piers Pressdee

John Vater

Frances Judd QC

Jonathan Baker QC

Harcourt Chambers (London & Oxford)
www.harcourtchambers.law.co.uk
0844 5617135

Family Law

Published by Family Law
A publishing imprint of Jordan Publishing Limited
21 St Thomas Street
Bristol BS1 6JS

British Library Cataloguing-in-Publication Data

A catalogue record for this book is available from the British Library.

ISBN 978 1 84661 118 6

Typeset by Letterpart Ltd, Reigate, Surrey

Printed in Great Britain by CPI Antony Rowe, Chippenham, Wiltshire

Foreword

The Protocol for Judicial Case Management in Public Law Children Act Cases, which came into operation in November 2003, adopted a new approach and provided a framework for case management, encouraging parties and the courts to tackle the causes of delay in resolving care cases. Subsequently the Child Care Proceedings Review recognised that, with the number and complexity of care cases increasing and the consequent strain upon resources, it was vital to improve pre-proceedings processes as well as the management of cases within the court system.

The Senior Judges of my Judicial Review Team (JRT), in consultation with the other key agencies in the Family Justice System, formulated the streamlined and simplified case management procedures now set out in the Public Law Outline (PLO). At the same time, the Department for Children, Schools and Families revised its statutory guidance for local authorities (The Children Act 1989 Guidance and Regulations), in liaison with the JRT, to ensure that the PLO and the Guidance complement each other, so as to focus on the key issues in the case when making the right decision within the Timetable for the Child.

Practitioners referring to this PLO Court Companion will find clear guidance and case-law on all the core legal principles which need to be considered in these often difficult cases. The key changes are described, in a logical and user-friendly way, with reference throughout to the relevant forms and paperwork.

A particular strength of the Court Companion is its careful explanation of the various parts of the reform package, putting the lawyers' role in context. The references to the Local Authority Children Act Guidance, to the policy and approach of Cafcass in the course of their guardianship, and to the Experts Practice Direction not only clarify what they can expect of each other, but serve to remind all disciplines of the need to co-operate in order to ensure the best possible outcome within the Timetable for the Child.

The authors are to be congratulated on the careful thought given to each section of the Companion, the comprehensive treatment of each subject heading, and on having produced this invaluable work so swiftly after the national implementation of the PLO.

Sir Mark Potter
President of the Family Division

Preface

The introduction from 1 April 2008 of the Public Law Outline signposts the most fundamental change to care proceedings for almost 20 years.

The PLO, its supporting Practice Direction, the Experts Practice Direction and the newly revised Children Act Guidance and Regulations all combine to transform the way in which local authorities, Children's Guardians, lawyers and courts operate in this area.

The rationale for this book can be easily explained from our own experiences as children lawyers who spend most of our time in court and who had all used the PLO in its draft form. Whenever there are major changes within your practice area, you want to know what they are and how they all fit together; you want to familiarise yourself not just with the text but also with the thinking that underpins that text; you want to understand your new role in the reformed system but also those of all the other participants within it; and you want to be able to assimilate and then refer to all of that information quickly and easily.

What we have sought to create is a portable and accessible book that puts the essentials of these reforms all in one place, making it as easy to use at court as out of it. Within Chapter 1, the key themes and core components of the Public Law Outline and its supporting Practice Direction are introduced. In Chapter 2, the focus is on pre-proceedings preparation by reference to the revised Children Act Guidance and Regulations. In Chapter 3, each of the four stages of the Public Law Outline is covered sequentially, whilst in Chapter 4 the spotlight is on the new Experts Practice Direction. Reflecting the desire inherent within these reforms for quicker and more efficient ways of working, the aim of Chapter 5 is to enable courts and practitioners to have at their fingertips the core legal principles applicable to the case management issues that habitually arise in these cases. The appendices then comprise the core materials of and associated with these reforms – the Practice Direction that houses the PLO, the subsequently produced PLO guideline documents, the key parts of the revised Children Act Guidance and Regulations, the Experts Practice Direction, the Bundles Practice Direction (as now adjusted) and the new policy produced by Cafcass that governs and explains its post-PLO reporting role in public law proceedings.

As practitioners, we are acutely aware that those who use this book will range from the comprehensive reader to the casual flicker. It is partly with the latter in mind that we have not worried too much about overlap and duplication between the chapters, taking the view that it is more important for something to be said twice than not to be read at all. Moreover, repetition does tend to breed familiarity; and familiarity invariably breeds good practice.

Will these reforms succeed? Only time will tell. But certain observations can be made at the outset. They will not succeed if local authorities are so over-stretched that they cannot fulfil their important new pre-proceedings role. Nor will they succeed if Cafcass is denied the means to discharge the numerous duties that it now carries in both public and private children law spheres. Equally these reforms will not succeed if local practice cultures are so entrenched that these new forms of practice are not given the chance to bed in. But Sir Mark Potter, President of the Family Division, is probably right, when commenting on the publication of the PLO, that 'its success will largely be dependent on the co-operation and expertise of the dedicated specialist lawyers who will operate it'.

The stakes in care proceedings could not be higher. A wrong decision one way could mean a child returned home only to be abused again, possibly fatally. A wrong decision the other way could mean a child removed permanently from their family of birth for no good reason. The premium in not getting these decisions wrong could not be greater; and the public interest in getting these decisions right could not be higher. Increasingly complex, stressful and time-consuming for all who have to deal with them, care proceedings inevitably are a burden on the public purse, but are a burden that the public can rationalise. Put simply, if it was you who stood to lose your child, you would want your corner fought by someone who knew exactly what they were doing. Especially when set against the millions of pounds of public money spent each year on lengthy and often fruitless criminal fraud trials, it is not so hard to justify that expended on care proceedings.

It is, of course, right that the growing public expenditure in this area should be brought under some form of control and that such public money should be spent in the best way possible. However, it also true that, if the PLO and its associated reforms succeed, then there will be fewer proceedings taken, those that are taken will be shorter and contain fewer experts, and savings will inexorably follow.

In their final report to accompany the introduction of the PLO's predecessor, the Protocol for Judicial Case Management in Public Law Children Act Cases, the Lord Chancellor's Advisory Committee said this:

> 'Publicly funded remuneration for the legal profession must reflect the fact that public law Children Act cases require the full input and co-operation of experienced, specialist practitioners. Without such practitioners the protocol will not work to its best advantage. Underpayment of the practitioners who do this work will inevitably lead to a shortage of such specialist lawyers (and accordingly in the future to a shortage of specialist judges, both part and full time) as the brightest and best turn to better remunerated fields of practice.'

Those self-evidently sensible points, made five years ago, sound perhaps with even greater force today. These reforms have entirely laudable aims – better and quicker resolutions for children, associated with a better and more constructive use of public money. But the best way to achieve those ends is through harnessing the support of those who have to implement these initiatives in practice, rather than by risking their departure from the field by imposing upon them that which is untried, unfair and unnecessary. The ball is in the government's court.

The law is stated as at 1 May 2008.

Piers Pressdee, John Vater,
Frances Judd QC & Jonathan Baker QC
Harcourt Chambers (London & Oxford)

Acknowledgements

Particular thanks are due to the President for his foreword, to the Jordans team (Greg Woodgate, Helen Pettet, Kate Hather and Gillian Wright) for their support, to our clerking team (Tim Wheeler, Judith Partington, Joseph Bernard, Chris Collins, Chris Luxmoore, Lynne Land and Denise Moles) for their understanding, to Penny Langdon and Chelsey Bonehill respectively for their assistance, and to Caroline Little, Alistair MacDonald and Liz Walsh for their perspectives on the PLO reforms.

This book is dedicated to our families, who bear the brunt of the work that we do.

By the same authors

Contact: The New Deal *(Family Law, 2006)*

An essential book for all those acting, advising and assisting on residence and contact issues, *Contact: The New Deal* remains the leading guide to the Children and Adoption Act 2006 and to the reforms associated with it.

'a truly excellent book … required reading for all in the Family Justice System'
(from the foreword by the Hon Mr Justice McFarlane)

'authoritative, comprehensive and well-written … easy to read and to use'
(Family Affairs – the magazine of the FLBA)

'the authors have usefully brought together a rigorous overview of research
and detailed analysis of the current law … stimulating …
a comprehensive guide that will effectively equip practitioners negotiating complex cases'
(Family Law journal)

'a timely and comprehensive addition to the family practitioner's library …
a book that should draw generous praise from all quarters'
(Association of Lawyers for Children)

'impressively wide-ranging … penetrative … rigorous … user-friendly …
deserves the widest readership from all those, lawyers and non-lawyers alike,
who have an interest in the past and future of family law'
(Counsel Magazine)

'This book is simply compulsory reading ….
All McKenzie friends and those representing themselves should have it.
All judges and family lawyers should have read it.'
(Families Need Fathers)

'A fundamental tool for court practice as well as an interesting read . . .
Full of useful quotations, research and up-to-date-minute law, this is certainly a text to dip in and out of. In particular, the substantial appendices offer an excellent single point of reference.'
(Seen and heard)

Available to buy in all good legal bookshops or via www.familylaw.co.uk.

Contents

CHAPTER ONE

INTRODUCING THE PUBLIC LAW OUTLINE

1.1 From 1 April 2008, the Public Law Outline ('the PLO') replaced the Protocol for Judicial Case Management in Public Law Children Act Cases ('the Protocol')[1] and, in doing so, heralded a new era in the management of and approach to care and supervision proceedings.

1.2 The Public Law Outline is the product of two reviews (the Thematic Review published by the Judicial Review Team in December 2005 and the government's *Child Care Proceedings Review* of May 2006),[2] both of which had identified areas where the Protocol had not achieved its objective and in which improvements in practice could be made.

1.3 Fundamentally a judicial initiative, the Public Law Outline represents the latest but probably the most concerted attempt to address the time-honoured problem of delay within public law proceedings, to improve the court's management of these difficult and sensitive cases and to do so within the constraints of a limited budget.

1.4 The Public Law Outline is not a stand-alone document, forming the table found within para 9 of the Practice Direction that supports it.[3] But a familiarity with the contents of that table represents the bare minimum for those who have to operate the PLO in practice. The PLO is only comprehensible by reference to the content of and thinking behind the Practice Direction[4] as a whole and the initiatives associated with it – namely the new Experts Practice Direction[5] and the new revised Children Act Guidance and Regulations.[6]

1.5 The purpose of this chapter is not to go through the four stages of the PLO, line by line, for that is the role of Chapter 3. Rather, this is a preparatory chapter, which seeks to equip the reader for the detail of new pre- and post-proceedings practice, by identifying the key themes and core components of the Public Law Outline and its supporting Practice Direction.

THE PLO – KEY THEMES AND CORE COMPONENTS

1.6 In a nutshell, the Public Law Outline aims to produce better outcomes for children subject to public law proceedings through the following means:

---

1 [2003] 2 FLR 719.

2 *Review of the Child Care Proceedings System in England and Wales* – published in May 2006 by the Department for Education and Skills and the Department for Constitutional Affairs (the forerunner of the Ministry of Justice).

3 Practice Direction: Guide to Case Management in Public Law Proceedings ('the PLO Practice Direction'), at para 4.1(1).

4 The PLO Practice Direction forms Appendix 1 to this book.

5 Practice Direction: Experts in Family Proceedings Relating to Children. Discussed in Chapter 4, and reproduced in full at Appendix 4 to this book.

6 Discussed in Chapter 2. The key parts of that guidance are reproduced at Appendix 3 to this book.

(1) simplifying the court process, with the four stages of the PLO (Issue and the First Appointment, Case Management Conference (CMC), Issues Resolution Hearing (IRH), and Final Hearing) replacing the six steps of the Protocol;[7]

(2) putting the court in greater control of the proceedings – giving it a more proactive interventionist role and charging it in particular with the ultimate identification of the issues to be resolved by them;

(3) creating a framework in which the management of cases can be improved, with a more problem-solving culture embedded, disproportionate hearings avoided, and unwarranted delay eradicated;

(4) setting the court's timetable for the proceedings by reference to the timetable(s) for the child(ren) concerned rather than to the somewhat arbitrary 40 week target time that the Protocol had introduced;

(5) ensuring that local authorities are better prepared when making applications to the court;

(6) front-loading the court process;

(7) bringing forward the input of the Children's Guardian to the start of that process;

(8) focusing on the issues that need to be resolved and determined by the court, with a clear emphasis at every stage of the process on issue identification, narrowing and resolution;

(9) replacing the Pre-Hearing Review (PHR) with the Issues Resolution Hearing (IRH) – a more court-interventionist, issue-focused hearing held much earlier in the proceedings than the PHR used to be;[8]

(10) avoiding the all too prevalent previous feature of discussions at the court door by providing that the parties should, collaboratively and in advance of the key case management hearings, have discussed and set out in writing for the court the issues for the court's consideration and determination.

1.7 All of the above will be apparent from this chapter's subsequent consideration of the Practice Direction itself, which has been ordered in a way that hopefully makes it most accessible. But, so as to make greater sense of the new and important earlier role for the Children's Guardian in the process, the chapter also covers the new Cafcass Reporting to Court policy.

THE PLO PRACTICE DIRECTION – SCOPE AND OVERRIDING OBJECTIVE

1.8 It will be with the field of care proceedings that the Public Law Outline will be most closely associated, but potentially its ambit is wider than that.

---

[7] Under the Protocol's Route Map, there were six steps: (1) The Application; (2) The First Hearing in the FPC; (3) Allocation Hearing & Directions; (4) The Case Management Conference; (5) The Pre-Hearing Review; and (6) The Final Hearing. In effect, PLO Stage 1 replaces Protocol Steps 1–3; PLO Stage 2 is what was formerly Protocol Step 4; PLO Stage 3 replaces Protocol Step 5; whilst PLO Stage 4 and Protocol Step 6 are essentially the same.

[8] There is no guidance as to how interventionist a court should be at this stage, though presumably the court will have to have in mind, in those cases where a very strong indication to the parties is given, the question of whether the same court should hear the final hearing (if there is to be one).

The scope of the Practice Direction

1.9 The PLO Practice Direction applies to care and supervision proceedings; but, insofar as practicable, the Practice Direction is also to be applied to all other public law proceedings.[9]

1.10 Within this context, public law proceedings are exhaustively defined, at para 25(29) of the Practice Direction, as meaning proceedings for:

(a) a residence order under Children Act 1989, s 8, with respect to a child who is subject of a care order;

(b) a secure accommodation order under Children Act 1989, s 25;

(c) a care order under Children Act 1989, s 31(1)(a), or the discharge of such an order under s 39(1);

(d) an order giving permission to change a child's surname or to remove a child from the United Kingdom under Children Act 1989, s 33(7);

(e) a supervision order under Children Act 1989, s 31(1)(b), the discharge or variation of such an order under s 39(2), or the extension or further extension of such an order under Sch 3, para 6(3);

(f) an order making provision for contact under Children Act 1989, s 34(2)–(4), or an order varying or discharging such an order under s 34(9);

(g) an education supervision order, the extension of an education supervision order under Children Act 1989, Sch 3, para 15(2), or the discharge of such an order under Sch 3, para 17(1);

(h) an order varying directions made with an interim care order or interim supervision order under Children Act 1989, s 38(8)(b);

(i) an order under Children Act 1989, s 39(3), varying a supervision order insofar as it affects a person with whom the child is living but who is not entitled to apply for the order to be discharged;

(j) an order under Children Act 1989, s 39(3A), varying or discharging an interim care order insofar as it imposes an exclusion requirement on a person who is not entitled to apply for the order to be discharged;

(k) an order under Children Act 1989, s 39(3B), varying or discharging an interim care order insofar as it confers a power of arrest attached to an exclusion requirement;

(l) the substitution of a supervision order for a care order under Children Act 1989, s 39(4);

(m) a child assessment order or the variation or discharge of such an order under Children Act 1989, s 43(12);

(n) an order permitting the local authority to arrange for any child within its care to live outside England and Wales under Children Act 1989, Sch 2, para 19(1);

---

[9] The PLO Practice Direction, at para 1.1.

(o) a contribution order, or the variation or revocation of such an order under Children Act 1989, Sch 2, para 23(8).

1.11 It will be plain from their exclusion from that list that a number of proceedings which might ordinarily be thought to be public in nature are not caught by the ambit of the PLO and its supporting Practice Direction. These include under the Children Act 1989 applications for an emergency protection order[10] and applications for a recovery order,[11] but also under the Adoption and Children Act 2002 applications for placement orders[12] and applications for adoption orders.[13]

1.12 It had been intended that a placement for adoption practice direction would accompany the advent of the Public Law Outline, and many practitioners were hoping that it would. For the many safeguards and procedures that characterise the process of the local authority advancing a care plan for adoption often sit uneasily with the declared need for speed within the care proceedings themselves. Particular guidance for those care cases where placement applications are required, with a view to a greater harmonising of the two sets of proceedings, would not have been unwelcome.[14]

1.13 In respect of the public law proceedings specified other than care and supervision proceedings, it will inevitably be the case that the obligation to apply 'insofar as practicable' the Practice Direction will bite with greater force in some proceedings more than in others. An application to discharge a care order, for example, might warrant a very similar approach to an application for a care order itself. But, by way of contrary example, given that a (final) secure accommodation order can be made at the first hearing within proceedings for it,[15] it is hard to discern why anything approaching four stages should be required in the vast majority of secure accommodation proceedings.

1.14 While the PLO Practice Direction came into effect on 1 April 2008 and therefore does not apply to applications issued before that date, in any individual case the court may direct that the Practice Direction Case Management Tools[16] and Case Management Documentation[17] will apply either wholly or partly to those applications.[18]

1.15 Paragraph 1.3 of The PLO Practice Direction provides that it is to be read with 'the Rules' and is subject to them. Defined as meaning 'the rules of court governing the practice and procedure to be followed in public law proceedings',[19] these are currently in the process of being completely revised with a view to there being a unified set of rules for family court practice at all levels of court.

The overriding objective

1.16 As with the Protocol, the PLO Practice Direction has an overriding objective. But, whereas with the former it was tucked away on page 82 of the combined Protocol documents, the

10 Under Children Act 1989, s 44.
11 Under Children Act 1989, s 50.
12 Under Adoption and Children Act 2002, s 21.
13 Under Adoption and Children Act 2002, s 46.
14 Placement for adoption is discussed at **5.244** et seq.
15 See *Re M (Secure Accommodation Order)* [1995] 1 FLR 418.
16 Discussed further at **1.24** and in Chapter 3.
17 Discussed further at **1.24** and in Chapter 3.
18 The PLO Practice Direction, at para 1.2, which adds, however, that this is subject to the Practice Direction's overriding objective and to the proviso that such a direction will neither cause further delay nor involve repetition of steps already taken or decisions already made in the case.
19 Ibid, at para 25(30).

overriding objective of the PLO Practice Direction, perhaps as an embodiment of a more front-loaded approach, is found on its first page.

1.17 The overriding objective of the PLO Practice Direction is to enable the court to deal with cases justly, having regard to the welfare issues involved.[20]

1.18 Paragraph 2.1 of the Practice Direction further provides that dealing with a case justly includes, so far as is practicable:

(1) ensuring that it is dealt with expeditiously and fairly;

(2) dealing with it in ways which are proportionate to the nature, importance and complexity of the issues;

(3) ensuring that the parties are on an equal footing;

(4) saving expense; and

(5) allotting to it an appropriate share of the court's resources, while taking into account the need to allot resources to other cases.

1.19 It will be seen, especially in its inclusion of the matters set out at sub-paras (4) and (5), that the terms of this new overriding objective are materially different from that which applied to the Protocol.[21]

1.20 The Practice Direction, at para 2.2, provides that the court must seek to give effect to the overriding objective when exercising the case management powers set out within it or interpreting any provision of it, whilst para 2.3 provides that the parties are required to help the court further the overriding objective.

THE ESSENTIALS OF COURT CASE MANAGEMENT

1.21 As befits an initiative that seeks to improve the court's management of these cases, the PLO Practice Direction contains a lengthy and detailed section on 'court case management', which:

- sets out the main principles of court case management;
- introduces the main case management tools to be used; and
- particularises the many aspects of active case management.

1.22 It also has a section setting out the Practice Direction's expectations, one which deals with how any variation of the court's case management timetable is to be handled, and ones which draw attention to the flexible powers of the court and to the use of technology.

---

20 Ibid, at para 2.1.

21 The Practice Direction supporting the Protocol provided, at para 3.1, as follows: 'The overriding objective is to enable the court to deal with every care case: (a) justly, expeditiously, fairly and with the minimum of delay; (b) in ways which ensure, so far as is practicable, that: (i) the parties are on an equal footing; (ii) the welfare of the children involved is safeguarded; and (iii) distress to all parties is minimised; (c) so far as is practicable, in ways which are proportionate (i) to the gravity and complexity of the issues; and (ii) to the nature and extent of the intervention proposed in the private and family life of the children and adults involved.

The main principles

1.23 There are four main principles now underlying court case management in public law proceedings:[22]

(1) *judicial continuity*: each case will be allocated to one or not more than two case management judges (in the case of magistrates' courts, case managers),[23] who will be responsible for every case management stage in the proceedings through to the Final Hearing – in the case of the High Court or county court, one of these case management judges may be, and where possible should be, the judge who will conduct the Final Hearing;

(2) *main case management tools*: each case will be managed by the court by using the appropriate main case management tools;

(3) *active case management*: each case will be actively case managed by the court with a view at all times to furthering the overriding objective;

(4) *consistency*: each case will, so far as compatible with the overriding objective, be managed in a consistent way and using the standardised steps provided for in the PLO Practice Direction.

The main case management tools

1.24 Having set out the main principles, the PLO Practice Direction, at paras 3.2–3.13, specifies eight 'main case management tools':

(1) *The Timetable for the Child* – this is a core component of the new procedure. The court is obliged to set an appropriate Timetable for the Child who is the subject of the proceedings.[24] That Timetable is to take account of all significant steps in the child's life that are likely to take place during the proceedings, and includes not only legal steps but also social, care, health and education steps.[25]

(2) *Case Management Documentation* – the Practice Direction introduces a number of new case management documents. These are defined and particularised within Chapter 3 of this book as and when they appear in the proceedings. It is important, however, to distinguish at the outset between those case management documents whose use in effect is prescribed[26] and those which are essentially guideline documents to be used or adapted locally as seen fit. The documents listed at para 3.5(1)–(8) of the Practice Direction (the Application form, the Supplementary Form PLO1,[27] the Schedule of Proposed Findings, the Allocation Record

---

22 The PLO Practice Direction, at para 3.1.

23 'Case manager' means the justices' clerk or assistant justices' clerk who manages the case in the magistrates' courts (the PLO Practice Direction, at para 25(11)). 'Justices' clerk' has the meaning assigned to it by the Courts Act 2003, s 27(1) (ibid, at para 25(25)). 'Assistant justices' clerk' has the meaning assigned to it by the Courts Act 2003, s 27(5) (ibid, at para 25(6)).

24 The PLO Practice Direction, at para 3.2.

25 Ibid, at para 3.3. Para 3.4 gives six examples of 'the dates the court will record and take into account when setting the Timetable for the Child': (1) any formal review by the local authority of the case of a looked after child (within the meaning of Children Act 1989, s 22(1)); (2) the child taking up a place at a new school; (3) any review by the local authority of any statement of the child's special educational needs; (4) an assessment by a paediatrician or other specialist; (5) the outcome of any review of local authority plans for the child (for example, any plans for permanence through adoption, special guardianship or placement with parents or relatives); and (6) a change or proposed change of the child's placement.

26 The PLO Practice Direction, provides, at para 3.6, that the court will encourage the use of those case management documents which are not prescribed by the Rules.

27 Annex A to the PLO Practice Direction.

and the Timetable for the Child, the Case Analysis and Recommendations provided by Cafcass or Cafcass Cymru, the Local Authority Case Summary,[28] the Other Parties' Case Summaries, and the Draft Case Management Order)[29] should all be seen as prescribed documents (whether in form, content or both). The following documents produced after the publication of the PLO – Form PLO4 (Allocation Record and Timetable for the Child(ren)), Form PLO5 (Standard Directions Form (on Issue) Menu) and Form PLO6 (Standard Directions Form (at First Appointment) Menu) – should all be seen as guideline documents.[30]

(3) *The Case Management Record* – this is the name for the court's filing system and will include the documents specified in para 3.7 of the Practice Direction.[31]

(4) *The First Appointment* – the first hearing in the proceedings, the purpose of which is to confirm allocation of the case and give initial case management directions.[32]

(5) *The Draft Case Management Order* – this is a special form of order containing terms of general application to be used as appropriate for each case. It is to be used for drawing up orders at the end of a hearing, but is also to be used as a case management checklist. The form contains standard provisions designed to help parties, their legal representatives and the court:
(i) identify the relevant issues and the procedural directions which may be required;
(ii) monitor changes to the relevant issues and compliance with the court's directions; and
(iii) focus on what the proceedings are intended to achieve.[33]

(6) *Advocates' Discussion/Meeting* – the advocates (together with any litigants in person) are to have discussions (whether by meeting or otherwise) before the CMC and the IRH, with a view to facilitating agreement and narrowing the issues for the court to consider.[34]

(7) *The Case Management Conference* – para 3.12 of the Practice Direction provides that, in each case, there will be a CMC to enable the case management judge or case manager, with the co-operation of the parties, actively to manage the case and, at the earliest practicable opportunity to:
(i) identify the relevant and key issues, and
(ii) give full case management directions including confirming the Timetable for the Child.

(8) *The Issues Resolution Hearing* – para 3.13 of the Practice Direction provides that, in each case there will be an IRH before the Final Hearing to:
(i) identify any remaining key issues; and
(ii) as far as possible, resolve or narrow those issues.

---

28 Annex B to the PLO Practice Direction. Also separately known as Form PLO2.

29 Annex C to the PLO Practice Direction. Also separately known as Form PLO3.

30 Forms PLO4, PLO5 and PLO6 are included at Appendix 2 to this book.

31 These documents are the Supplementary Form PLO1 (which will be the index of documents on the Record); in care and supervision proceedings, any Letter Before Proceedings and any related subsequent correspondence confirming the local authority's position to parents and others with parental responsibility for the child; the Case Management Documentation; Standard Directions on Issue and on First Appointment; and the Draft Case Management Orders approved by the court. The parties or their legal representatives are also expected to retain their own record containing copies of the documents on the court's Case Management Record (the PLO Practice Direction, at para 3.8).

32 Ibid, at para 3.9.

33 Ibid, at para 3.10.

34 Ibid, at para 3.11.

1.25 The advocates' discussion/meeting and the four PLO hearings itemised above are all considered in greater detail within Chapter 3.

Active case management

1.26 The concept of active case management lies at the heart of the PLO Practice Direction.

1.27 Paragraph 3.14 specifies that the court must further the overriding objective by actively managing cases.

1.28 Paragraph 3.15 then particularises 20 ways in which that active case management can occur:

(1) identifying the Timetable for the Child;

(2) identifying the appropriate court to conduct the proceedings and transferring the proceedings as early as possible to that court;

(3) encouraging the parties to co-operate with each other in the conduct of the proceedings;

(4) retaining the Case Management Record;

(5) identifying all facts and matters that are in issue at the earliest stage in the proceedings and at each hearing;

(6) deciding promptly which issues need full investigation and hearing and which do not;

(7) deciding the order in which issues are to be resolved;

(8) identifying at an early stage who should be a party to the proceedings;

(9) considering whether the likely benefits of taking a particular step justify any delay which will result and the cost of taking it;

(10) directing discussion between advocates and litigants in person before the CMC and IRH;

(11) requiring the use of the Draft Case Management Order and directing advocates and litigants in person to prepare or adjust the draft order where appropriate;

(12) standardising, simplifying and regulating:
  (a) the use of Case Management Documentation and forms;
  (b) the court's orders and directions;

(13) controlling:
  (a) the use and cost of experts;
  (b) the nature and extent of the documents which are to be disclosed to the parties and presented to the court;
  (c) whether and, if so, in what manner the documents disclosed are to be presented to the court;
  (d) the progress of the case;

(14) where it is demonstrated to be in the interests of the child, encouraging the parties to use an alternative dispute resolution[35] procedure if the court considers such a procedure to be appropriate and facilitating the use of such procedure;

(15) helping the parties to reach agreement in relation to the whole or part of the case;

(16) fixing the dates for all appointments and hearings;

(17) dealing with as many aspects of the case as it can on the same occasion;

(18) where possible dealing with additional issues which may arise from time to time in the case without requiring the parties to attend at court;

(19) making use of technology; and

(20) giving directions to ensure that the case proceeds quickly and efficiently.

The Expectations

1.29 Following the bespoke 'Court case management' section within the Practice Direction, there is then a short section entitled 'The Expectations'.

1.30 As if to reinforce the message of what has gone before, the stated expectations are that proceedings should be:

(1) conducted using the Case Management Tools and Case Management Documentation referred to in the Practice Direction in accordance with the Table known as the Public Law Outline;[36]

(2) finally determined within the timetable fixed by the court in accordance with the Timetable for the Child, the PLO target times being adhered to and being taken as the maximum permissible time for the taking of each step referred to in the PLO.[37]

1.31 Paragraph 4.2, however, recognises that there may be cases where the court considers that the welfare of the child requires a different approach from the one contained in the PLO. In those cases, the court will:

(1) determine the appropriate case management directions and timetable; and

(2) record on the face of the order the reasons for departing from the approach in the Public Law Outline.

Variation of the case management timetable

1.32 Paragraph 21 of the Practice Direction emphasises that a party or the Children's Guardian must apply to the court at the earliest opportunity if they wish to vary by extending the dates set by the court for a directions appointment, a First Appointment, a CMC, an IRH, the Final

---

35 'Alternative dispute resolution' is defined by the PLO Practice Direction, at para 25(5), as meaning the methods of resolving a dispute other than through the normal court process.

36 The PLO Table is contained in para 9 of the PLO Practice Direction.

37 The PLO Practice Direction, at para 4.1.

Hearing, the period within which the Final Hearing of the application is to take place, or any discussion between advocates or for the filing of the Draft Case Management Orders.

Flexible powers of the court

1.33 Paragraph 17.1 of the Practice Direction draws attention to the flexible powers of the court either following the issue of the application in that court, the transfer of the case to that court or at any other stage in the proceedings.

1.34 These flexible powers include the following:

- giving directions without a hearing including setting a date for the Final Hearing or a period within which the Final Hearing will take place;[38]
- if the circumstances of the case merit such an approach, taking steps ordinarily taken at the various PLO stages at another stage in the proceedings;[39]
- cancelling or repeating a particular hearing.[40]

Technology

1.35 Paragraph 23 of the Practice Direction provides that, where the facilities are available to the court and the parties, the court will consider making full use of technology, including electronic information exchange and video or telephone conferencing.

HELPING THE COURT AND CO-OPERATION

1.36 The allied concepts of helping the court and co-operation are key to practice under the Public Law Outline.

Helping the court

1.37 Indeed, para 5 of the Practice Direction is headed 'How the parties should help court case management', with seven 'main methods of helping' then specified:

(1) *Good Case Preparation* – the applicant should prepare the case before proceedings are issued, and, in care and supervision proceedings, the local authority should use the Pre-Proceedings Checklist.[41]

---

38 Ibid, at para 17.2.

39 Ibid, at para 17.2.

40 Ibid, at para 17.3, which adds, by way of example, that, if the issue on which the case turns can with reasonable practicability be crystallised and resolved by having an early Final Hearing, then in the fulfilment of the overriding objective, such a flexible approach must be taken to secure compliance with Children Act 1989, s 1(2).

41 Ibid, at para 5.1.

(2) *The Allocation Record and The Timetable for the Child* – the applicant must prepare and file the Allocation Record and the Timetable for the Child, should provide information to update the Timetable regularly and is responsible for updating the Allocation Record including the Timetable after each hearing.[42]

(3) *Case Management Documentation* – the parties[43] must use the Case Management Documentation.[44]

(4) *Co-operation* – the parties and their representatives should co-operate with the court in case management, including the fixing of timetables to avoid unacceptable delay, and in the crystallisation and resolution of the issues on which the case turns.[45]

(5) *Directions* – the parties or their legal representatives[46] will monitor compliance with the court's directions and tell the court or court officer about any failure to comply with a court direction or any other delay in the proceedings.[47]

(6) *The Case Management Record* – (repeating in effect the terms of para 3.8) the parties or their legal representatives are expected to retain a record containing copies of the documents on the court's Case Management Record.[48]

(7) *The Draft Case Management Order*, in respect of which paras 5.7–5.9 of the Practice Direction make the following provisions:
- Parties should start to consider the content of the Draft Case Management Order at the earliest opportunity either before or in the course of completing applications to the court or the response to the application.[49]
- Parties should in any event consider the Draft Case Management Order after the First Appointment.[50]
- There should be ongoing consideration of the Draft Case Management Orders throughout the proceedings.[51]
- The Draft Case Management Orders should serve as an aide memoire to everyone involved in the proceedings of the Timetable for the Child, the case management decisions and the identified issues.[52]
- Only one Draft Case Management Order should be filed with the court for the CMC and the IRH.[53]
- It is the responsibility of the advocate for the applicant, which in care and supervision proceedings will ordinarily be the local authority, to prepare those drafts and be responsible for obtaining comments from the advocates and the parties.[54]

---

42 Ibid, at para 5.2, which adds that the Allocation Record must contain the applicant's allocation proposal and a record of the court's allocation decision and reasons, and that the Timetable for the Child will be part of the Allocation Record.
43 'Parties' includes their legal representatives (ibid, at para 5.10).
44 Ibid, at para 5.3.
45 Ibid, at para 5.4.
46 'Legal representative' means a barrister or solicitor, solicitor's employee or other authorised litigator (as defined in the Courts and Legal Services Act 1990) who has been instructed to act for a party in relation to the proceedings (the PLO Practice Direction, at para 25(22).
47 Ibid, at para 5.5.
48 Ibid, at para 5.6.
49 Ibid, at para 5.7.
50 Ibid, at para 5.7.
51 Ibid, at para 5.8.
52 Ibid, at para 5.8.
53 Ibid, at para 5.9.
54 Ibid, at para 5.9.

Co-operation

1.38 Similarly, at para 19 of the Practice Direction, there is a section entitled 'Co-operation'.

1.39 In general terms, it provides that throughout the proceedings the parties and their representatives should co-operate wherever reasonably practicable to help towards securing the welfare of the child as the paramount consideration.[55]

1.40 But it provides further that at each court appearance the court will ask the parties and their legal representatives:

(1) what steps they have taken to achieve co-operation and the extent to which they have been successful;

(2) if appropriate the reason why co-operation could not be achieved; and

(3) the steps needed to resolve any issues necessary to achieve co-operation.[56]

1.41 In like vein, para 20.1 provides that the parties, their advisers and the Children's Guardian, are encouraged to try to agree directions for the management of the proceedings.

1.42 To obtain the approval of the court, the agreed directions must set out a Timetable for the Child by reference to calendar dates for the taking of steps for the preparation of the case, and also include a date when it is proposed that the next hearing will take place.[57]

FURTHER PROVISIONS

1.43 The paragraphs of the PLO Practice Direction addressing and particularising the four stages of the Public Law Outline are covered within Chapter 3; but the Practice Direction contains a number of further sections with which courts and practitioners will need to be familiar.

Ethnicity, language, religion and culture

1.44 Paragraph 6 of the Practice Direction provides that:

- at each case management stage of the proceedings (particularly at the First Appointment and CMC), the court will consider giving directions regarding the obtaining of evidence about the ethnicity, language, religion and culture of the child and other significant persons involved in the proceedings;

- the court will subsequently consider the implications of this evidence for the child in the context of the issues in the case.

---

[55] Ibid, at para 19.1.
[56] Ibid, at para 19.2.
[57] Ibid, at para 20.2.

Adults who may be protected parties

1.45 Paragraphs 7.1–7.4 of the Practice Direction deal with adults who may be protected parties, with the following in particular to be noted:

- The court will investigate as soon as possible any issue as to whether an adult party or intended party to the proceedings lacks capacity (within the meaning of the Mental Capacity Act 2005) to conduct the proceedings.[58]
- An adult who lacks capacity to conduct the proceedings is a protected party and must have a representative (a litigation friend, next friend or guardian ad litem) to conduct the proceedings on his or her behalf.[59]
- Any issue as to the capacity of an adult to conduct the proceedings must be determined before the court gives any directions relevant to that adult's role within the proceedings.[60]
- Where the adult is a protected party, his or her representative should be involved in any instruction of an expert, including the instruction of an expert to assess whether the adult, although a protected party, is competent to give evidence.[61]
- If at any time during the proceedings, there is reason to believe that a party may lack capacity to conduct the proceedings, then the court must be notified and directions sought to ensure that this issue is investigated without delay.[62]

Child likely to lack capacity to conduct the proceedings when reaching 18

1.46 The PLO Practice Direction also makes provision for the child likely to lack capacity to conduct the proceedings when he or she reaches the age of 18.

1.47 Paragraph 8 provides that, where it appears that a child is:

(1) a party to the proceedings and not the subject of them;

(2) nearing his or her eighteenth birthday; and

(3) considered likely to lack capacity to conduct the proceedings when he or she reaches 18,

the court will consider giving directions relating to the investigation of a child's capacity in this respect.

---

58 Ibid, at para 7.1.
59 Ibid, at para 7.1.
60 Ibid, at para 7.2.
61 Ibid, at para 7.3, which recognises that the instruction of an expert is a significant step in the proceedings and adds that the representative will wish to consider (and ask the expert to consider), if the protected party is competent to give evidence, their best interests in this regard, may wish to seek advice about 'special measures' and may put forward an argument on behalf of the protected party that the protected party should not give evidence. For a discussion of special measures, see **5.201** et seq.
62 Ibid, at para 7.4.

Alternative dispute resolution

1.48 Paragraph 18 of the Practice Direction makes provision for alternative dispute resolution.

1.49 The court will encourage the parties to use an alternative dispute resolution procedure and facilitate the use of such a procedure where it is readily available, demonstrated to be in the interests of the child, and reasonably practicable and safe.[63]

1.50 The parties can ask the court for advice about alternative dispute resolution at any stage in the proceedings.[64]

1.51 At any stage in the proceedings the court itself will consider whether alternative dispute resolution is appropriate. If so, the court may direct that a hearing or proceedings be adjourned for such specified period as it considers appropriate to enable the parties to obtain information and advice about alternative dispute resolution, and, where the parties agree, to enable it to take place.[65]

1.52 Reflecting the position in private law, however, para 18.4 expressly recognises that no party can or should be obliged to enter into any form of alternative dispute resolution if they are unwilling to do so.

Performance of the court's function and application of the Bundles Practice Direction

1.53 Paragraph 22 of the PLO Practice Direction specifies in detail who should perform the function of the court at High Court, county court and family proceedings court level.

1.54 Attention is particularly drawn to the terms of para 22.3 and 22.4:

- In proceedings in a magistrates' court, where a party considers that there are likely to be issues arising at a hearing (including the First Appointment, CMC and IRH) which need to be decided by a family proceedings court, rather than a justices' clerk, then that party should give the court written notice of that need at least two days before the hearing.[66]
- Family proceedings courts may consider making arrangements to ensure a properly constituted court[67] is available at the same time as IRHs are being heard by a justices' clerk.[68]

---

63 Ibid, at para 18.1.

64 Ibid, at para 18.2.

65 Ibid, at para 18.3.

66 Ibid, at para 22.3. This provision makes clear that in the family proceedings court the IRH should be heard by a justices' clerk rather than a bench. The MOJ Care Proceedings Reforms website (www.justice.gov.uk/docs/faqs-care-proceedings-reforms.pdf) provides the rationale for this approach: 'While the IRH is in principle capable of producing a final order if the circumstances warrant, and that is a highly desirable outcome, its primary function and purpose is that of a case management exercise to be dealt with by the legal advisers. Legal advisers will be capable, and required, to scrutinise filed evidence and draw attention to failings to deal with or respond to issues raised by other parties. Legal advisers will be able to fulfil the objective of the IRH "to resolve and narrow issues; to identify any remaining key issues". In the few cases where the case can be finally resolved by the time of the IRH or where interim issues/directions require the determination of a bench at IRH stage, it is most unlikely that the parties, or at least one of them, will be unaware of this and will thus be expected to inform the court. The legal adviser will ensure that any such hearings are listed before a bench as necessary.'

67 One constituted in accordance with the Magistrates' Courts Act 1980, s 66.

68 The PLO Practice Direction, at para 22.4, which explains that thereby any delay so caused should be minimal. See further footnote 66.

1.55 Paragraph 24.1 of the Practice Direction provides that it must be read with the Bundles Practice Direction,[69] which does not apply in the family proceedings court.

1.56 Paragraph 24.2 then provides that the Bundles Practice Direction is to be applied to High Court and county court public law proceedings subject to the following adjustments:

(1) excluded from the ambit of hearings to which the Bundles Practice Direction applies are the First Appointment, the CMC and the IRH referred to in the PLO Practice Direction where there are no contested applications being heard at those hearings;

(2) the references in the Bundles Practice Direction (at paras 6.1 and 15) to the Protocol and to the Practice Direction: Care Cases: Judicial Continuity and Judicial Case Management are to be read as if they were references to the PLO Practice Direction.

1.57 The Bundles Practice Direction, as adjusted, forms Appendix 5 to this book.

THE CAFCASS REPORTING TO COURT POLICY

1.58 A key aspect of the new practice regime lies in the changed role for the Children's Guardian within proceedings.

1.59 The Cafcass[70] Reporting to Court Policy, issued to its staff in April 2008, explains how Cafcass will report to court in individual cases. It covers private as well as public children law cases, though the focus here inevitably is only on the public law side.

1.60 The Policy explains how the process of reporting is a cumulative one, starting from the early stages of Cafcass involvement in the case; it appends the 'Analysis and Recommendations' templates to be used by Cafcass officers, and also provides guidance about how these templates should be completed.

1.61 The Cafcass Reporting to Court Policy, including its appendices, forms Appendix 6 to this book. It should be stressed that the version reproduced here is that which Cafcass has issued to its staff for use in public law proceedings. It is finalised insofar as public law proceedings are concerned, but, at the time of writing, is subject to amendment in respect of private law proceedings pending finalisation of the integrated private law pathway.

Key features

1.62 The following features of this new Reporting Policy are highlighted below.

1.63 The Policy has been formulated to comply with the PLO, and the templates that it attaches are to be used for all new public law cases from April 2008. There are three templates (initial, interim and final), but the Policy also appends a verbal checklist for the First Appointment.

1.64 Cafcass will now provide information to the court from the earliest stages of a case. There had been some concern about how the Children's Guardian could do this with limited

---

[69] Practice Direction Family Proceedings: Court Bundles (Universal Practice to be Applied in all Courts other than Family Proceedings Court) of 27 July 2006 (the PLO Practice Direction, at para 24.2).

[70] Practitioners will note that CAFCASS is now styled Cafcass.

information and without in some cases compromising the formation of a working relationship with the parents. The Policy makes the following clear:[71]

> 'In the early stages, it is unlikely that you will have a full overview. The aim is to provide an initial analysis of what is "safe and sensible" for the child(ren), recognising that your analysis will change and develop in situations where you are involved for a longer period. For public law cases where the First Appointment is within days of your appointment, you may prefer to provide the information verbally and only write the Initial Analysis for the Case Management Conference. We have produced a "verbal information" checklist for this situation.'

1.65 The templates are not 'stand-alone' documents. They should avoid repeating any information from a previous Analysis and should only include information which is both new and relevant. The aim is for the court to receive the Cafcass analysis as it develops through the life of the case.[72]

1.66 The Analysis should not repeat information held elsewhere, for example within an expert's report. The Cafcass officer should use cross-references, so that the analysis 'contributes to the full picture rather than re-painting it'.[73]

1.67 The templates do not set out the welfare checklist in full, but require the worker to include the relevant sections in their analysis. However, for contested final hearings or for any other contested hearing, the checklist should be used in full.[74]

1.68 Paragraph 4.5 of the Policy explains the focus and priorities of the templates:

> 'The templates are child-centred, emphasising what information means for the child. The templates prioritise: the child's timetable; the child's views, including providing information from direct work with the child; and the child's right to find out what has happened at each stage of the court process.'

1.69 Paragraph 4.5 also adds that, on the occasions when it is not possible for the Children's Guardian to see the child before the First Appointment, the reasons for this should be explained.

1.70 The aim is for much shorter and sharper Cafcass documents, reflecting the court's perceived desire for Cafcass to focus on relevant analysis not description, to emphasise 'sorting' not 'reporting', and to be brief and specific in style not discursive.[75]

1.71 Paragraph 5 of the Policy explains which documents are to be used at which stage of the process. The 'initial' template is to be used for the first written document. Thus, where at First Appointment, a verbal rather than a written report is provided,[76] the initial template should be used for the CMC and should recap the information previously provided verbally. If there had previously been an initial written report, then the interim template should be used for the CMC. The interim template should always be used for the IRH.

1.72 Part 7 of the Policy explains what fits under each of the template headings.[77] It should be read together with the 'funnel model', which the Policy appends and which usefully sets out a

---

71 The Cafcass Reporting to Court Policy, at para 4.1.

72 Ibid, at para 4.2.

73 Ibid, at para 4.3.

74 Ibid, at para 4.4.

75 Ibid, at paras 4.6 and 4.7. Paras 4.8 and 4.9 explain the process of internal quality assurance of these reports.

76 The decision as to whether the Children's Guardian provides a spoken summary or written document for the First Appointment is for the Children's Guardian to make, based on the circumstances of the case.

77 In what will doubtless be seen as a controversial piece of guidance, the Cafcass policy comments: 'In some areas there has been a tradition of including the Children's Guardian's length of experience and qualifications. This should not be included as it risks allowing discrimination against more recently appointed practitioners. Where the court asks for this information, all that should be included is that the author is a qualified social worker and

number of pertinent questions for the Children's Guardian to consider at each successive stage of the case and which narrows down towards its final resolution.

1.73 Although created for the use of the Children's Guardian, courts and non-Cafcass practitioners alike will find that the 'funnel model' contains a very helpful summary of the issues to be considered by all at First Appointment, CMC, IRH and Final Hearing.

1.74 Many will mourn the passing of the traditional Children's Guardian final report. It was a comprehensive document that often provided an excellent summary of the case, as informative to the child in the future as it was to the parties in the present. For many courts, the Guardian's report was the first document read in preparation for the final hearing. With some courts, the suspicion was that it was the only document read. Such was its importance in the case that many litigants simply gave way in the face of the depth of its analysis and the strength of its recommendations.

1.75 There can, however, be little doubt that Cafcass's new style of reporting is more in keeping with the spirit as well as the letter of the Public Law Outline, with its emphasis on the front-loading of information and on the earlier identification and resolution of issues, and with the early expert input of the Children's Guardian necessary to the success of that process.

---

registered with the General Social Care Council.' It is hard to see how the court can determine (as it has to under the Experts Practice Direction) the question of whether any area of expert evidence required could be covered by the social worker or Children's Guardian without knowing the extent of their experience. Further, almost inevitably, courts charged with taking difficult welfare decisions will be likely to place more weight on the recommendations of a Children's Guardian with much rather than little experience.

CHAPTER TWO

PRE-PROCEEDINGS PREPARATION

2.1 While the Public Law Outline is principally geared towards improving the management of public law proceedings once issued, that initiative goes hand in hand with the simultaneous changes to local authority practice in the pre-proceedings phase upon which this chapter focuses. Indeed, the success or otherwise of the former will inevitably be informed by the success or otherwise of the latter.

2.2 These changes are to be found within the newly revised Volume 1 of the Children Act 1989 Guidance and Regulations and reflect the particular concerns of the *Child Care Proceedings Review*[1] to improve families' understanding of and engagement with the system, to encourage (where safe and desirable) the exploration of alternatives to court proceedings, and to improve the quality and consistency of applications for care and supervision orders.

2.3 The key changes can be summarised under four headings:

(1) *Core assessments* – the expectation is that core assessments, as a matter of routine, will have been carried out prior to making an application for a care or supervision order.

(2) *Placement with relatives and friends* – as part of the above, the expectation is that, in advance of any proceedings, consideration will have been given to the possibility of the placement of the child with relatives and friends, whether as an alternative to proceedings or as a care placement.

(3) *'Letter Before Proceedings'* – the expectation is that, as a means of involving and engaging parents in the process, they will, in advance of any application, be sent a 'letter before proceedings' (save where it would be unsafe for the child for that to occur).

(4) *Better preparation of applications* – the aim is for improved preparation of materials to support applications for care and supervision orders.

2.4 It will swiftly be seen that the main cumulative objective of these changes is to shift a large amount of work that currently takes place once proceedings are issued to the pre-proceedings phase – so as to make any subsequent care or supervision proceedings quicker and more focused, or even to avoid those proceedings altogether.

2.5 The guidance appends The PLO Practice Direction[2] as its Annex 2, and has as its Annex 3 the two flowcharts that appear at the back of that Practice Direction. Practitioners should familiarise themselves with the content of the Pre-Proceedings Flowchart which helpfully sets out the steps that are to be taken by local authorities in the pre-proceedings phase.

---

1 *Review of the Child Care Proceedings System in England and Wales* – published in May 2006 by the Department for Education and Skills and the Department for Constitutional Affairs (the forerunner of the Ministry of Justice).

2 Practice Direction: Guide to Case Management in Public Law Proceedings. Discussed in Chapters 1 and 3, and reproduced at Appendix 1 to this book.

2.6 The content of the guidance relevant to the changes in local authority pre-proceedings practice is extracted below.[3] Where appropriate, it has been added to with information available from the Ministry of Justice's Care Proceedings Reforms website,[4] produced in answer to practitioner queries.

THE SCOPE OF THE REVISED GUIDANCE

2.7 Volume 1 of the Children Act Guidance and Regulations was first published in 1991, and provided guidance, primarily addressed to local authorities and their staff, about the court-related provisions set out in the 1989 Act. Following the *Child Care Proceedings Review*, and subsequent public consultation on the draft guidance, a revised volume of guidance has now been prepared, replacing the 1991 edition and, like the PLO, coming into effect from 1 April 2008.

2.8 Volume 1, issued as guidance under the Local Authority Social Services Act 1970, s 7, requires local authorities, in exercising their social services functions, to act under the general guidance of the Secretary of State. Indeed, the guidance should be complied with by local authorities when exercising these functions, unless local circumstances indicate exceptional reasons that justify a variation. The guidance is primarily addressed to children services practitioners and front-line managers who, supported by their legal advisers, have particular responsibilities for safeguarding and promoting the welfare of children. It is also highly relevant to Directors of Children's Services and other senior local authority managers, who together oversee the exercise by local authorities of their functions under the Children Act 1989, in relation to safeguarding and promoting the welfare of children.

2.9 The purpose of this chapter is not to provide an exhaustive summary of the guidance itself,[5] which plainly exceeds the remit of this book, rather to focus on what the local authority should do before, and potentially as an alternative, to care and supervision proceedings.

THE ASSESSMENT PROCESSES

2.10 Paragraphs 3.12–3.18 of the guidance detail the various assessment processes to be undertaken by the local authority in the pre-proceedings phase.

The initial assessment

2.11 Where a child is referred to the local authority as a child who may be in need, para 3.12 of the guidance provides that the local authority should decide, within one working day of the referral, whether to undertake an initial assessment. This decision would normally follow discussion with the person who has made the referral, together with consideration of other information which the local authority may hold or obtain.

---

3 The following parts of the guidance, being those most relevant to care and supervision proceedings, are reproduced at Appendix 3 to this book: chapter 1, chapter 3, chapter 4 (paras 4.73–4.82) and annex 1.

4 To be found at www.justice.gov.uk/docs/faqs-care-proceedings-reforms.pdf.

5 The guidance provides a complete account of the range of Children Act 1989 orders (private as well as public), and describes too the key principles underpinning the Act and the roles of the police and of Cafcass in relation to it.

2.12 The following should be noted in respect of initial assessments:[6]

- Any assessment should be undertaken in accordance with the *Framework for the Assessment of Children in Need and Their Families* (the 'Assessment Framework'), produced in 2000 by the Department of Health et al.[7]
- The initial assessment should be completed within seven working days of the date of the referral.
- Information should be gathered and analysed using the dimensions and domains set out in the Assessment Framework, namely:
  - the child's developmental needs;
  - the capacity of the parents or other caregivers to respond appropriately to those needs; and
  - the wider family and environmental factors.

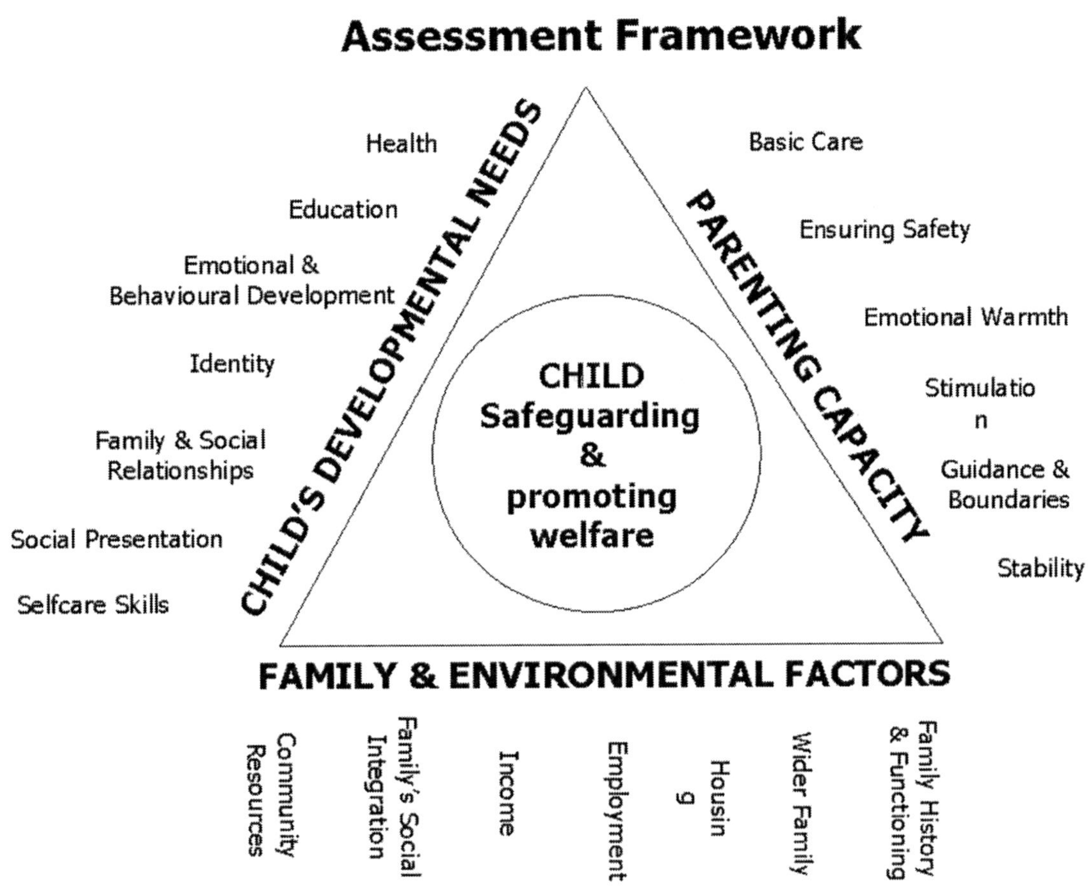

2.13 It is recognised that in urgent safeguarding situations the initial assessment may be very brief.[8]

---

6 The guidance, at para 3.12.

7 To be found at www.archive.official-documents.co.uk/document/doh/facn/fw-00.htm.

8 The guidance, at para 3.12.

2.14 The initial assessment may then enable the local authority to ascertain whether:

- the child is a child in need;[9] and
- there is reasonable cause to suspect that the child is suffering, or is likely to suffer, significant harm.[10]

2.15 Where concerns about significant harm do not emerge or are not substantiated, but the child is assessed as being a 'child in need', the local authority may have sufficient information to determine what services (if any) should be provided, on the basis of the initial assessment, and to agree a 'child in need' plan with the child and that child's family.[11]

2.16 In determining what services to provide, the local authority is required (*so far as is reasonably practicable and consistent with the child's welfare)* to ascertain and, having regard to his/her age and understanding, to give due consideration to the wishes and feelings of that child.[12]

2.17 If, however, the child is assessed as being in need and the local authority is concerned that the child is suffering, or is at risk of suffering, significant harm, then the position is different.

2.18 In that scenario, the local authority is under a duty to make, as soon as practicable and, in any event, within 48 hours of receiving the information, such enquiries as it considers necessary to enable it to decide:

- whether it should take action to safeguard or promote the welfare of the child; and
- (if so) what action may be appropriate in the circumstances.[13]

2.19 Emergency action, in the form of an emergency protection order (EPO)[14] or the exercise of police protection powers,[15] may be required to secure the immediate protection of the child; and, where emergency action has been taken, such section 47 enquiries as may be necessary should follow quickly.

The core assessment

2.20 The core assessment is the means by which section 47 enquiries[16] are carried out by local authorities.

2.21 Paragraph 3.15 of the guidance provides with appropriate emphasis:

---

9 Children Act 1989, s 17(10), provides that, for the purposes of Part III of the Act, 'a child shall be taken to be in need if: (a) he is unlikely to achieve or maintain, or to have the opportunity of achieving or maintaining, a reasonable standard of health or development without the provision for him of services by a local authority under this Part; (b) his health or development is likely to be significantly impaired, or further impaired, without the provision for him of such services; or (c) he is disabled'.

10 The criteria to be found under Children Act 1989, s 47(1)(b).

11 The guidance, at para 3.13.

12 Children Act 1989, s 17(4A).

13 The guidance, at para 3.14; and see Children Act 1989, s 47.

14 Children Act 1989, s 44.

15 Children Act 1989, s 46.

16 The duty of local authorities to make enquiries under Children Act 1989, s 47, is covered within the guidance, at paras 4.73–4.82.

> 'In all cases where an initial assessment concludes that there is cause to suspect that a child is suffering or is likely to suffer significant harm, a *core assessment should be completed*, informed by the information obtained through the initial assessment.'

2.22 Paragraph 3.15, however, goes on to make clear that the need to complete a core assessment should not deter necessary safeguarding action from being taken. It also highlights that, under the PLO Practice Direction, compliance with the requirement to complete the core assessment will be scrutinised by the responsible court as part of the court's first consideration of any application for a care or supervision order.[17]

2.23 The following should be noted in respect of core assessments:[18]

- A core assessment is defined by the Assessment Framework, at para 3.11, as 'an in-depth assessment which addresses the central or most important aspects of the needs of a child and the capacity of his or her parents or caregivers to respond appropriately to these needs within the wider family and community context'.

- The core assessment therefore has to assess, as well as the needs of the child, the needs and capacities both of the child's parents and those to be found in the wider family and community.[19]

- The core assessment should build on the initial assessment, utilise any prior specialist assessments that may have been carried out and should be completed within 35 working days of its commencement.[20]

- The core assessment forms the central part of the evidence supporting any application that the local authority may make for a care or supervision order. Local authorities must ensure that an up-to-date core assessment is available in relation to any child who is the subject of such an application.

The care plan for the child

2.24 It is upon the findings from the initial and core assessments that the plan for the care of the child should be based.[21]

2.25 The plan should set out its aims and the intended outcomes for the child, informed by the findings from the assessments.[22]

---

17 See PLO Stage 1.

18 The guidance, at paras 3.2, 3.16 and 3.17.

19 Considered at **2.29** et seq.

20 The guidance recognises that newly-commissioned specialist assessments from other agencies or independent professionals will not necessarily be completed within this 35 day period, but clear timescales for their completion should have been agreed with those bodies from which they have been commissioned, which should be specified in the core assessment. Once these specialist assessments are available, they will need to be taken into account and, depending on their relevance, may influence the local authority's planning for the child. The MOJ Care Proceedings Reforms website adds that local authorities, as part of the core assessment process, will need to consider to what extent specialist or independent assessments may or may not be appropriate.

21 The guidance, at para 3.18.

22 Namely, the identified developmental needs of the child and the capacity of the parents to respond to the child's needs in the context of their wider family and environmental context.

2.26 In structure, the plan should follow the Assessment Framework domains and dimensions in accordance with the Integrated Children's System (ICS) care plan exemplar and be explicit about the services which will be provided by which agency and at what frequency in relation to the dimension headings.[23]

2.27 The plan should also set out the outcomes which are being sought in relation to the needs and services identified.[24]

2.28 Paragraph 3.18 of the guidance also highlights the provisions of Children Act 1989, s 31A. Under that provision, where an application is made from which a care order might be made, the local authority must within the timetable directed by the court prepare a care plan, and no care order can be made until the court has considered a section 31A plan.[25]

PLACEMENT WITH RELATIVES AND FRIENDS

2.29 Paragraph 3.7 of the guidance starts with the reminder of the local authority's general duty, under Children Act 1989, s 17, to promote the upbringing of children in need by their families (so far as is consistent with its duty to safeguard and promote the welfare of such children), and to do so through the provision of family support services to children in need and their families.

2.30 But para 3.7 then goes on to make clear the implications of that general duty for the consideration of potential alternative carers within the pre-proceedings phase:

> 'This means that voluntary arrangements for the provision of services to the child and his family including the consideration of potential alternative carers should always be fully explored ahead of the making of any application under section 31, provided that this does not jeopardise the child's safety and welfare. The local authority should ensure, when assessing the wider family and environmental factors within the core assessment . . . that it considers the capacity and willingness of the wider family to provide care for the child on a short or a longer-term basis.'

2.31 As part of their recognition of the 'no order principle' under Children Act 1989, s 1(5), local authorities should keep in mind the possibility that care proceedings could be avoided altogether or that a different application, such as for a special guardianship order or a residence order (made by a relative or carer), may be more appropriate, rather than a care order application by the local authority.[26]

2.32 Paragraph 3.8 of the guidance acknowledges that a family group conference (FGC) can be an important opportunity to engage friends and members of the wider family at an early stage of concerns about a child – either to support the parents or to provide care for the child, whether in the short or longer term. In either scenario, it is felt that a FGC can reduce or eliminate the need for the child to become looked after.

2.33 Social workers will need to consider whether, and if so when, it is appropriate to hold a FGC depending on the circumstances of an individual case. As the pre-proceedings flowchart sets out, FGCs may be used at any point following the initial assessment.[27]

---

[23] The guidance, at para 3.18.

[24] LAC (99) 29 provides further guidance on the preparation of care plans in applications under Children Act 1989, s 31. See **5.112**.

[25] Children Act 1989, s 31(3A). See **5.108** et seq.

[26] The guidance, at para 3.7.

[27] See the MOJ Care Proceedings Reforms website.

2.34 In presenting a care plan to the court in any application for a care order, the local authority will be required to demonstrate that it has considered family members and friends as potential carers at each stage of its decision making.[28]

2.35 In practice, the process of approaching members of the wider family without antagonising the child's parents can present quite a challenge to local authorities. Hence, the following advice should be borne in mind:[29]

> 'The most important thing is to work closely with parents at each stage so they are fully engaged with the process. This is likely to be much more productive than covert approaches to members of the wider family which would be inappropriate. It is accepted that in many cases some relatives will not put themselves forward at an early stage to avoid conflict with the parents. The focus on working with the parents before proceedings is an attempt to overcome some of these issues. In many cases, though, it is accepted that it may only be possible to pursue "family and friends" options once proceedings have started.'

2.36 In terms of the depth and timing of any assessment of the wider family and the extent of the search of it, the following should also be noted:[30]

- The level of detail required within the assessment will depend on the role that is envisaged for the family member. A high level of detail is likely to be needed if, for example, a family member is to be assessed with a view to being approved as a local authority foster parent.
- Whether all relevant kinship assessments can be completed before the issue of proceedings will depend on the circumstances of each case. In some it will be possible, but in others the need to safeguard the child may preclude this from occurring.
- The extent of the search for relatives will need to be considered on a case-by-case basis.
- When to end the search should be a matter for the exercise of professional judgement. Particularly without the authority of the court, a final deadline for potential carers to come forward should not be set.

INVOLVING AND ENGAGING THE FAMILY

2.37 A further concern of the *Child Care Proceedings Review* was to see better inter-agency working in this area, and, at para 3.23, the guidance recognises the imperative of this occurring:

> 'Full inter-agency co-operation, including the sharing of information for the purpose of safeguarding children is essential whenever a potential care or supervision order case is identified, both because of the need to obtain as complete as possible a picture of actual or likely harm to the child but also to plan appropriate provision to meet the child's needs, if the order is made. Information from health professionals is likely to be of particular importance.'

2.38 But the desire for full inter-agency co-operation should not blind the local authority to the need, wherever possible, to involve and engage the family concerned in the pre-proceedings assessment and decision-making process:

---

[28] The guidance, at para 3.8.
[29] See the MOJ Care Proceedings Reforms website.
[30] Ibid.

> 'Parents, the child (if they are of sufficient age and understanding) and others with a legitimate interest in the child's future should, as far as possible, be involved in the pre-application assessment processes and should, to the extent that it is possible to do so, be consulted on the local authority's plans for the child.'[31]

2.39 Three important consequences for the pre-proceedings phase flow from this general principle, though they should all be understood to be subject to the general proviso that, if the safety of the child indicates otherwise, then they will not ensue:

(1) Even before the local authority reaches a decision that it should apply for a care or supervision order, parents should already have been made aware of their concerns about the relevant child.

(2) Before reaching such a decision, the local authority:
- should have taken such steps as are possible, perhaps through a family group conference or other family meeting, to explore whether care for the child can be safely provided by a relative or friend;
- should have assessed the suitability of such possible arrangements; and
- should have considered the most appropriate legal status of them.

(3) Where the local authority decides, having sought and considered legal advice, that it intends to apply for a care or supervision order, it must immediately notify that decision to the parents and others with parental responsibility for the child. Further, it must do so using language and methods of communication, both in writing and orally, that will be understood by them. In particular the local authority should consider whether the parent (or other person with parental responsibility) appears to have the capacity to instruct their legal representative.[32]

2.40 The guidance also deals with the issue of informing the child, and in this context the following should be noted:[33]

- Where any affected child is of a sufficient age and level of understanding, the intention to initiate care or supervision proceedings must also be explained to that child, subject to there being parental consent to that step being taken, and unless to do so would exacerbate any significant harm that the child might already be suffering, have suffered or be likely to suffer.

- However, the guidance recognises that, in a number of cases, there may be parental sensitivity about the local authority's involvement with the child, leading to parental consent for such involvement being withheld. In such scenario, such information can only be provided after the start of proceedings, at which point the Cafcass Children's Guardian will also have a role to play. In this connection, the guidance indicates that it will be helpful for Cafcass planning purposes for the local authority to notify it of the prospect of the commencement of proceedings at the point at which parents are notified, though identifying details of the child should only be disclosed to Cafcass with the parents' consent.

---

31 The guidance, at para 3.24.

32 Ibid, at para 3.25, reflects the position that the Official Solicitor may act as guardian ad litem/Next Friend/Litigation Friend for parties who lack litigation capacity (within the meaning of the Mental Capacity Act 2005) to represent themselves in proceedings, where there is no other person willing or suitable to do so. See **5.53** et seq.

33 The guidance, at para 3.28.

The 'Letter Before Proceedings'

2.41 The notification to the parents and others with parental responsibility (of the decision to commence proceedings) should, in its written version, take the form of a 'Letter Before Proceedings'.[34]

2.42 Such a letter should be sent in all cases 'where the short term safety and welfare of the child permits'.[35]

2.43 A very helpful standard template letter has been devised (and is included as Annex 1 to the guidance);[36] but the letter, where used, will need to be adjusted to fit the particular circumstances of the case.[37]

2.44 By way of content, the guidance provides that the 'Letter Before Proceedings' should include the following:[38]

- a summary of the local authority's concerns about the actual or likely harm to the child and the evidence upon which these concerns are based;
- information about the following matters:
  - what the local authority has done to safeguard and promote the welfare of the child;
  - what needs to be addressed;
  - what support will be provided; and
  - what the outcome will be if the problems are not addressed;
- information about how to obtain legal help (on a non-means tested basis) and advice (with details of appropriate local solicitors included), together with encouragement to seek such advice as soon as possible.

2.45 The standard template letter is broken down in the following way:

- At the top of the letter, the recipient is told in capitals not to ignore it and to take it to a solicitor now.
- The letter then identifies the relevant local authority and is headed, again in capitals: 'Concerns about [the named child(ren)] – Letter Before Proceedings'.
- The first subject heading, again in capitals, is: 'How to Avoid Going to Court'. It lets the recipient know how concerned the local authority has become about the care of the child(ren), and that it is thinking about starting care proceedings in respect of them, meaning that it may apply and that the child(ren) may be taken into care, if the court decides this to be best for them.
- The next subject heading, again in capitals, is: 'An Important Meeting About What Will Happen Next'. It asks the recipient to come to a meeting with the local authority to talk about these concerns and, again in capitals, implores the recipient to bring a solicitor to the meeting.

---

34 Ibid, at para 3.29.

35 Ibid, at para 3.3.

36 The standard template letter annexed is based on the prototype developed during the currency of the draft PLO by Yvonne Gibson, principal solicitor (child care) at Buckinghamshire County Council.

37 The guidance, at para 3.29.

38 Ibid.

- The next block capital heading is: 'What Will Happen if You Do Nothing'. It lets the recipient know that, if they do nothing, then the local authority will go to court as soon as possible to secure the safety of the relevant child(ren).

- The final block heading within the body of the letter is: 'Your Wider Family'. It prepares the recipient to discuss at the meeting who might look after the child(ren), if the court decides that it is no longer safe for the recipient to do so.

- Appended to the standard template letter is a grid, by which the local authority should set out its main concerns. The local authority should enumerate their concerns and give examples of when they have manifested themselves, which 'should capture chronic ongoing concerns as well as acute episodes/incidents'.

- Next comes a section which records 'What Children's Services Have Done to Try to Help'.

- The letter then ends with a three point reminder to the recipient under the block heading: 'What You Have to Do so that We Will Not Go to Court'.

2.46 The primary purpose of the 'Letter Before Proceedings' is to enable the parents or others with parental responsibility to obtain legal assistance and advice, prior to the meeting identified within it. The guidance interprets the intention of such a meeting as being either to deflect proceedings or, at least, to narrow and focus the issues of concern.[39] There is no provision for the child to be represented at this meeting.[40]

2.47 On receipt of such a letter, the parents (and any others with parental responsibility) are entitled to non-means tested publicly funded legal advice at 'Level 2', which covers liaison and negotiations with the local authority.[41]

2.48 Save where urgent court action is needed to safeguard the child, the guidance provides that the local authority should liaise with the parents (and those with parental responsibility) with a view to considering what steps, if any, can be taken to avoid proceedings. These should include steps to improve parental engagement with the local authority (where this is in the interests of the child), to explain further the local authority's position and concerns, and, where proceedings cannot be avoided, to narrow the issues.[42]

2.49 If the intended meeting takes place, then at or immediately after it, the local authority should provide in writing to the parents or others with parental responsibility (PR) (and their legal representatives) any revised plan for the child, setting out what the parents and the local authority are to do to safeguard the child and the steps that the local authority will take if this action is not effective in safeguarding the child. The local authority should also explain the outcome of the meeting orally to the parents (or others with PR).[43]

2.50 The follow-up letter and, as relevant, the plan for the child should make explicit the consideration that has been given to the possibility, in the light of the needs of the child (as identified by the core assessment), of the child living with a relative or a friend. This plan:

---

39 The guidance, at para 3.3.

40 See the MOJ Care Proceedings Reforms website, which does however stress that 'it is of course important, and part of the local authority's role, to consider the voice of the child throughout a properly undertaken core assessment'.

41 The guidance, at para 3.26. Once the application for a care or supervision order has been made, parents are entitled to 'Level 3' legal representation, also available on a non-means tested basis (ibid, at para 3.27).

42 Ibid, at para 3.27.

43 Ibid, at para 3.31.

- will be based on findings from the up-to-date core assessment and any other current assessments or previous plans and the outcome of any previous family group conference or other family meeting;
- will reflect also the outcome of the meeting triggered by the 'Letter Before Proceedings';
- will identify how the child's short term needs will be met (and will also set out any longer term plans if information to support these is available).[44]

2.51 The plan should be reviewed regularly, and the safety of the child should be a paramount consideration in that process. Local authorities will need to introduce their own procedures and systems for monitoring whether progress is being made with the family; and, if at any point, the risk to the child is such that court proceedings should be taken, then an application should be made immediately.[45]

2.52 Indeed, para 3.33 of the guidance emphasises that, if, notwithstanding the 'Letter Before Proceedings' and any meeting following it, the local authority continues to be concerned (or again becomes concerned) that the child is suffering, or is likely to suffer, significant harm, then it remains responsible for making an application to the court for a care or supervision order.

2.53 It cannot be stressed enough, however, that the sending of a 'Letter Before Proceedings' and the discussions that it is intended to prompt are not mandatory in all scenarios. Nor could they be. The guidance, at para 3, makes the following clear:

> 'It is recognised, of course, that there will be some emergency and other situations where the welfare of the affected child will not permit even a brief period for such correspondence and direct discussions to take place.'

2.54 At para 3.30, the guidance then expressly acknowledges that there will be some cases which, while inappropriate to be the subject of an EPO application, will nevertheless need to be the subject of an immediate section 31 application by the local authority. This is likely to occur where the scale, nature and urgency of the local authority's safeguarding concerns are such that it considers that it is not in the interests of the child for a 'Letter Before Proceedings' to be sent.

2.55 The decision about whether to send a 'Letter Before Proceedings' should be taken at a legal planning/gateway meeting.[46]

2.56 The 'Letter Before Proceedings' can be sent pre-birth in respect of an unborn child.[47]

BETTER PREPARATION OF APPLICATIONS

2.57 The *Child Care Proceedings Review* identified unnecessary delay as a serious concern and identified poorly presented court applications as a cause of such delay.

2.58 In an effort to address that problem, the Public Law Outline provides for certain specified documents – the Checklist Documents – to be filed by the local authority alongside its application for a care or supervision order.

---

44 The guidance, at para 3.32.

45 See the MOJ Care Proceedings Reforms website.

46 Ibid.

47 Ibid.

2.59 They entail specific documents to be disclosed from the local authority's files, together with additional documents that the local authority has to prepare for the proceedings.

2.60 The requirement to append these documents is highlighted within the guidance, at paras 3.4 and 3.34, but is dealt with in depth within the PLO Practice Direction. Consequently the provisions relating to the Checklist Documents are addressed in full within the next chapter.[48]

2.61 The guidance also recognises, as does the PLO Practice Direction itself,[49] that in the kind of situation where the 'Letter Before Proceedings' procedure may not be possible,[50] it may also be that not all of the other pre-proceedings steps will have been completed. In such circumstances, the guidance indicates,[51] the local authority's application to the court will need to make explicit the reasons for any missing documentation or absent steps.

DISCUSSION – DUTIES AND DELAY

2.62 Shortly after the finalisation of the updated Volume 1 of the Children Act 1989 Guidance and Regulations, the results of the *Care Profiling Study*, carried out by Prof Judith Masson and her colleagues, were published by the Ministry of Justice.[52]

The implications of the Masson Research

2.63 The research makes particularly interesting reading in the context of the changes in local authority practice covered by this chapter.

2.64 The *Care Profiling Study* was jointly commissioned by the Department for Constitutional Affairs[53] and the Department of Education and Skills[54] in September 2006 to look at the functioning of child protection proceedings in the family courts. The objective of the study was to provide 'baseline data' on proceedings brought under Children Act 1989, s 31, against which reforms to the care proceedings system could be evaluated, and to do so through a detailed analysis of court records for a sample of 300–500 completed cases resulting from section 31 applications made in 2004.

2.65 Among the main points emerging from this research are the following:

- There is no evidence that the local authorities involved brought care proceedings without good reason, with many of the families studied having lost the care of children in previous proceedings.
- Over a quarter of care proceedings involve babies.
- Neglect was the basis for concern in three-quarters of cases.

---

48 At **3.11** et seq.
49 The PLO Practice Direction, at para 10.3 (considered at **3.15**).
50 See **2.53–2.54**.
51 The guidance, at para 3.30.
52 J Masson, J Pearce & K Bader with O Joyner, J Marsden & D Westlake *Care Profiling Study* (MOJ, March 2008). The research in full can be found at www.justice.gov.uk/docs/care-profiling-study.pdf. A summary of the research is available at www.justice.gov.uk/docs/care-profiling-summary.pdf.
53 Now known as the Ministry of Justice.
54 Now known as the Department for Children, Schools and Families.

- Fewer than 10% of cases involved major injuries to children, but 40% of cases resulted from a crisis.
- Over 90% of the families in the sample had been known to Children's Social Services Departments prior to the current proceedings studied, and in 45% of cases that knowledge extended for five years or more. In 85% of cases there had been active social work leading up to the application in question.
- Nevertheless core assessments had been completed, at some point, in less than half (approximately 43%) of the cases studied, and in only 15% of cases had the core assessment been carried out in the three month period immediately preceding the date of the application.
- The two most commonly occurring factors contributing to delay in proceedings were completion of reports, followed by exploring family placements.

2.66 While the research brief for this study sought baseline data rather than a policy-oriented analysis, those findings would seem to justify the focus within the revised guidance on shifting work hitherto undertaken too often post-proceedings to the pre-proceedings phase. However, the study does sound a cautionary note of some importance:

> 'The expectations of local authority practice in preparation for care proceedings under the PLO far exceed what was undertaken or could have been undertaken before action to protect the child in most of the sample cases.'

2.67 That perhaps should not surprise, given the already stretched nature of many local authorities (both in terms of personnel and resources). But it does highlight the need for courts to show some degree of latitude to local authorities if in individual cases they fall short of what is expected of them within the pre-proceedings phase.

Delay

2.68 Equally, however, it does highlight the potential downsides if too much is invested in the goal of avoiding proceedings and in the ability of local authorities to discharge, fairly and efficiently, the duties upon them.

2.69 The avoidance of delay in decision-making for children lies at the heart of the reform package, but it is important not to focus artificially solely on delay within proceedings themselves.

2.70 For in practice some of the worst delays for children have been seen in the pre-proceedings phase. Local authorities closing files for no good reason, giving parents too many chances before initiating proceedings, allowing drift to occur whilst the child is voluntarily accommodated, and failing at the relevant time to seek court-based findings where non-accidental injury is suggested but not accepted – these are all features that are already seen in practice and which have regularly and rightly drawn criticism from Children's Guardians and courts alike.

2.71 It is important therefore for local authorities to recognise the significant responsibilities that come with their increased burdens within the pre-proceedings phase.

2.72 The first remains not to delay the bringing of proceedings where proceedings are genuinely warranted.[55]

2.73 A second, inter-related, is to keep a watchful eye on the timetable for the child within and whilst they are carrying out work in the pre-proceedings phase.

2.74 A third is to undertake any assessment and to commission any expert assessment in a way that is demonstrably fair and above criticism. For, inevitably, that will remain the most effective way to avoid the need for any 'second opinion' further assessment within proceedings, with the delay to decision-making that such inexorably causes. Indeed, the words of Wall J (as he then was) in *Re JC (Care Proceedings: Procedure)*[56] have never been more apposite:

> 'All parties have a duty in family proceedings not to be tendentious in the presentation of their evidence. That duty is, however, particularly acute in relation to local authority evidence, and never more so than when the local authority is advising the court of its view of the outcome of an assessment of parental capacity or otherwise setting out its recommendations and plans. The duty of local authorities to be objective, fair and balanced cannot be over-emphasised. ...
>
> In my judgment . . . the very difficulties inherent in the performance of the social work role make it all the more important that the evidence of the social worker should be demonstrably fair, balanced and objective. In particular this means, where value judgements are concerned, that the social worker must include in his or her evidence all the material upon which the judgement is based, both negative and positive, and be able to demonstrate that the judgement which has been reached is a fair one objectively based on all the disclosed material.'

2.75 It is plain that the new regime created by the revised guidance will not be so apposite for the acute crisis kind of care case. But it clearly does have the potential to improve the management of the more chronic neglect-based form of care case, which the Masson research would indicate is the most prevalent sort. Provided that local authorities are not overwhelmed by the extent of the new challenge facing them, are given the resources to enable them to meet that challenge, and are able to exercise their judgement in individual cases sensibly, efficiently and fairly, then improvements in practice should be seen.

---

55 In this context, it is to be hoped that the recent huge increase in the cost to local authorities of bringing section 31 applications does not (as many practitioners fear) discourage local authorities from issuing where issuing is warranted. This highly controversial measure has drawn widespread criticism (see *The Times*, 28 April 2008, and G Eddon & J Ward *Increases to Court Fees* [2008] Fam Law 416).

56 [1995] 2 FLR 77, at p 80.

CHAPTER THREE

THE PLO IN STAGES

3.1 In Chapter 1 the core themes and key components of the Public Law Outline Practice Direction[1] were identified. The purpose of this chapter is to take the reader sequentially through the PLO's four stages, and to provide the reader at each point with all the information required to navigate each stage. For ease of reference, therefore, the definitions to be found in the PLO Practice Direction's comprehensive glossary[2] are set out appropriately within the body of the text or within the footnotes to it. As with Chapter 2, where relevant, information available from the Ministry of Justice's Care Proceedings Reforms website,[3] produced in answer to practitioner queries, has also been included.

3.2 The preparation of documents for issue apart, the pre-proceedings stage was addressed within the preceding chapter. The focus of this chapter is upon the development and management of proceedings, once the decision to issue has been taken, from commencement to conclusion, progressing through the PLO's four stages:

(1) Issue and the First Appointment;

(2) Case Management Conference (CMC);

(3) Issues Resolution Hearing (IRH);

(4) Final Hearing.

3.3 The PLO is set out in the tabular form[4] familiar to those who used the draft PLO in the initiative courts,[5] with the PLO Table containing an outline of:

(1) the order of the different stages of the process;

(2) the purposes of the main case management hearings and matters to be considered at them; and

(3) the latest timescales within which the main stages of the process should take place.[6]

---

1 Practice Direction: Guide to Case Management in Public Law Proceedings.
2 Ibid, at para 25.
3 To be found at www.justice.gov.uk/docs/faqs-care-proceedings-reforms.pdf.
4 The Public Law Outline is the table found within para 9 of its supporting Practice Direction (ibid, at para 4.1(1)). It is also briefly summarised in flowchart form at the back of the Practice Direction.
5 The PLO was tested in draft form in the following Care Centres and the FPCs feeding into them (known collectively as the PLO initiative courts) – Birmingham, London, Liverpool, Warrington/Chester, Newcastle/Sunderland, Exeter/Plymouth, Leicester, Milton Keynes/Oxford, Swansea and Portsmouth.
6 The PLO Practice Direction, at para 9.1.

STAGE 1 – ISSUE AND THE FIRST APPOINTMENT

3.4 Stage 1 of the Public Law Outline comprises both the issue of proceedings and the first court hearing within them – the First Appointment[7] (referred to within the PLO Table as the 'FA')[8].

3.5 The Issue part of Stage 1 comprises the various steps that should be taken on day 1 and by day 3 of the proceedings, with the objectives being threefold:[9]

(1) in care and supervision proceedings, to ensure compliance with the Pre-proceedings checklist;[10]

(2) to allocate the proceedings; and

(3) to obtain the information necessary to enable initial case management by the court at the First Appointment.

Starting the proceedings

3.6 To start the proceedings, the applicant must file the following documents:[11]

- the Application Form;
- the Supplementary Form PLO1;[12]
- an Allocation Record and Timetable for the Child, which is to include the applicant's allocation proposal.

The Allocation Record and Timetable for the Child

3.7 The Allocation Record and Timetable for the Child means a document containing: (a) the local authority's proposal for allocation; (b) the local authority's proposed Timetable for the Child; (c) the court's allocation decisions and reasons; and (d) the court's approved Timetable for the Child.[13]

3.8 The court is obliged to set an appropriate Timetable for the Child who is the subject of the proceedings.[14] That Timetable is to take account of all significant steps in the child's life that are likely to take place during the proceedings, and includes not only legal steps but also social, care, health and education steps.[15]

---

7 Ibid, at para 12.1.

8 Ibid, at para 9.2(2).

9 Ibid, at para 11.1.

10 See **3.11** et seq.

11 The PLO Practice Direction, at para 10.1. At the present time, proceedings will ordinarily be issued in the family proceedings court.

12 This means the form set out at Annex A to the PLO Practice Direction, to be filed with the application form and then used as the index to the court's Case Management Record (the PLO Practice Direction, at para 25(38)).

13 Ibid, at para 25(4)).

14 Ibid, at para 3.2.

15 Ibid, at para 3.3. Para 3.4 gives six examples of 'the dates the court will record and take into account when setting the Timetable for the Child': (1) any formal review by the local authority of the case of a looked after child (within the meaning of Children Act 1989, s 22(1)); (2) the child taking up a place at a new school; (3) any review by the local authority of any statement of the child's special educational needs; (4) an assessment by a paediatrician or other

3.9 The following further practice points in relation to the Timetable for the Child should be borne in mind:

- In case of proceedings involving more than one child, the Timetable may be different for different children. If one child's case will be ready well in advance of another's, it may be appropriate to deal with that child first.[16]

- The court is responsible for reviewing the Timetable for the Child at all stages of the case and will need to consider if it needs to be altered. There may well be competing considerations faced by the court (such as the availability of expert witnesses) which will affect the timetable, and this will need to be addressed on a case by case basis.[17]

- If Adoption Panel consideration of care plans is a factor in individual cases, then this should be flagged as a consideration for the court in setting the Timetable for the Child.[18]

- Although the 40 week target time enshrined within the Protocol has been replaced, care cases should still not exceed 40 weeks without good welfare reasons.[19]

3.10 A guideline Allocation Record and Timetable for the Child(ren) (Form PLO4) has been produced and is included within Appendix 2 to this book. It is to be used or adapted locally as practitioners and courts see fit. Somewhat surprisingly, given the Practice Direction's definition,[20] it contains no part within which to record the court's approved Timetable for the Child.

The Pre-proceedings checklist – content and compliance

3.11 Where the application is for a care or supervision order, it is expected that the applicant (invariably the local authority)[21] will file with/attach to the application form a number of additional documents. These are collectively known as the Checklist Documents, being those identified in the PLO Table's Pre-proceedings checklist.[22] The Checklist 'will promote good case preparation' and 'should be used at the earliest opportunity as a guide to what documents the court will expect to see at the start of the proceedings'.[23]

3.12 The Checklist Documents fall into two categories:

- documents to be disclosed from the local authority's files;

- documents to be prepared specifically for the proceedings that are consequent upon the application.

---

specialist; (5) the outcome of any review of local authority plans for the child (for example, any plans for permanence through adoption, special guardianship or placement with parents or relatives); and (6) a change or proposed change of the child's placement.

16 See the MOJ Care Proceedings Reforms website.

17 Ibid.

18 Ibid.

19 Ibid.

20 See **3.7**.

21 As the PLO Practice Direction recognises, at para 10.1.

22 Ibid, at para 25(28).

23 Ibid, at para 10.2.

3.13 The documents to be disclosed from the local authority's files comprise the following:

- previous court orders and judgments/reasons;[24]
- any relevant assessment materials – to include initial[25] and core[26] assessments, reports provided pursuant to Children Act 1989, s 7[27] or s 37,[28] assessments of relatives and friends,[29] and any other assessment materials (such as a genogram);[30]
- other relevant reports and records – to include single, joint or inter-agency materials (for example, health & education/Home Office and immigration documents), records of discussions with the family, and key local authority minutes and records for the child (including strategy discussion records);[31]
- any pre-existing care plans (for example, a child in need plan, a looked after child plan and a child protection plan);
- the social work chronology – defined in the PLO Practice Direction as meaning a schedule containing:
  - (a) a succinct summary of the significant dates and events in the child's life in chronological order – a running record to be updated during the proceedings;
  - (b) information under the following headings:
    - (i) serial number;
    - (ii) date;
    - (iii) event-detail;
    - (iv) witness or document reference (where applicable);[32]
- letters before proceedings – meaning any letter from the local authority containing written notification to the parents and others with parental responsibility for the child of the local authority's plan to apply to court for a care or supervision order.[33]

3.14 The following documents are to be specifically prepared for the proceedings by the applicant (local authority):

---

[24] Where leave is required to disclose such previous orders/judgments preventing their filing at the outset, the MOJ Care Proceedings Reforms website indicates that local authorities should alert the court to the fact that there have been previous orders and summarise what happened in these cases and why they are relevant.

[25] 'Initial assessment' means the assessment undertaken by the local authority in accordance with *The Framework for the Assessment of Children in Need and their Families* (Department of Health, 2000) (the PLO Practice Direction, at para 25(20)). See **2.11** et seq.

[26] 'Core assessment' means the assessment undertaken by the local authority in accordance with *The Framework for the Assessment of Children in Need and their Families* (Department of Health, 2000) (the PLO Practice Direction, at para 25(13)). See **2.20** et seq.

[27] A 'report to the court on such matters relating to the welfare of that child as are required to be dealt with in the report' (Children Act 1989, s 7(1)).

[28] A report resulting 'where, in any family proceedings in which a question arises with respect to the welfare of any child, it appears to the court that it may be appropriate for a care or supervision order to be made with respect to [that child]' and the court directs the appropriate authority to undertake an investigation of the child's circumstances (Children Act 1989, s 37(1)).

[29] A key aspect of the reform package is to seek (wherever possible) to have relatives and friends assessed prior to proceedings, which may avoid the need for them. See **2.29** et seq.

[30] 'Genogram' means a family tree, setting out in diagrammatic form the family's background (the PLO Practice Direction, at para 25(18)).

[31] 'Strategy discussion record' means a note of the strategy discussion within the meaning of *Working Together to Safeguard Children* (2006) (the PLO Practice Direction, at para 25(37)).

[32] Ibid, at para 25(34).

[33] Ibid, at para 25(23).

- the Schedule of Proposed Findings – defined as the schedule of findings of fact prepared by the local authority sufficient to satisfy the threshold criteria under Children Act 1989, s 31(2), and to inform the care plan;[34]

- the Initial Social Work Statement – this is a statement prepared by the local authority strictly limited to the following evidence:
  (a) the precipitating incident(s) and background circumstances relevant to the grounds and reasons for making the application, including a brief description of any referral and assessment processes that have already occurred;
  (b) any facts and matters that are within the social worker's personal knowledge limited to the findings sought by the local authority;
  (c) any emergency steps and previous court orders that are relevant to the application;
  (d) any decisions made by the local authority that are relevant to the application;
  (e) information relevant to the ethnicity, language, religion, culture, gender and vulnerability of the child and other significant persons in the form of a 'family profile' together with a narrative description and details of the social care and other services that are relevant to the same;
  (f) where the local authority is applying for an interim order: the local authority's initial proposals for the child (which are also to be set out in the care plan) including placement, contact with parents and other significant persons and the social care services that are proposed;
  (g) the local authority's initial proposals for the further assessment of the parties during the proceedings including twin track/concurrent planning (where more than one permanence option for the child is being explored by the local authority);[35]

- the care plan;[36]

- the Allocation Record and Timetable for the Child.[37]

3.15 While the expectation is that the Checklist Documents will be filed at the outset, the PLO Practice Direction makes clear that the child's safety and welfare override any such procedural requirement. It expressly recognises that the absence of any or all of the Checklist Documents at the point of issue should not prohibit the commencement of proceedings if to do so would jeopardise the safety and welfare of the child concerned. There is also an acknowledgment that not all of the Checklist Documents may or even could exist. These matters are addressed in para 10.3 of the Practice Direction, which provides as follows:

> 'It is recognised that in some cases the circumstances are such that the safety and welfare of the child may be jeopardised if the start of proceedings is delayed until all of the documents appropriate to the case and referred to in the Pre-proceedings checklist are available. The court recognises that the preparation may need to be varied to suit the circumstances of the case. The court is likely to make directions relating to the preparation of any missing documentation at the start of the proceedings and at the First Appointment. The court also recognises that some documents on the Pre-proceedings checklist may not exist and may never exist, for example, the section 37 report, and that in urgent proceedings no Letter Before Proceedings may have been sent.'

---

34 Ibid, at para 25(31).
35 Ibid, at para 25(21).
36 Meaning a 'section 31A plan', as referred to in Children Act 1989, s 31A (ibid, at para 25(12)). Care plans are discussed at **5.107** et seq.
37 See **3.7** et seq.

Issue of proceedings

3.16 A number of steps are to be taken on day 1 of the proceedings consequent on the issue by the court officer of the application received that day.

3.17 Paragraph 11.3 of the PLO Practice Direction specifies that the court will at this very early stage consider allocation of the case and 'transfer those cases to the county court which are obviously suitable for immediate transfer'.[38]

3.18 Paragraph 11.4(1)(a) then provides for the court to give directions appropriate to the case including Standard Directions on Issue. These include those set out at Stage 1 of the PLO,[39] which are in turn set out in fuller fashion at paras 11.4–11.6 of the Practice Direction.

3.19 This involves the court:

- in care and supervision proceedings, considering giving directions relating to the preparation and filing of any Checklist Documents which are not yet available;[40]
- considering giving directions relating to the representation of any protected party and, where appropriate, inviting the Official Solicitor to act for a protected party or any child who is a party to, but is not the subject of, the proceedings and, where appropriate, inviting the Official Solicitor to act as his or her guardian ad litem;[41]
- appointing a Children's Guardian in specified proceedings[42] (in relation to care and supervision proceedings the court will expect that Cafcass or Cafcass Cymru will have received notice from the local authority that proceedings were going to be started);[43]
- appointing a solicitor for the child under Children Act 1989, s 41(3), where appropriate;[44]
- making arrangements for a contested hearing, if necessary;[45]
- setting a date for the First Appointment, normally no later than six days from the date of issue of the proceedings and in any event in line with the draft Timetable for the Child;[46]
- requesting the Children's Guardian or, if appropriate, another Cafcass officer or Welsh family proceedings officer to prepare a Case Analysis and Recommendations for the First Appointment.[47]

---

38 A case 'where there is evidence that a parent may be a protected party and require representation which currently cannot be obtained in the magistrates' court' is given as an example of a case of this kind.

39 The PLO Practice Direction, at para 25(36).

40 Ibid, at para 11.4(1)(b).

41 Ibid, at para 11.4(1)(c).

42 'Specified proceedings' are those assigned by Children Act 1989, s 41(6) (ibid, at para 25(35)).

43 Ibid, at para 11.4(2).

44 Ibid, at para 11.4(3). The MOJ Care Proceedings Reforms website adds: 'It is imperative that a solicitor is appointed to the child in good time for the first hearing. On day one the court should appoint a Children's Guardian. Cafcass/Cafcass Cymru will allocate the case and a Children's Guardian should appoint a solicitor on the child's behalf by day three. In cases where Cafcass/Cafcass Cymru are not in a position to do this, the court should appoint a solicitor for the child under section 41 of the Children Act 1989 and in accordance with the guidelines for courts for appointing a solicitor for the child in specified proceedings, April 2007. The court should follow the same procedure whether or not a court duty guardian scheme is in operation.'

45 The PLO Practice Direction, at para 11.4(5).

46 Ibid, at para 11.5.

47 Ibid, at para 11.4(4).

3.20 The 'Case Analysis and Recommendations' is a key component of the new procedure. It means a written or oral outline of the case from the child's perspective prepared by the Children's Guardian (or other Cafcass officer or Welsh family proceedings officer) at different stages of the proceedings, requested by the court, to provide:

(a) an analysis of the issues that need to be resolved in the case including:
   (i) any harm or risk of harm;
   (ii) the child's own views;
   (iii) the family context including advice relating to ethnicity, language, religion and culture of the child and other significant persons;
   (iv) the local authority work and proposed care plan;
   (v) advice about the court process including the Timetable for the Child; and
   (vi) identification of work that remains to be done for the child in the short and longer term; and

(b) recommendations for outcomes, in order to safeguard and promote the best interests of the child in the proceedings.[48]

3.21 Cafcass has a new Reporting to Court Policy that gives guidance on the completion of the 'Case Analysis and Recommendations' and provides templates for them.[49]

3.22 Paragraph 11.6 of the PLO Practice Direction provides that, in the magistrates' courts, the justices' clerk may nominate one but not more than two case managers.[50]

3.23 The issue part of Stage 1 of the PLO deals with two other matters. It is expected that a Children's Guardian will have been allocated by day 3 of the proceedings. Also by day 3, the local authority has to serve on the other parties the Application Form, the Supplementary Form PLO1 and the Checklist Documents.

3.24 A guideline Standard Directions Form (on Issue) Menu (Form PLO5) has been produced and is included within Appendix 2 to this book. It is to be used or adapted locally as practitioners and courts see fit.

The First Appointment

3.25 As para 12.1 of the PLO Practice Direction makes clear, there are two main objectives of the First Appointment:

(1) to confirm allocation; and

(2) to give initial case management directions having regard to the Public Law Outline.

3.26 A guideline Standard Directions Form (at First Appointment) Menu (Form PLO6) has been produced and is included within Appendix 2 to this book. As with Forms PLO4 and PLO5, it is to be used or adapted locally as practitioners and courts see fit.

---

48 Ibid, at para 25(8).

49 Summarised at **1.58** et seq. Set out in full at Appendix 6 to this book.

50 'Case Manager' means the justices' clerk or assistant justices' clerk who manages the case in the magistrates' courts (the PLO Practice Direction, at para 25(11)). 'Justices' clerk' has the meaning assigned to it by the Courts Act 2003, s 27(1) (ibid, at para 25(25)). 'Assistant justices' clerk' has the meaning assigned to it by the Courts Act 2003, s 27(5) (ibid, at para 25(6)).

3.27 Paragraph 12.3 of the Practice Direction particularises and fleshes out most of what is contained within the First Appointment part of Stage 1 of the PLO. It stipulates that the court will:

(1) confirm the Timetable for the Child;

(2) make arrangements for any contested interim hearing such as an application for an interim care order (and the PLO indicates that the other parties should by this point have notified the local authority and the court of the need for such a hearing);

(3) confirm the allocation of the case or, if appropriate, transfer the case;

(4) request the Children's Guardian or, if appropriate, another Cafcass officer or Welsh family proceedings officer to prepare a Case Analysis and Recommendations for the CMC or IRH;

(5) scrutinise the care plan;

(6) consider giving directions relating to:
  (a) those matters in the Public Law Outline which remain to be considered;
  (b) the joining of a person who would not otherwise be a respondent under the Rules[51] as a party to the proceedings;
  (c) where any person to be joined as a party may be a protected party, an investigation of that person's capacity to conduct the proceedings and the representation of that person, and if appropriate invite the Official Solicitor to act for that person;
  (d) the identification of family and friends as proposed carers and any overseas, immigration, jurisdiction and paternity issues;
  (e) in public law proceedings other than care and supervision proceedings, the documents to be filed with the court;
  (f) evidence to be obtained as to whether a parent who is a protected party is competent to make his or her own statement.

3.28 The matters within the First Appointment part of Stage 1 of the PLO which should be considered, but which are not specified within para 12.3, include the following matters:[52]

- a direction for the preparation of the Local Authority Case Summary;[53]
- a direction for the preparation of the Other Parties' Case Summaries;[54]
- a direction for the parties' initial witness statements;[55]
- a direction for the taking place of an advocates' meeting – para 12.6 of the Practice Direction provides that the court will consider directing a discussion between the parties' advocates and any litigant in person and the preparation of a Draft Case Management Order;[56]

---

51 Being the rules of court governing the practice and procedure to be followed in public law proceedings (ibid, at para 25(30)).

52 Within the PLO Table, standard directions on FA are stated to include these directions, together with the direction for the preparation of a Case Analysis and Recommendations for PLO Stages 2 and 3.

53 The contents of the Local Authority Case Summary are prescribed by the PLO Practice Direction, at para 25(24), and are set out at **3.33**.

54 The contents of the Other Parties' Case Summaries are indicated by the PLO Practice Direction, at para 25(27), and are set out at **3.34**.

55 Although not defined within the PLO Practice Direction, the initial witness statements of the parties presumably mean witness statements by parties other than the local authority and those children represented by a Children's Guardian in response to the local authority's initial social work statement.

56 See **3.46**.

- a direction listing the Case Management Conference (unless the case is suitable for an Early Final Hearing) – this will normally be no later than 45 days from the date of issue of the proceedings and will in any event be in line with the Timetable for the Child;[57]

- directions upon transfer.

Early Final Hearing cases

3.29 Although also not specified within para 12.3 of the Practice Direction, Stage 1 of the PLO requires the court to identify 'early Final Hearing' cases.

3.30 In the run-up to the finalisation of the Public Law Outline there was much concern as to what would constitute an 'early Final Hearing' case, the anxiety being that the court might make too early a judgment on the merits of the case. That anxiety has been largely laid to rest by para 12.4 of the Practice Direction, which provides as follows:

> 'Cases which are suitable for an early Final Hearing are likely to be those cases where the child has no parents, guardians, relatives who want to care for the child, or other carers. Examples are those cases where the child is an abandoned baby or where a child has been brought into this country and abandoned.'

3.31 Paragraph 12.4(1) and (2) of the Practice Direction provides that the court will identify at the First Appointment whether the case is one which is suitable for an early Final Hearing, and, if so, set a date for that Final Hearing.

The Local Authority and Other Parties' Case Summaries

3.32 Directions for the preparation of the Local Authority Case Summary and of the Other Parties' Case Summaries form part of the standard directions made by the court at First Appointment.

3.33 The 'Local Authority Case Summary' is a comprehensive document, covering 14 separate categories of information. It is a summary for each case management hearing in the form prescribed by Annex B to the Practice Direction[58] which must include the following information:

(a) the applications which have been issued in the current proceedings;

(b) any previous proceedings in relation to the child(ren) and any orders made in previous proceedings or in the current proceedings to which the child(ren) is/are subject;

(c) the present living arrangements for the child(ren) and arrangements for contact between the child(ren) and parent(s) or other relevant adult or child;

(d) a very brief summary of the incident(s) or circumstances giving rise to the application and of the background to the proceedings;

(e) a summary of any concerns the local authority may have about the mental capacity of an adult to care for the child or the capacity of the adult to prepare for the proceedings;

---

[57] PLO Practice Direction, at para 12.5.

[58] Although not known as such within the PLO Practice Directions itself, this form has separately been called Form PLO2.

(f) the key issues in the case;

(g) any agreements that there are as to the key issues or the findings of fact sought by the local authority;

(h) whether an application for placement for adoption is among the range of options that will have to be considered;

(i) any current or proposed proceedings (for example criminal proceedings, other family proceedings, disciplinary, immigration or mental capacity/health determinations) which are relevant to the determination of the application(s);

(j) the issues and directions which the court will need to consider at the CMC/IRH, including any interim orders sought;

(k) any steps which have not been taken or directions not complied with, an explanation of the reasons and the effect, if any, on the Timetable for the Child;

(l) a recommended reading list and suggested reading time;

(m) any additional information relevant to the Timetable for the Child or for the conduct of the hearing or the proceedings;

(n) the contact details of all advocates, their solicitors (where appropriate) and other significant persons (for example, the local authority key worker or team manager and the Children's Guardian).

3.34 'Other Parties' Case Summaries' means summaries by parties other than the local authority containing:

(a) the party's proposals for the long term future of the child (to include placement and contact);

(b) the party's reply to the local authority's Schedule of Proposed Findings;

(c) any proposal for assessment/expert evidence; and

(d) the names, addresses and contact details of any family or friends who it is suggested be approached in relation to long term care/contact or respite.

Early Consideration of Expert Evidence

3.35 Finally, within the context of Stage 1 of the PLO, the terms of para 12.7 of the PLO Practice Direction should be noted:

> 'A party who wishes to instruct an expert should comply with the Experts Practice Direction.[59] Where the parties are agreed on any matter relating to experts or expert evidence, the draft agreement must be submitted for the court's approval as early as possible in the proceedings.'

---

[59] Practice Direction: Experts in Family Proceedings Relating to Children. See Chapter 4 and Appendix 4 to this book.

3.36 In other words, while the provision of expert evidence is ordinarily a matter that will be dealt with by the court at the Case Management Conference, it is something that the court can, and indeed should, address at the First Appointment if the parties are at that point agreed on the issue.

STAGE 2 – THE CASE MANAGEMENT CONFERENCE

3.37 As will be apparent from the face of the PLO, there are two parts to Stage 2:

(1) the advocates' preparation for the Case Management Conference; and

(2) the Case Management Conference itself (abbreviated as before to the CMC),[60] which ought to take place no later than day 45 of the proceedings.

Advocates' discussions/meeting and the Draft Case Management Order

3.38 In terms of the former, while this part is represented within the PLO Table by the words 'advocates' meeting' (as was the case with the original draft PLO), it is suggested that this should be read subject to the terms of para 3.11 of the PLO Practice Direction, which provides as follows:

> 'The court will consider directing advocates to have discussions before the Case Management Conference and the Issues Resolution Hearing. Advocates may well find that the best way to have these discussions is to meet. Such discussion is intended to facilitate agreement and to narrow the issues for the court to consider. Advocates and litigants in person may take part in the advocates' meeting or discussions.'

3.39 'Advocate' is defined as 'a person exercising a right of audience as a representative of, or on behalf of, a party'.[61] Although not expressly stated within the PLO Practice Direction itself, the guidance that has accompanied its introduction has made clear that such advocates' discussions or meetings are limited to advocates, and therefore ought not to be attended, for example, by social workers or the Children's Guardian.[62] In cases involving counsel as well as a solicitor or legal executive, there would seem to be no bar to either or both being involved within the discussions or meeting. Indeed, given the common difficulty of finding a date to meet suitable for advocates on all sides, there is clearly a need for some degree of flexibility.

3.40 As para 13.1 of the Practice Direction makes clear, the main objective of the advocates' meeting or discussion is to prepare the Draft Case Management Order.

---

60 The PLO Practice Direction, at para 9.2(1).

61 Ibid, at para 25(3).

62 The MOJ Care Proceedings Reforms website provides the following rationale: 'As legal representatives the role of advocates at these meetings is to clarify and where possible, resolve issues in order to assist the court to manage the case in line with the PLO. This is a new and separate task and attendance of people who will not be making a case before the court may obscure the issues.During the course of preparing the necessary documentation for the court, the advocates should be fully instructed regarding their client's position in order to participate effectively in the meeting. They may also find it useful to ensure their clients are in a nearby room and/or can be contacted should further instructions be needed during the meeting itself. If professionals were to attend these meetings it may be seen as unfair to parents if they are the only people excluded (unless they are a litigant in person) or intimidating if they were there with the professionals.' If, however, the child has sought separate representation from the Children's Guardian, and the Children's Guardian no longer has legal representation, then the Children's Guardian is able to participate in the advocates meeting, as he or she 'would be in a position analogous to that of a litigant in person'.

3.41 As the PLO itself indicates, the secondary objective is to identify experts and draft questions for them.

3.42 Recognising that not every party to the proceedings may be legally represented, para 13.2 of the Practice Direction provides that, where there is a litigant in person, the court will consider the most effective way in which that person can be involved in the advocates' discussions and give directions as appropriate including directions relating to the part to be played by any McKenzie friend.[63]

3.43 Whereas, under the Protocol, it was permissible to have the advocates' meeting on the day of the Case Management Conference, up to an hour before it, there is a clear steer under the new PLO regime away from that form of case management.

3.44 Paragraph 13.3 of the Practice Direction makes clear that the timing of the advocates' discussions is of the utmost importance, and that the need for discussions outside the 'court room door' of matters which could have been discussed at an earlier time, is to be avoided. Discussions are to take place no later than two days before the CMC or the IRH (as the case may be), but may take place earlier than two days before those hearings, for example, up to seven days before them.

3.45 Those participating in the advocates' discussions are expected to consider the Case Summaries and Case Analysis and Recommendations that have been provided. Thereafter, and following discussion, the advocates are required to prepare or adjust the Draft Case Management Order, the intention being that the advocate for the applicant will take the lead in preparing and adjusting it following discussion with the other advocates.[64]

3.46 The 'Draft Case Management Order' means the draft case management document in the form of an order set out at Annex C to the Practice Direction.[65] As para 3.10 of the Practice Direction makes clear:

- the Draft form of Case Management Order is a special form of order containing terms of general application to be used as appropriate for each case;
- the form of order is not only to be used for drawing up orders in the form prescribed by the Rules at the end of a hearing, but is also to be used as a case management checklist;
- the form contains standard provisions designed to help parties, their legal representatives and the court:
  - identify the relevant issues and the procedural directions which may be required;
  - monitor changes to the relevant issues and compliance with the court's directions;
  - focus on what the proceedings are intended to achieve.

3.47 Stage 2 of the PLO indicates that the parties should notify the court in advance of the CMC of any need for a contested hearing, and this ought to be apparent from the face of the Draft Case Management Order.

---

63 A 'McKenzie friend' means any person permitted by the court to sit beside an unrepresented litigant in court to assist the litigant by prompting, taking notes and giving advice to the litigant (the PLO Practice Direction, at para 25(26). For a discussion of the McKenzie friend procedure and the terms of the President's new Guidance, see **5.62** et seq.

64 The PLO Practice Direction, at para 13.4.

65 Ibid, at para 25(16). Although not known as such within the PLO Practice Direction itself, it is separately called Form PLO3.

3.48 Where it is not possible for the advocates to agree the terms of the Draft Case Management Order, para 13.5 of the Practice Direction provides that the advocates should specify on the Draft Case Management Order, or on a separate document if more practicable, those provisions on which they agree and those on which they disagree.

3.49 Unless the court directs otherwise, the Draft Case Management Order must be filed with the court no later than 11am on the day before the CMC or the IRH (as the case may be).[66]

3.50 Recognising the secondary objective of the advocates' meeting or discussion before the CMC,[67] para 13.7 of the Practice Direction stipulates that the advocates participating in them should also try to agree the questions to be put to any proposed expert (whether jointly instructed or not) if not previously agreed. This provision entails an acknowledgement that, under the Experts Practice Direction,[68] the questions on which the proposed expert is to give an opinion are a crucial component of the expert directions which the court is required to consider at the CMC.

Case Management Conference

3.51 The Case Management Conference is the main hearing at which the court manages the case, and in consequence it has two main objectives:

(1) to identify key issues; and

(2) to give full case management directions.[69]

3.52 Paragraph 14.3 of the PLO Practice Direction provides for nine steps to be taken by the court at the Case Management Conference, and these include all those specified in Stage 2 of the PLO under the heading 'Detailed case management by the court'. The court is required to:

(1) review and confirm the Timetable for the Child;

(2) confirm the allocation or the transfer of the case;

(3) scrutinise the care plan;

(4) identify the key issues;

(5) identify the remaining case management issues;

(6) resolve remaining case management issues by reference to the Draft Case Management Order;

(7) identify any special measures such as the need for access for the disabled or provision for vulnerable witnesses;[70]

---

[66] The PLO Practice Direction, at para 13.6.
[67] See **3.41**.
[68] For a full discussion of the Experts Practice Direction, see Chapter 4.
[69] The PLO Practice Direction, at para 14.1.
[70] The issue of special measures is considered in depth at **5.201** et seq.

(8) scrutinise the Case Management Record[71] to check whether directions have been complied with and if not, consider making further directions as appropriate;

(9) where expert evidence is required, check whether the parties have complied with the Experts Practice Direction, in particular section 4 (Preparation for the relevant hearing)[72] and consider giving directions as appropriate.

3.53 Once in a position to do so, the court will issue the approved Case Management Order, and the parties or their legal representatives are expected to submit in electronic form the final approved Case Management Order on the conclusion of, and the same day as, the CMC.[73]

Further listing of hearings

3.54 Under para 14.5 of the PLO Practice Direction, the court is required:

(1) to set a date for the Issues Resolution Hearing, normally at any time between 16 and 25 weeks from the date of issue of the proceedings and in any event in line with the Timetable for the Child; and

(2) if necessary, specify a period within which the Final Hearing of the application is to take place unless a date has already been set.

3.55 The latter provision makes clear that, whatever may have been thought to be the position in respect of the draft PLO, the listing of the final hearing may take place before the Issues Resolution Hearing.[74]

3.56 Paragraph 16 of the Practice Direction provides that an advocate who has conduct of the Final Hearing should ordinarily attend the CMC. If that is not possible, then an advocate who is familiar with the issues in the proceedings should attend instead.

STAGE 3 – THE ISSUES RESOLUTION HEARING

3.57 As will similarly be apparent from the face of the PLO, there are two parts to Stage 3:

(1) the advocates' preparation for the Issues Resolution Hearing; and

(2) the Issues Resolution Hearing itself (abbreviated to the IRH),[75] which ought to take place between 16 and 25 weeks from the date of issue of the proceedings.

---

71 The 'Case Management Record' means the court's filing system for the case, which will include the following main documents: (1) the Supplementary Form PLO 1 which will be the index of documents on the Record; (2) in care and supervision proceedings, any Letter Before Proceedings and any related subsequent correspondence confirming the local authority's position to parents and others with parental responsibility for the child; (3) the Case Management Documentation; (4) Standard Directions on issue and on First Appointment; (5) the Draft Case Management Orders approved by the court (the PLO Practice Direction, at para 3.7).

72 See **4.58** et seq.

73 The PLO Practice Direction, at para 14.4.

74 One of the downsides of the Protocol was that the early listing requirement within it led in practice to a listing on a 'worst case scenario' basis (rather than on the basis of a reasonable time estimate) and to the consequent blocking of the court lists. The experience of the draft PLO in Liverpool was that, by listing the final hearing at the IRH, final hearings could be listed in around eight weeks from that point. Clearly individual courts will need to work out sensibly and flexibly what suits them and individual cases best.

75 The PLO Practice Direction, at para 9.2(3).

Advocates' preparation for the IRH

3.58 The terms of paras 3.11 and 13.1–13.6 of the Practice Direction[76] apply as much to the advocates' preparation for the IRH as they do to the advocates' preparation for the CMC.

3.59 Consistent with that proposition, the PLO itself identifies the objective of this part of Stage 3 as being to prepare or update the draft Case Management Order, with the parties required to undertake the following:

- to consider all other parties' Case Summaries and Case Analysis and Recommendations;
- to prepare/update the Draft Case Management Order;
- to notify the court of the need for a contested hearing/time for oral evidence to be given;
- to file the Draft Case Management Order with the case manager/case management judge by 11am one working day before the IRH.

Issues Resolution Hearing

3.60 The Issues Resolution Hearing is likely to be the last hearing before the Final Hearing, and in consequence final case management directions and other preparations for the Final Hearing will be made at this hearing.[77]

3.61 The objectives and purpose of the IRH are set out within paras 15.1 and 15.4 of the PLO Practice Directions.

3.62 The objectives are stated as being to:

(1) resolve and narrow issues;

(2) identify key remaining issues requiring resolution.[78]

3.63 Paragraph 15.4 then adds 'for the avoidance of doubt' that the purpose of an IRH is to:

(1) identify key issues which are not agreed;

(2) examine if those key issues can be agreed; and

(3) where those issues cannot be agreed, examine the most proportionate method of resolving those issues.

3.64 Following on from para 15.4(3), para 15.5 then provides as follows:

> 'The expectation is that the method of resolving the key issues which cannot be agreed will be at a hearing (ordinarily the Final hearing) where there is an opportunity for the relevant oral evidence to be heard and challenged.'

3.65 In terms of the steps to be taken by the court at the IRH in pursuance of its stated objectives, para 15.3 of the Practice Direction provides that the court will:

---

76 Considered above at **3.38** et seq.
77 The PLO Practice Direction, at para 15.2.
78 Ibid, at para 15.1.

(1) identify the key issues (if any) to be determined;

(2) review and confirm the Timetable for the Child;

(3) consider giving case management directions relating to:
   (a) any outstanding matter contained in the Draft Case Management Order;
   (b) the preparation and filing of final evidence including the filing of witness templates – consistent with the PLO itself, this should include the final local authority care plan(s) and an updated Case Analysis and Recommendations;
   (c) skeleton arguments;
   (d) preparation and filing of bundles in accordance with the Bundles Practice Direction;[79]
   (e) any agreement relating to the satisfaction of the threshold criteria under Children Act 1989, s 31, or facts and issues remaining to be determined in relation to it or to any welfare question which arises;
   (f) time estimates;
   (g) the judicial reading list and likely reading time and judgment writing time;

(4) issue the Case Management Order, which on its face should provide (if applicable) for the listing or conformation of the Final Hearing.

3.66 To those steps should be added the following two, apparent from the face of the PLO (which otherwise itemises the steps above) – scrutinising compliance with directions already given and scrutinising the care plan.

3.67 As with the CMC, para 16 of the Practice Direction provides that an advocate who has conduct of the Final Hearing should ordinarily attend the IRH. If that is not possible, then an advocate who is familiar with the issues in the proceedings should attend instead.

3.68 In the family proceedings court, the IRH will ordinarily be conducted by the legal adviser.[80]

STAGE 4 – FINAL HEARING

3.69 Although on the face of the PLO, the Final Hearing is simply referred to as 'Hearing', it is plain from the many references within the Practice Direction itself that what is meant and contemplated is a Final Hearing.

3.70 Unlike with the previous stages of the PLO, there is no supplementary section within the Practice Direction explaining or amplifying what occurs at Stage 4. Accordingly, it is to the PLO itself that attention must solely be given.

3.71 That provides that the final hearing should take place in accordance with the Timetable for the Child, and that the objective of this hearing is to determine the remaining issues within the proceedings. The following are then itemised:

- the obligation on the parties to file and serve updated case management documents and for the applicant to file the trial bundle;

---

[79] The Practice Direction (Family Proceedings: Court Bundles) (Universal Practice to be Applied in all Courts other than the Family Proceedings Court) of 27 July 2006 (ibid, at para 25(7)), to be found, as adjusted by this PLO Practice Direction at Appendix 5 to this book.

[80] The rationale for this approach is set out at Chapter 1, footnote 66.

- the drafting of the final order(s) in approved form;
- judgment/reasons;
- disclosure of documents as required after the hearing.[81]

[81] See **5.196** et seq.

CHAPTER FOUR

THE TREATMENT OF EXPERTS

4.1 The use – or more accurately over-use – of experts within public law children's cases has long been a major problem for the family justice system. Expert evidence is costly and its commissioning often contributes significantly to delays within proceedings.

4.2 In certain cases, especially those turning on medical evidence, the provision of expert evidence is absolutely essential to the fair resolution of the issues entailed. But in many others it is unnecessary, duplicating the expertise already available or simply reinforcing the opinions of other professionals involved, and at considerable price – not just in terms of time and cost, but also in terms of the value ascribed to the views of the professionals already within the proceedings. Indeed, such has been the courts' reliance on independent expert evidence that increasingly social workers and also Children's Guardians have themselves become over-reliant on such expert evidence to form their own opinions and inhibited from trusting and pushing their own judgements.[1]

4.3 The Practice Direction: Experts in Family Proceedings Relating to Children ('The Experts Practice Direction')[2] came into force on 1 April 2008. It is an essential component of the Public Law Outline scheme, providing comprehensive guidance on the instruction of experts, and superseding the Code of Guidance for Expert Witnesses in Family Proceedings[3] and the Practice Direction to Part 17 (Experts) of the Family Procedure (Adoption) Rules 2005.

4.4 The objectives of the Experts Practice Direction and of the PLO Practice Direction itself in this regard are clear. The intention is plainly to promote a more rigorous approach to the instruction of experts. Expert evidence should be necessary and proportionate, and, where commissioned, should be more focused and issue-driven. That in turn will lead to narrower disputes on expert evidence, with any such disputes being identified sooner rather than later within the process.

4.5 The content of the new Experts Practice Direction, insofar as it impacts on public law children's cases, provides the primary focus of this chapter. Where appropriate, the text has been supplemented by references to relevant case-law.

---

1 Particularly marked has been the greater prevalence of and court reliance on adult psychiatric and psychological opinions, a product largely of care proceedings having become more dynamic and future-orientated. It is striking to recall that, when the Children Act 1989 was born, the intention was that care proceedings would be completed within 12 weeks. However, rather than determining a case on the basis of the local authority's evidence and the parents' response to it, courts have tended to supervise the investigation of the family's ability to meet the child's needs and the assessment of alternative plans for the child. See further J Masson, J Pearce & K Bader with O Joyner, J Marsden & D Westlake *Care Profiling Study* (MOJ, March 2008).

2 Reproduced in full at Appendix 4 to this book.

3 Appendix C to the 2003 Protocol for Judicial Case Management in Public Law Children Act Cases.

THE COURTS' NEW APPROACH TO EXPERTS: GENERAL PRINCIPLES

4.6 There are a number of general principles underpinning the PLO Practice Direction which will dominate the court's approach to the instruction of experts. More rigorous control over the instruction of experts and the deployment of expert evidence is an explicit and important purpose of a number of its key concepts.

4.7 Firstly, the overriding objective requires the court to deal with cases 'justly, having regard to the welfare issues involved',[4] and provides further that such includes so far as is practicable:

(1) ensuring that the case is dealt with expeditiously and fairly;

(2) dealing with it in ways which are proportionate to the nature, importance and complexity of the issues;

(3) ensuring that the parties are on an equal footing;

(4) saving expense; and

(5) allotting to it an appropriate share of the court's resources, while taking into account the need to allot resources to other cases.

4.8 Secondly, it is a 'main principle' of the PLO Practice Direction that 'each case will be actively case managed by the court with a view at all times to furthering the overriding objective'.[5]

4.9 Thirdly, the first (and probably most important) case management tool is the Timetable for the Child. The instruction and deployment of any expert evidence will doubtless be as guided by the application of that case management tool as by any other step in the process.

4.10 Fourthly, active case management includes, amongst other things:

- 'deciding promptly which issues need full investigation and hearing and which do not';[6]
- 'considering whether the likely benefits of taking a particular step justify any delay which will result and the cost of taking it';[7] and
- (most importantly of all) 'controlling the use and cost of experts'.[8]

4.11 Fifthly, the Public Law Outline, as supported by its Practice Direction, is designed and drafted to promote 'issue-driven' litigation. One of the major purposes of it is to focus minds at an early stage upon the real issues in the case, and to direct resources towards the resolution of those issues.

---

4 The PLO Practice Direction, at para 2.1.
5 Ibid, at para 3.1(3).
6 Ibid, at para 3.15(6).
7 Ibid, at para 3.15(9).
8 Ibid, at para 3.15(13)(a).

4.12 Although many practitioners would argue that hitherto the instruction of experts has been issue-driven and focused, and determined with reference to the twin principles of necessity and proportionality, the conjunction of the PLO and Experts Practice Directions is likely to lead to more explicit concentration upon:

(1) identifying (with significant input from the court itself):
- what the issues are; and
- (given their importance) whether and to what extent expert evidence is likely to assist with their resolution, and, if so, how;

(2) whether the particular issues can be resolved by social work assessment or assessment by the Children's Guardian without reference to expertise external to the case; and

(3) whether and to what extent the instruction of an expert is reasonable, necessary and proportionate, having particular regard to the overriding objective and the case management tools.

4.13 The conjunction of the PLO and Experts Practice Directions will also produce:

(1) greater input from the court on the question of instructing an expert at all; and

(2) significant intervention from the court in deciding whether and to what extent and why it is necessary for an agreed medical expert opinion to be challenged.

THE EXPERTS PRACTICE DIRECTION: APPLICABILITY AND AIMS

4.14 The Experts Practice Direction applies in any 'family proceedings relating to children', including:[9]

- placement and adoption proceedings;
- family proceedings held in private which:
  - are brought under the Children Act 1989 in any family court, or
  - relate to the exercise of the inherent jurisdiction of the High Court with respect to children, or
  - are brought in the High Court or county court and otherwise relate wholly or mainly to the maintenance or upbringing of a minor.

4.15 The Practice Direction is therefore of wide application, covering all conceivable proceedings which have as their primary focus the welfare of children. As it recognises, at para 1.4, the guidance does not aim to cover all possible eventualities, but it 'should be complied with so far as consistent in all the circumstances with the just disposal of the matter'.

4.16 The aim of the Practice Direction is to provide the court with early information to determine whether an expert[10] or expert evidence will assist the court to:

- identify, narrow and where possible agree the issues between the parties;

---

9 The Experts Practice Direction, at para 1.2.

10 Any reference within the Experts Practice Direction to 'an expert' or 'the expert' includes a reference to an expert team (ibid, at para 1.1).

- provide an opinion about a question which is not within the skill or experience of the court;
- encourage the early identification of questions that need to be answered by an expert; and
- encourage disclosure of full and frank information between the parties, the court and any expert instructed.[11]

4.17 It is notable that, in expressing its aim, the Experts Practice Direction seems to intend the provision of a framework within which a court can decide whether expert evidence is necessary at all. That is a clear indication of one of the main purposes of the guidance: to focus the minds of the court and representatives on the necessity and proportionality of expert opinion in any particular case.

TIMING OF APPLICATIONS TO INSTRUCT EXPERTS

4.18 Applications for permission either to instruct an expert or to use expert evidence should be made at the earliest possible date, and in public law proceedings under the Children Act 1989 no later than the Case Management Conference (being the 'relevant hearing' for this purpose).[12]

4.19 In considering whether expert evidence is necessary, and, if so, when to make an application to instruct an expert, courts and practitioners will inevitably have to have in mind the Timetable for the Child. In many cases, this may mean having to raise the issue of expert evidence before the CMC or listing the CMC much sooner than the limit of day 45 of the proceedings.[13]

GENERAL AND PRELIMINARY MATTERS

4.20 The following topics are covered under this heading:

- expert evidence obtained pre-proceedings;
- emergencies; and
- capacity issues.

Expert evidence obtained pre-proceedings

4.21 Local authorities will occasionally commission expert opinion prior to the issue of proceedings, as part of pre-proceedings preparation and/or as part of the core assessment. In such circumstances, the relevant expert should consider themselves bound by the provisions of the guidance and must always be commissioned by a letter of instruction drafted in accordance with it.[14]

---

11 Ibid, at para 1.3

12 Ibid, at para 1.9. The 'relevant hearing' in private law proceedings is the First Hearing Dispute Resolution Appointment, and, in placement and adoption proceedings, the First Directions Hearing.

13 The PLO stipulates that this is the latest day for the CMC to take place.

14 The Experts Practice Direction, at para 2.3.

4.22 There are a number of situations in which local authorities in particular will find themselves in possession of expert reports prior to the commencement of proceedings. These will include the following scenarios:

- where children have been treated by an expert, either therapeutically or as part of some medical intervention, possibly over a number of years or as an emergency;
- where local authorities have instructed a particular expert to undertake a particular type of work with a family – for example, work on parenting skills or child protection issues;
- where an expert has been commissioned to assess some aspect of family functioning.

4.23 There will also be a number of reasons why expert reports will have been produced, and it will not always be the case that such reports have been 'commissioned'. For example, reports from experts treating a child might be produced, not primarily for use in court but simply to provide feedback or information to social workers and authorities, whilst reports might also be produced for the purposes of a child's medical records.[15]

4.24 The question inevitably arises as to whether the Experts Practice Direction guidance applies to the pre-proceedings evidence of any expert, on any issue, howsoever the evidence was obtained.

4.25 There is an important distinction to be drawn here between treating experts and forensic experts, which is not just confined to the pre-proceedings phase. The therapeutic role of an expert who is treating a child should not be muddled with the role of an expert providing a forensic report, particularly where that treatment is of a psychological or psychiatric nature.[16] The court should be astute to analyse the different purposes for which treating and forensic experts give their reports and weigh the relative cogency of the reports in accordance with that analysis.[17]

4.26 However, treating experts often provide the court with essential clinical, contemporaneous material about the precipitating circumstances of a case:

> 'They are and should be the first port of call for the local authority when it needs to commission specialist assessments and reports to inform its knowledge of the background and precipitating circumstances and its core assessment. They are often called upon by the court to provide such materials when, for whatever reason, they are missing from the proceedings.'[18]

4.27 For that reason, treating experts should not be dissuaded from providing opinion and evidence to the court; but it is essential that they are fully involved in the whole process and properly instructed to provide their evidence within the parameters of the relevant guidance.[19]

4.28 It is suggested that, where a local authority commissions a report from an expert (whether treating or otherwise) prior to the commencement of proceedings, and that expert is invited to express an opinion on the issues which might be relied upon in any later proceedings, the Experts Practice Direction should apply with full effect.

---

15 Such as a report from a consultant paediatrician to a child's General Practitioner.

16 *Re B (Sexual Abuse: Expert's Report)* [2000] 1 FLR 871.

17 See *Oldham Metropolitan Borough Council v GW and PW* [2007] EWHC 136 (Fam), [2007] 2 FLR 597, at paras [96]–[98].

18 Ibid, at para [98].

19 See also *Oxfordshire County Council v DP, RS and BS* [2005] EWHC 2156 (Fam) (as yet unreported), at paras [104]–[107].

4.29 It is further suggested that, if a local authority comes into possession of a report without commissioning it, then the Practice Direction should apply with full effect at and from the point when reliance is sought to be placed upon any opinion expressed within it by any of the parties to the case (for whatever purpose). At that point the expert should be treated as an 'expert' for all purposes and should be invited to provide their opinion in accordance with the guidance.[20]

Emergencies

4.30 A party seeking to adduce expert evidence in emergencies, where there is a sudden and unforeseen need for expert evidence, need not comply with the Experts Practice Direction. In those circumstances, an urgent application should be made to court for further directions.[21]

Capacity Issues

4.31 Paragraphs 2.6–2.9 and 2.10 of the Experts Practice Direction, which are in terms identical to those set out in paras 7 and 8 of the PLO Practice Direction, provide as follows:

- The court will investigate as soon as possible any issue as to whether an adult party or intended party to the proceedings lacks capacity (within the meaning of the Mental Capacity Act 2005) to conduct the proceedings.[22]
- An adult who lacks capacity to conduct the proceedings is a protected party and must have a representative (a litigation friend, next friend or guardian ad litem) to conduct the proceedings on his or her behalf.[23]
- Any issue as to the capacity of an adult to conduct the proceedings must be determined before the court gives any directions relevant to that adult's role in the proceedings.[24]
- Where the adult is a protected party, his or her representative should be involved in any instruction of an expert, including the instruction of an expert to assess whether the adult, although a protected party, is competent to give evidence.[25]
- If at any time during the proceedings, there is reason to believe that a party may lack capacity to conduct the proceedings, then the court must be notified and directions sought to ensure that this issue is investigated without delay.[26]
- Where it appears that a child is a party to the proceedings and not the subject of them, nearing his or her eighteenth birthday, and considered likely to lack capacity to conduct the

---

20 Ibid, at paras [104]–[107].
21 The Experts Practice Direction, at para 2.4.
22 Ibid, at para 2.6.
23 Ibid, at para 2.6.
24 Ibid, at para 2.7.
25 Ibid, at para 2.8, which recognises that the instruction of an expert is a significant step in the proceedings and adds that the representative will wish to consider (and ask the expert to consider), if the protected party is competent to give evidence, their best interests in this regard, may wish to seek advice about 'special measures' and may put forward an argument on behalf of the protected party that the protected party should not give evidence (which argument will presumably depend upon the expert opinion obtained). It is not without interest that the guidance plainly envisages circumstances in which a 'protected party' might nevertheless be expected to give oral evidence. As a matter of practice, once a certificate of incapacity is obtained in relation to a party, it is extremely unusual for anyone to expect that party to give evidence. The new guidance seems to anticipate a shift in emphasis here, and invites representatives always to consider (with expert opinion) competence to give evidence with and without special measures. For a discussion of special measures, see **5.201** et seq.
26 Ibid, at para 2.9.

proceedings when he or she reaches 18, the court will consider giving directions relating to the investigation of a child's capacity in this respect.[27]

THE DUTIES OF EXPERTS

4.32 The Experts Practice Direction defines the duties of experts, as court-appointed experts and in the compilation of their reports.

Overriding and Particular Duties

4.33 The overriding duty of an expert in family proceedings relating to children is owed to the court and takes precedence over any obligation to the person instructing or paying that expert.[28]

4.34 Additionally, the expert has a number of particular duties:[29]

- to assist the court in accordance with the overriding duty;
- to provide advice to the court that conforms to the best practice of the expert's profession;
- to provide an independent opinion;
- to confine the opinion to matters material to the issues between the parties and within the expert's expertise;
- where a question has been put which falls outside the expert's expertise, to state this at the earliest opportunity and to volunteer an opinion as to whether another expert is required to bring expertise not possessed by those already involved or ('in the rare case') as to whether a second opinion is required on a key issue and, if possible, what questions should be asked of the second expert;
- in expressing an opinion, to take into consideration all of the material facts (including any relevant factors arising from ethnic, cultural, religious or linguistic contexts);
- to inform those instructing the expert without delay of any change in the opinion and of the reason for the change.

4.35 There is nothing particularly new about these duties, which amount to an amalgam of previous and long-standing good practice and recent case-law.[30]

---

27 Ibid, at para 2.10.

28 Ibid, at para 3.1. This provision mirrors that contained within appendix C to the Protocol. In *Re J (Application for a Shadow Expert)* [2008] Fam Law 406, HHJ Anthony Hughes, sitting as a Judge of the Family Division, rejected as being inconsistent with the expert's overriding duty to the court an application made by the father (against whom findings of NAHI were sought) for permission to instruct a 'shadow expert' (a paediatric neuro-radiologist) to obtain assistance in analysing the existing expert evidence, to receive guidance on framing questions for cross-examination, and to allow the shadow expert to have anonymity so that he would be protected from being called to give oral evidence or prepare a report. Permission to appeal in respect of this novel point was given but not pursued.

29 Ibid, at para 3.2.

30 See in particular *Oldham MBC v GW and PW* (above).

The contents of the expert's report

4.36 The content of the expert's report is dealt with in detail at para 3.3 of the new guidance.

General matters

4.37 The report must be prepared and filed in accordance with the court's timetable,[31] and should:

- include details of the expert's qualifications and experience;[32]
- contain a statement setting out the substance of the expert's instructions (whether written or oral), summarising the facts stated and instructions given which are material to the conclusions and opinions expressed in their report;[33]
- make clear which of the facts stated in the report are within the expert's own knowledge;[34]
- state the identity and qualifications of any person carrying out any test, examination or interview which the expert has used for the report and indicate whether such has been carried out under the expert's supervision;[35]
- contain a summary of the expert's conclusions and opinions;[36]
- contain a statement that the expert understands his or her duty to the court and has complied and will continue to comply with that duty;[37]
- contain a 'conflict of interest' statement;[38]
- be verified by a statement of truth.[39]

Issues of disclosure and source material

4.38 The expert's report should also:

- identify materials that have not been produced either as original medical or other professional records or in response to an instruction from a party;[40]

---

31 The Experts Practice Direction, at para 3.3.
32 Ibid, at para 3.3(1).
33 Ibid, at para 3.3(2).
34 Ibid, at para 3.3(5).
35 Ibid, at para 3.3(6)–(7).
36 Ibid, at para 3.3(10).
37 Ibid, at para 3.3(11).
38 Ibid, at para 3.3(12) – a statement that the expert: (a) has no conflict of interest of any kind, other than any conflict disclosed in his or her report; (b) does not consider that any interest disclosed affects his or her suitability as an expert witness on any issue on which he or she has given evidence; and (c) will advise the instructing party if, between the date of the expert's report and the final hearing, there is any change in circumstances which affects the expert's answers to (a) or (b).
39 Ibid, at para 3.3(13) – the statement should be in the following form: 'I confirm that insofar as the facts stated in my report are within my own knowledge I have made clear which they are and I believe them to be true, and that the opinions I have expressed represent my true and complete professional opinion.'
40 Ibid, at para 3.3(3), which explains that this is because such materials may contain an assumption as to the standard of proof, the admissibility or otherwise of hearsay evidence, and other important procedural and substantive questions relating to the different purposes of other enquiries (for example, criminal or disciplinary proceedings).

- identify all requests to third parties for disclosure and their responses.[41]

4.39 These provisions are a direct reflection of the case-law.[42] They are also a response to the requirement, imposed in particular by ECHR,[43] Art 6, that parties to the instruction of experts should be able to participate effectively in the process by which the report is produced.[44]

4.40 Self-evidently, if an opinion is expressed on the basis of partial disclosure, or material about which any party has no knowledge, the ability to participate effectively in the process by which a report is produced and an opinion formed is fundamentally undermined.

Expression of opinion

4.41 Furthermore, the expert report should, in expressing an opinion to the court:

- take into consideration all of the material facts including any relevant factors arising from ethnic, cultural, religious or linguistic contexts at the time the opinion is expressed, identifying the facts, literature and any other material including research material that the expert has relied upon in forming an opinion;
- describe their own professional risk assessment process and process of differential diagnosis, highlighting factual assumptions, deductions from the factual assumptions, and any unusual, contradictory or inconsistent features of the case;
- highlight whether a proposition is an hypothesis (in particular a controversial hypothesis), or an opinion deduced in accordance with peer-reviewed and tested technique, research and experience accepted as a consensus in the scientific community;
- indicate whether the opinion is provisional (or qualified, as the case may be), stating the qualification and the reason for it, and identifying what further information is required to give an opinion without qualification.[45]

4.42 This again is a direct reflection of guidance provided in recent case-law.[46]

---

41 Ibid, at para 3.3(4), which indicates that this is 'in order to avoid partial disclosure which tends only to prove a case rather than give full and frank information'.

42 See *Oldham MBC v GW and PW* (above).

43 European Convention for the Protection of Human Rights and Fundamental Freedoms, as incorporated into domestic law by the Human Rights Act 1998.

44 See *Mantovanelli v France (Application No 21497/93)* (1997) 24 EHRR 370. In *Re L (Care: Assessment: Fair Trial)* [2002] EWHC 1379 (Fam), 2 FLR 730, particularly at para [113], Munby J held that, where an expert's report (whether instructed jointly or solely) is likely to have a preponderant influence on the court's assessment, there may be a breach of Art 6 if a litigant is denied the opportunity, before the expert produces the report, to examine and comment on the documents being considered by the expert, and cross-examine witnesses interviewed by the expert and on whose evidence the report is based. His comments must, however, be viewed in light of the subsequent Court of Appeal decision in *Re V (Care: Pre-Birth Actions)* [2004] EWCA Civ 1575, [2005] 1 FLR 627. In determining whether or not there has been an Art 6 breach, the court had to ascertain whether the proceedings, taken as a whole, were fair and it was manifestly impermissible to isolate one alleged incident and use it as a basis for a finding that there had been a breach of Art 6 rights. Trial judges should be extremely cautious in reading too much into the judgment in *Re L*, which was merely intended to draw attention to certain principles of practice that deserved emphasis.

45 The Experts Practice Direction, at para 3.3(8).

46 See *Oldham MBC v GW and PW* (above), at para [90]. In *Re AB (Child Abuse: Expert Witnesses)* [1995] 1 FLR 181, Wall J (as he then was) held that, where an expert advances an hypothesis to explain a given set of facts, he owes a very heavy duty to explain to the court that what he is advancing is an hypothesis, that it is controversial (if it is) and to place before the court all the material which contradicts the hypothesis; that the expert must make available to the other experts in the case all material upon which he has relied; and that, where the medical evidence points overwhelmingly to non-accidental injury, an expert advancing an innocent explanation has a heavy duty to ensure that he has considered the available material carefully and is expressing an objectively justifiable opinion.

4.43 This part of the Experts Practice Direction is designed not only to guard against the under-reasoned innocent explanation. It is also crucial to ensure that, where there is complete unanimity about an abusive aetiology, the court and the parties are in a position objectively to analyse the basis of that opinion and to engage effectively in the process described by Stuart-Smith LJ in *Loveday v Renton*:[47]

> 'In reaching my decision a number of processes have to be undertaken. The mere expression of opinion or belief by a witness, however eminent, ... does not suffice. The court has to evaluate the witness and soundness of his opinion. Most importantly this involves an examination of the reasons given for his opinions and the extent to which they are supported by the evidence. The judge also has to decide what weight to attach to a witness's opinion by examining the internal consistency and logic of his evidence; his precision and accuracy of thought as demonstrated by his answers; how he responds to searching and informed cross-examination and in particular the extent to which a witness faces up to and accepts the logic and proposition put in cross-examination or is prepared to concede points that are seen to be correct; the extent to which a witness has conceived an opinion and is reluctant to re-examine it in light of later evidence, or demonstrates a flexibility of mind which may involve changing or modifying opinions previously held; whether or not a witness is biased or lacks independence.'

4.44 Without some clearly ascertainable indication of the processes of reasoning and deduction which have led an expert to reach a particular conclusion, the ability of the court and the parties to examine and evaluate the soundness of that conclusion is fundamentally undermined. The purpose of this particular part of the guidance is therefore to ensure that reasoning processes and deductions are transparent and susceptible to forensic examination.

The nature of the opinion

4.45 In many cases, experts are likely to be expressing an opinion which arises in the context of a range of possible opinions. Where there is a range of opinion on any question to be answered by the expert, the Experts Practice Direction provides that the expert report must:

- summarise the range of opinion;
- highlight and analyse within the range of opinion an 'unknown cause', whether on the facts of the case (for example, there is too little information to form a scientific opinion) or because of limited experience, lack of research, peer review or support in the field of expertise which the expert professes;
- give reasons for any opinion expressed, the guidance indicating that 'the use of a balance sheet approach to the factors that support or undermine an opinion can be of great assistance to the court'.[48]

4.46 Again, some transparent analysis of the range of opinion from which a particular one is drawn, and the reasons for its selection, is essential to facilitate the forensic process by which courts evaluate expert opinions.

4.47 In this context, the guidance of Charles J in *A County Council v K, D and L*[49] is of particular importance. Rather than medical experts expressing a view as to the cause of the relevant death, injuries or harm on the balance of probabilities, he felt that it would be preferable if they were asked to:

---

[47] [1990] 1 Med LR 117 at p 125.

[48] The Experts Practice Direction, at para 3.3(9).

[49] [2005] EWHC 144 (Fam), [2005] 1 FLR 851, at para [89].

(1) identify possible causes of the relevant death, injuries or harm, setting out in respect of each the reasons why it might be a cause and thus why it should be considered;

(2) state their views as to the likelihood of each possibility being the cause of the relevant death, injuries or harm and the reasons why they include or reject it as a reasonable (as opposed to a fanciful or merely theoretical) possible cause;

(3) compare the likelihood of the cause (or causes) identified as reasonable possibilities being the actual cause of the relevant death, injuries or harm;

(4) state whether they consider that a cause (or causes) is (are) the most likely cause (or causes) of the relevant death, injuries or harm and their reasons for that view; and

(5) state whether they consider that a cause (or causes) is (are) more likely than not to be the cause (or causes) of the relevant death, injuries or harm and their reasons for that view.

4.48 Such an approach, Charles J felt, would:

(a) assist all involved,

(b) better reflect the roles of the expert and the judge, and

(c) demonstrate that the expert is not the decision-maker as to whether the relevant death, injuries or harm is the result of non-accidental human agency and whether the threshold is satisfied, and does not have all the relevant information.

4.49 Espousing the balance sheet approach and guarding against too great a focus on reaching agreed solutions to difficult problems, the guidance of Ryder J in *Oldham Metropolitan Borough Council v GW and PW*[50] is of equal importance:[51]

> '[E]xperts should be asked not only whether their opinion is mainstream or orthodox (as they were in this case) and what the range of orthodox opinions might be, but also whether within that range of opinions the answer might be that the cause of an injury is unknown, highlighting the unusual features of the case that may indicate contrary interpretations. In essence, they should take the court through the differential diagnosis highlighting any contradictory or inconsistent features. This balance sheet approach is used in many expert disciplines and areas of litigation and is almost universally of assistance. The court and experts generally may have become too focused in trying to reach agreed solutions to difficult problems. Experts are asked to inform the court of their agreements and their disagreements: the latter can often be as important as the former.'

The differing functions of experts and court

4.50 Paragraphs 3.3(8) and 3.3(9) of the Experts Practice Direction are focused upon how expert opinions should be expressed in reports. That focus is aimed not only at encouraging the expression of expert opinion in a way which is of optimum assistance to the forensic analytical process, but also in a way which reduces the danger of confusion between the respective roles of judge and expert.

4.51 As explained by Thorpe LJ in *Re B (Non-Accidental injury)*,[52] an expert opinion to the effect that an injury was probably inflicted, or that the cause of a particular problem was probably poor parental care, is not to be equated with a finding of either on the balance of probabilities. A

---

50 Above.
51 Above, at para [83].
52 [2002] EWCA Civ 752, [2002] 2 FLR 1133, particularly at para [17].

medical opinion is just that, bounded by medical convention and scientific language: the court's very different task is to decide whether an allegation is made out to the requisite standard of proof and within the meaning of the Children Act 1989, s 31.

4.52 Per Ward LJ in *Re B (Care: Expert witnesses)*:[53]

> 'The court invariably needs and invariably depends upon the help it receives from experts in this field . . .. The expert advises, but the judge decides. The judge decides on the evidence.'

4.53 The expert evidence is one (albeit important) component of the overall evidential jigsaw, within which the court decides whether a particular allegation is made out on the balance of probabilities.[54] The court invariably surveys a wide canvas, which includes a detailed history of the parents' lives, their relationship and their interaction with professionals, with many contributions to this context – family members, neighbours, health records, as well as the observation of professionals such as social workers, health visitors and the Children's Guardian.[55] It is within the context of that 'wide canvas' of evidence from various sources that any expert opinion, and its cogency, falls to be considered.

4.54 Assessing the credibility of lay witnesses is the function of the court.[56] Expert evidence as to the propensity of any lay party to cause harm to a child will not normally be admissible during any causation hearing, and should not be obtained unless on the facts of a particular case that opinion is directly relevant or likely to be directly relevant to the factual issue to be tried.[57] Courts should not rely on psychological personality tests when assessing credibility save in exceptional circumstances and where the conclusions of those tests had been validated by other evidence in the case.[58]

Rejecting or departing from expert evidence

4.55 It is accordingly open to the court to come to a conclusion which is contrary to a body of expert evidence, where the evidence in a case permits it and subject to the need for the court to give reasons.[59] Where the expert evidence indicates a number of possible causes of harm, it is open to the court to find either that the cause identified by the expert as the most likely cause has not been proved, or that one of the causes identified by the expert as possible but not likely is in fact the most likely cause.[60] In those circumstances, the court is not rejecting that expert's evidence, but reaching conclusions with a changed emphasis.

4.56 Nevertheless, where the expert evidence is capable of logical analysis and has withstood the rigours of the forensic process, and where the expert evidence reaches a clear conclusion that

---

53 [1996] 1 FLR 667, at p 670.

54 Ibid, per Butler Sloss LJ at p 674. See also the dicta of Bracewell J in *Re A (A minor) (Retinal Haemorrhages: Non-accidental injury)* [2001] 3 FCR 262, at para [10]: 'Although the medical evidence is of very great importance it is not the only evidence in the case. Explanations given by carers and the credibility of those involved with the child concerned are of great significance. All the evidence, both medical and non-medical, has to be considered in assessing whether the pieces of the jigsaw form into a clear, convincing picture of what happened.'

55 *Re U (Serious Injury: Standard of Proof); Re B* [2004] EWCA Civ 567, [2004] 2 FLR 263, particularly at para [26].

56 *A County Council v K, D and L* (above); *A County Council v A Mother, A Father, X, Y and Z (By Their Guardian)* [2005] EWHC 31 (Fam), [2005] 2 FLR 129.

57 Per Wall J (as then was) in *Re CB and JB (Care Proceedings: Guidelines)* [1998] 2 FLR 211, at pp 217–219; see also *Re U; Re B* (above), at paras [146]–[147].

58 *Re S (Care: Parenting Skills: Personality Tests)* [2004] EWCA Civ 1029, [2005] 2 FLR 658.

59 *Re B (Care: Expert Witnesses)* [1996] 1 FLR 667; *Re J (Expert Evidence: Hearsay)* [1999] 2 FLR 661.

60 See *A County Council v K, D and L* (above).

a particular cause is overwhelmingly likely to be the cause of harm, a court is not entitled to reject that opinion on the basis of the credibility of the lay witnesses alone. Per Butler-Sloss LJ in *Re B (Split Hearing: Jurisdiction)*:[61]

> 'The credibility or otherwise of the lay witnesses on the facts of the case… cannot stand so high as to make the evidence of the two consultant radiologists of no effect.'

4.57 Where experts disagree, with one opinion declining to exclude a reasonable possibility of natural causes for the alleged harm, particular caution is necessary.[62] Notwithstanding disagreement between the experts, it remains the responsibility of the court to scrutinise the evidence and reach a decision on the evidence: in so doing, the court is entitled to prefer the evidence of one expert to another as long as it gives reasons for doing so.[63] Per Ryder J in *Oldham Metropolitan Borough Council v GW and PW*:[64]

> 'Agreements and disagreements have to be scrutinised for what they are: an exercise in skilled and pragmatic deductive reasoning, not a substitute for the court's duty to make its own decision.'

PREPARATION FOR THE RELEVANT HEARING

4.58 The requirements to make early and appropriate preliminary enquiries of the proposed expert and to obtain suitable confirmation from that expert are dealt with at paras 4.1–4.2 of the Experts Practice Direction.

Preliminary enquiries of the expert

4.59 In good time for the information requested to be available for the relevant hearing or for the preceding advocates' meeting or discussion, the solicitor for the party proposing to instruct the expert[65] shall approach the expert with the following information:

- the nature of the proceedings and the issues likely to require determination by the court;
- the questions about which the expert is to be asked to give an opinion (including any ethnic, cultural, religious or linguistic contexts);
- the date when the court is to be asked to give permission for the instruction (or if, unusually, permission has already been given, the date and details of that permission);
- whether permission is to be asked of the court for the instruction of another expert in the same or any related field (that is, to give an opinion on the same or related questions);
- the volume of reading which the expert will need to undertake;
- whether or not permission has been applied for or given for the expert to examine the child;

---

61 [2000] 1 FLR 334, at p 339. Cited with approval by the Court of Appeal in *Re B (Non-Accidental Injury: Compelling Medical Evidence)* [2002] EWCA Civ 902, [2002] 2 FLR 599.

62 *Re U; Re B* (above), at para [23].

63 *Re J (Expert Evidence: Hearsay)* (above); *Re U; Re B* (above); *A Local Authority v S, W and T (by his Guardian)* [2004] EWHC 1270 (Fam), [2004] 2 FLR 129; *Oldham MBC v GW and PW* (above).

64 Above, at para [95].

65 Or the lead solicitor or solicitor for the child if the instruction proposed is joint.

- whether or not it will be necessary for the expert to conduct interviews, and, if so, with whom;
- the likely timetable of legal and social work steps;
- when the expert's report is likely to be required;
- whether and, if so, what date has been fixed by the court for any hearing at which the expert may be required to give evidence (in particular the Final Hearing).[66]

4.60 The obvious purpose of these preliminary enquiries is to identify at an early stage availability and other logistical issues, but more importantly the nature and range of the issues to which the evidence should be addressed. The guidance specifically emphasises the need for co-ordination between the court and expert in drawing up the case management timetable, so that a balance can be struck between the needs of the court and the other professional duties of the expert. It also indicates that the expert should be informed at this stage of the possibility of making, through his or her instructing solicitor, representations to the court about being named or otherwise identified in any public judgment given by the court.[67]

Expert's response to preliminary enquiries

4.61 It is the responsibility of the solicitors intending to instruct the expert to obtain, in good time for the relevant hearing or preceding advocates' meeting or discussion, confirmation from the expert:

- that acceptance of the proposed instructions will not involve the expert in any conflict of interest;
- that the work required is within the expert's expertise;
- that the expert is available to do the relevant work within the suggested timescale;
- when the expert is available to give evidence, of the dates and times to avoid and, where a hearing date has not been fixed, of the amount of notice the expert will require to make arrangements to come to court (or to give evidence by video link) without undue disruption to his or her normal professional routines;
- of the cost, including hourly or other charging rates, and likely hours to be spent, attending experts' meetings, attending court and writing the report (to include any examinations and interviews);
- of any representations which the expert wishes to make to the court about being named or otherwise identified in any public judgment given by the court.[68]

4.62 Where the parties cannot agree upon the identity of experts, this information is to be sought of each of the contenders.

---

66 The Experts Practice Direction, at para 4.1.

67 Ibid, at para 4.1.

68 Ibid, at para 4.2. The provision of such information will obviously depend upon the co-operation from the expert involved, and a lack of such co-operation ought not to be the responsibility of the solicitor seeking it.

The proposal to instruct an expert

4.63 By 11am on the business day before the relevant hearing, the party seeking permission to instruct an expert has to file and serve a proposal to instruct the expert containing the following details:

- the name, discipline, qualifications and expertise of the expert (by way of CV where possible);
- the expert's availability to undertake the work;
- the relevance of the expert evidence sought to be adduced to the issues in the proceedings and the specific questions upon which it is proposed that the expert should give an opinion (including the relevance of any ethnic, cultural, religious or linguistic contexts);
- the timetable for the report;
- the responsibility for instruction;
- whether or not the expert evidence can properly be obtained by the joint instruction of the expert by two or more of the parties;
- whether the expert evidence can properly be obtained by only one party (for example, on behalf of the child);
- why the expert evidence proposed cannot be given by social services undertaking a core assessment or by the Children's Guardian in accordance with their respective statutory duties;
- the likely cost of the report on an hourly or other charging basis: where possible, the expert's terms of instruction should be made available to the court;
- the proposed apportionment (at least in the first instance) of any jointly instructed expert's fee; when it is to be paid; and, if applicable, whether public funding has been approved.[69]

4.64 This part of the guidance seeks to promote the primary aim of ensuring that expert evidence is necessary, reasonable and proportionate in any particular case, having careful regard to the range and nature of the issues in dispute.

4.65 In particular, it requires the party seeking to instruct an expert to identify, prior to the instruction itself, the questions to be asked of any expert and their relevance to the forensic issues in the case.

4.66 Importantly, it also makes the parties address their minds to the expertise already available within the proceedings before assuming that further expert evidence is required.[70]

---

[69] Ibid, at para 4.3.

[70] By way of example, expert evidence has in the past been obtained on issues of attachment or placement. Yet, in many cases, the social workers and/or Children's Guardian will be more than equipped to address these questions.

Joint instruction of experts

4.67 In general, it is preferable for one expert to be instructed by all the parties to provide an opinion for the assistance of the court.[71] Although there may be circumstances in which the court gives permission for one of the parties to instruct another expert for a second opinion,[72] parties will not routinely be permitted unilaterally to instruct experts at the outset of proceedings in addition to those already jointly instructed to provide expert opinion in the case.[73]

4.68 It is wholly inappropriate for a party unilaterally to instruct an expert without the knowledge of the court and the other parties. Experts should not accept instructions unless they have received permission from the court to accept them and know the terms of the court order pursuant to which their instruction has been permitted.[74]

Sharing the cost

4.69 In *Calderdale MBC v S and the Legal Services Commission*,[75] Bodey J held that, as a general rule, the approach of sharing the costs of all joint expert reports between all parties was to be preferred to the 'moiety' approach proposed by the Legal Services Commission (in that case, a moiety of 50% and 50% to be paid for by the local authority). In giving judgment, he identified the following considerations for a court deciding how costs of jointly instructed experts should be apportioned:

- the court should apportion the relevant costs fairly and reasonably, bearing in mind all the circumstances of the particular case;
- the court would have regard to the reasonableness of how the local authority had conducted the information-gathering process and with what degree of competence and thoroughness;
- competence and thoroughness were relevant because there might be cases where a local authority had done little preparation or had prepared poorly;
- the court would have regard to the extent to which the report went merely to satisfying the 'threshold' for state intervention, as distinct from helping the court to decide more generally what overall 'disposal' would best serve the interests of the child's welfare;
- 'treating experts' and others who had had a 'hands on' role with the family were more likely to be paid for by the local authority, whereas the fees of a purely forensic expert were more likely to be ordered to be shared in principle between the parties;
- the sharing of the costs of a forensic expert gave each party confidence in the integrity of the forensic process, but if a party had genuinely opposed the commissioning of the joint report, then this would be a relevant factor;

---

71 *Re B (Sexual Abuse: Expert's Report)* [2000] 1 FLR 871. See also the *Best Practice Guide for Instructing a Single Joint Expert* [2003] 1 FLR 573.

72 See **4.84** et seq.

73 *Re S; WSP v Hull City Council* [2006] EWCA Civ 981, [2007] 1 FLR 90.

74 *Re A (Family Proceedings: Expert Witness)* [2001] 1 FLR 723.

75 [2004] EWHC 2429 (Fam), [2005] 1 FLR 751.

- the fact that a party was publicly funded was not a reason for making a different decision about costs from that which would otherwise have been made.[76]

Draft order for the relevant hearing

4.70 In addition to filing the detailed proposal to instruct an expert, the party proposing such instruction shall, by 11am on the business day before the relevant hearing, submit to the court a draft order dealing particularly with the following matters:

- the party who is to be responsible for drafting the letter of instruction and providing the documents to the expert;
- the issues identified by the court and the questions about which the expert is to give an opinion;
- the timetable within which the report is to be prepared, filed and served;
- the disclosure of the report to the parties and to any other expert;
- the organisation of, preparation for and conduct of an experts' discussion;
- the preparation of a statement of agreement and disagreement by the experts following an experts' discussion;
- making available to the court at an early opportunity the expert reports in electronic form;
- the attendance of the expert at court to give oral evidence (alternatively, the expert giving his or her evidence in writing or remotely by video link), whether at or for the Final Hearing or another hearing, unless agreement about the opinions given by the expert is reached at or before the Issues Resolution Hearing, or, if no IRH is to be held, by a specified date prior to the hearing at which the expert is to give oral evidence ('the specified date').[77]

THE LETTER OF INSTRUCTION

4.71 The solicitor instructing the expert shall, within five business days of the relevant hearing, prepare (in agreement with the other parties where appropriate), file and serve a letter of instruction to the expert which must:

- set out the context in which the expert's opinion is sought (including any ethnic, cultural, religious or linguistic contexts);
- set out the specific questions which the expert is required to answer, ensuring that they:
  (a) are within the ambit of the expert's area of expertise;

---

[76] Ibid, at para [35]. These principles were applied to assessments under Children Act 1989, s 38(6), in *Lambeth London Borough Council v S, C, V and J (by his Guardian); Legal Services Commission intervening* [2005] EWHC 776 (Fam), [2005] 2 FLR 1171. Following subsequent changes to the LSC Funding Code, however, the burden of those assessments now falls on the local authority alone.

[77] The Experts Practice Direction, at para 4.4. Although the Practice Direction should in any event make such orders obsolete, courts should not (even if departing from the guidance) make orders granting permission for a report from 'experts' or 'an expert'. The expert(s) should be identified by name, or at least by area of expertise, in any order authorising expert evidence (see *Re G (Minors) (Expert Witnesses)* [1994] 2 FLR 291; *H v Cambridgeshire County Council* [1996] 2 FLR 566).

(b) do not contain unnecessary or irrelevant detail;
(c) are kept to a manageable number and are clear, focused and direct; and
(d) reflect what the expert has been requested to do by the court;

- list the documentation provided, or provide for the expert an indexed and paginated bundle which shall include:
  - a copy of the order (or those parts of the order) which gives permission for the instruction of the expert (to be sent immediately the order becomes available);
  - an agreed list of essential reading; and
  - a copy of the Experts Practice Direction;

- identify materials that have not been produced either as original medical (or other professional) records or in response to an instruction from a party;[78]

- identify all requests to third parties for disclosure and their responses;[79]

- identify the relevant people concerned with the proceedings (for example, the treating clinicians) and inform the expert of his or her right to talk to them provided that an accurate record is made of the discussions;

- identify any other expert instructed in the proceedings and advise the expert of his or her right to talk to the other experts provided that an accurate record is made of the discussions;

- subject to any public funding requirement for prior authority, define the contractual basis upon which the expert is retained and in particular the funding mechanism including how much the expert will be paid (an hourly rate and overall estimate should already have been obtained), when the expert will be paid, and what limitation there might be on the amount the expert can charge for the work which he or she will have to do.[80]

4.72 These requirements for the letter of instruction advance two main principles:

(1) the importance of identifying, with precision, the issues to be addressed by the expert and their relevance to the disputed issues in the case; and

(2) the importance of ensuring that the instruction of an expert and the process by which the report is produced is fair and transparent at all times – that, where in particular the expert report is likely to have a preponderant influence on the decision of the court, a party should be allowed effectively to engage in the process by which the report is produced.[81]

---

78 For the reasons identified at footnote 40.

79 For the reasons identified at footnote 41.

80 The Experts Practice Direction, at para 5.1. In cases where the parties are publicly funded, there should also be a brief explanation of the costs and expenses excluded from public funding by the Funding Code, criterion 1.3, and the detailed assessment process.

81 See footnote 44. It is difficult to see how a party can be 'effectively engaged' in the process by which an expert report is produced without knowing what material has contributed to the opinions given, or without access to accurate notes of conversations which have contributed to those opinions. Furthermore, a failure by an expert to set out precisely the facts and deductions drawn therefrom in reaching his or her conclusions hampers the forensic process by which the soundness of those conclusions can be scrutinised.

4.73 Where the parties cannot agree the terms of the proposed letter of instruction, a request may be made in writing to the court to settle the letter, and this will usually be dealt with without the need for a hearing.[82] Experts should be promptly sent copies of any new documents filed at court, together with any new indices.[83]

THE COURT'S CONTROL OF EXPERT EVIDENCE: CONSEQUENTIAL ISSUES

4.74 Paragraph 6 of the Experts Practice Direction deals briefly with the issue of supplementary clarificatory written questions to the expert, and addresses in rather more depth experts' discussions or meetings.

Written questions

4.75 Any party wishing to put written questions to an expert for the purpose of clarifying the expert's report must do so not later than ten business days after receipt of the report, and the court will specify the timetable for the expert's response.[84]

Experts' discussions or meetings

4.76 By the 'specified date',[85] the court may direct (if it has not already done so) that the experts are to meet or communicate for the following purposes:

- to identify and narrow the issues in the case;
- where possible, to reach agreement on the expert issues;
- to identify the reasons for disagreement on any expert question and what, if any, action needs to be taken to resolve any outstanding disagreement or question;
- to explain or add to the evidence in order to assist the court to determine the issues;
- to limit, wherever possible, the need for the experts to attend court to give oral evidence.[86]

4.77 In accordance with the court's directions, the guidance provides, at para 6.3, that 'the nominated professional'[87] shall, within 15 business days of receipt of the experts' reports, arrange for the experts to meet or communicate. Where applicable, the following matters should be considered in this context:

- Where permission has been given for the instruction of experts from different disciplines, a global discussion may be held relating to those questions that concern all or most of them.

---

82 The Experts Practice Direction, at para 5.2.
83 Ibid, at para 5.3.
84 Ibid, at para 6.1.
85 Defined by the Experts Practice Direction, at para 4.4(8), as 'a specified date prior to the hearing at which the expert is to give oral evidence'.
86 Ibid, at para 6.2.
87 'The nominated professional' is the solicitor or other professional who is given the appropriate responsibility by the court (ibid, at para 6.3).

- Separate discussions may have to be held among experts from the same or related disciplines, but care should be taken to ensure that the discussions complement each other so that related questions are discussed by all relevant experts.

- Five business days prior to a discussion or meeting, the nominated professional should formulate an agenda including a list of questions for consideration:
  - the agenda should contain only those questions which are intended to clarify areas of agreement or disagreement;
  - questions which repeat questions asked in the letter of instruction[88] or which seek to rehearse cross-examination in advance of the hearing should be rejected as likely to defeat the purpose of the meeting;
  - the agenda may usefully take the form of a list of questions to be circulated among the other parties in advance;
  - the agenda should comprise all questions that each party wishes the experts to consider;
  - the agenda and list of questions should be sent to each of the experts not later than two clear business days before the discussion.

- The nominated professional may exercise his or her discretion to accept further questions after the agenda (with list of questions) has been circulated to the parties. Only in exceptional circumstances should questions be added to the agenda within the two day period before the meeting, and under no circumstances should any question received on the day of or during the meeting be accepted.[89]

- The discussion should be chaired by the nominated professional. A minute must be taken of the questions answered by the experts, and a Statement of Agreement and Disagreement must be prepared which should be agreed and signed by each of the experts who participated in the discussion. The statement should be served and filed not later than 5 business days after the discussion has taken place.

- In each case, consideration should be given as to whether some or all of the experts should participate by telephone conference or video link to ensure that minimum disruption is caused to professional schedules and that costs are minimised.[90]

4.78 This clear and detailed approach to meetings or discussions between experts with a view to producing a Statement of Agreement and Disagreement reflects the caution with which the process should be undertaken. But courts and practitioners should also appreciate the actual, somewhat limited, status of what is said or agreed in any such meeting or discussion. Per McFarlane J in *Oxfordshire County Council v DP, RS and BS*:[91]

> '[I]t must in any event be borne in mind that what is said at an experts meeting is not strictly evidence in the case. Experience shows that the manner in which experts express themselves at such meetings is less guarded than when they are writing reports for the court or giving oral evidence. The meeting and the dialogue are an important event in the preparation for the hearing, but any record of the meeting does not have evidential status. [The submission] that the experts meeting in this case

---

88 It is assumed that the reference here to 'questions' is to specific questions. The approach suggested by Charles J in *A County Council v K, D and L* (above) (set out at **4.47**) can in practice often provide a very useful framework for the experts' discussion or meeting, even though the questions that he suggests will probably have appeared already in the letters of instruction to some or all of the experts involved.

89 The Experts Practice Direction, at para 6.3(4). The guidance indicates that strictness in this regard is vital, for adequate notice of the questions enables the parties to identify and isolate the issues in the case before the meeting so that the experts' discussion at the meeting can concentrate on those issues.

90 Ibid, at para 6.3(6). The suggestions for telephone conference and video link reflect the desire within the PLO Practice Direction (at para 23) to promote the greater use of techonology.

91 Above, at para [109].

> resulted in 'trial by expert' . . . might be a sound submission if the result of the meeting were treated by the courts as having a verdict-like status, but it does not have that status or anything approaching it. The trial of these issues has taken place in this court. The evidence upon which any judicial conclusion is based will be the written and oral evidence that has been submitted and thoroughly tested by the forensic process rather than any note of an experts meeting, the purpose of which is limited to clarifying issues and flagging up areas of agreement or dispute.'

4.79 Furthermore, agreement between experts on particular aspects of a case does not of itself add cogency to the scientific evidence on that point. Experts might agree with each other for various reasons, influenced by factors such as professional standing and deference. Whatever the agreement appears to be, it is still subject to the rigour of the court's forensic process.[92]

4.80 Although the guidance should avoid this particular problem arising at all, where it is proposed that treating clinicians are invited to any experts' meeting, they should first be properly and fully instructed in accordance with the Experts Practice Direction.[93]

4.81 Unless the parties have agreed or the court has directed otherwise, jointly instructed experts should not attend any meetings which are not 'joint' within the meaning of the guidance.[94] Any meeting or conference attended by a jointly instructed expert should be proportionate to the case.[95]

4.82 Where the court gives a direction that the local authority should be entitled to meet any expert with a view to future planning for a child, it should also give directions for the arranging, chairing and minuting of such a meeting.[96]

4.83 Where a party refuses to be bound by any agreement reached at an experts' meeting, that party must inform the court and the parties in writing of the reasons for that refusal within ten business days after the discussion or meeting or, where an IRH is to be held, not less than five business days before the IRH.[97]

The instruction of experts to provide a second opinion

4.84 Although the guidance is silent on the point at which a party may apply to instruct another expert to provide a 'second opinion' in a case, it can be assumed that the guidance applies to any such application, and that sound, issue-led justification will have to be given before the court is likely to accede to such an application. A party seeking further expert evidence may not necessarily have to wait until after the experts' meeting or discussion, but justifying the need for a further opinion before it might be difficult.

4.85 In *Daniels v Walker*,[98] Lord Woolf MR suggested the following process be undertaken before the instruction of a second expert was sought:

- instruction of the first expert on the basis of an agreed letter; then
- separate written questions from any party discontented with the report for 'reasonable reasons';

---

92 For an example of apparent consensus at an experts' meeting being permitted to distort the forensic process (and leading to a miscarriage of justice), see *Oldham MBC v GW and PW* (above).

93 *Oxfordshire County Council v DP, RS and BS* (above), at paras [104]–[109].

94 The Experts Practice Direction, at para 6.4.

95 Ibid, at para 6.4.

96 Ibid, at para 6.5.

97 Ibid, at para 7.

98 [2000] 1 WLR 1382.

- if the answers to those questions remained unsatisfactory, then a party could apply for further expert evidence which would be considered on the basis of proportionality.

4.86 In view of the guidance, it is likely that the necessity for and proportionality of further expert evidence will be rigorously scrutinised by the court.

4.87 In *W v Oldham Metropolitan Borough Council*,[99] the Court of Appeal held that, in cases in which certain medical evidence became pivotal, for example, in cases involving non-accidental head injury or pathologically 'unascertained' infant death, and in which such evidence was, by its nature, difficult to challenge in the absence of further expert opinion, the court should be slow to decline an application for a second expert. In that case, the expert evidence which was the subject of challenge went to the issue of critical importance.

4.88 *W v Oldham MBC*,[100] however, is not authority for the proposition that parties are entitled routinely to instruct a selection of experts in the same disciplines as those already destined to give evidence at the outset of a case.[101] The justification for a second opinion lies in the existence of a report which is the 'pivot' around which the case turns. The question is whether the critical issue has been answered by the first report in such a way that a second is justified by fairness to the party against whom an adverse finding might be made.

Fairness, best evidence and proportionality

4.89 In the context of further expert evidence being sought, the principle of fairness can be of great importance. In *Re B (Care Proceedings: Expert Witness)*[102] the Court of Appeal held, in circumstances where the local authority sought to rely on expert evidence given in proceedings relating to an older child, and where as a consequence the parents' case on a subsequent child appeared hopeless, that the parents ought to be permitted to instruct an expert of their own. In taking that course, Thorpe LJ explained that it was very important that parents at risk of losing their child forever should have confidence in the fairness and even-handed nature of the proceedings, and added that, if the parents' expert reached the same conclusions as the local authority's, his or her instruction might shorten or avoid the final hearing.[103]

4.90 In similar vein, the commissioning of further expert evidence is often justified not only on the grounds of fairness, but also by reference to the inter-related perceived need of the court to take decisions based on the best evidence.[104] But there are limits. Per Thorpe LJ in *Re M (Care Proceedings: Best Evidence)*:[105]

> 'There has to be a point at which the garnering of evidence is sufficiently full and thorough to enable the court to arrive at a conclusion, even on the elevated balance of probabilities standard of proof.'

4.91 The balance and potential tension in individual cases between on the one hand the principle of fairness (incorporating the best evidence rule) and on the other the principle of proportionality, both reflected in the PLO Practice Direction's overriding objective,[106] will doubtless keep courts at first instance and appellate level busy for some time to come.

---

99 [2005] EWCA Civ 1247, [2006] 1 FLR 543.
100 Ibid.
101 *Re S; WSP v Hull City Council* (above).
102 [2007] EWCA Civ 556, [2007] 2 FLR 979.
103 Ibid, at para [8]. A refusal to permit a party to instruct an expert in support of his or her case might contribute or amount to a breach of that party's Art 6 or 8 ECHR rights (see *Elsholz v Germany (Application No 25735/94)* [2002] 34 EHRR 58, [2000] 2 FLR 486).
104 See *Re L and H (Residential Assessment)* [2007] EWCA Civ 213, [2007] 1 FLR 1370, cited at **5.98**.
105 [2007] EWCA Civ 589, [2007] 2 FLR 1006.
106 The PLO Practice Direction, at para 2.1.

THE EXPERTS PRACTICE DIRECTION: ANCILLARY PROVISIONS

4.92 The remaining provisions of the Experts Practice Direction deal with the following:

- arrangements for experts to give evidence;
- matters after the final hearing;
- sample letters of instruction.

Arrangements for experts to give evidence

4.93 Paragraph 8.1 of the Practice Direction provides that, where the court has directed the attendance of an expert witness, the party responsible for the expert's instruction shall, by the specified date or by the IRH (if held), make sure:

- that a date and time (if possible, convenient to the expert) are fixed for the court to hear the expert's evidence – this is to be fixed substantially in advance of the hearing at which the expert is to give oral evidence and no later than a specified date prior to that hearing or the IRH (if held);
- that, if the expert's oral evidence is not required, the expert is notified as soon as possible;
- that the witness template accurately indicates how long the expert is likely to be giving evidence;[107]
- that consideration is given in each case to whether some or all of the experts participate by telephone conference or video link, or submit their evidence in writing.[108]

4.94 By the same date, all parties shall ensure:

- that the parties' advocates have identified (whether at an advocates' meeting or by other means) the issues which the experts are to address;
- that, wherever possible, a logical sequence to the evidence is arranged, with experts of the same discipline giving evidence on the same day;
- that the court is informed of any circumstance where all experts agree but a party nevertheless does not accept the agreed opinion – this is so that directions can be given for the proper consideration of the experts' evidence and of the party's reasons for not accepting the agreed opinion;
- that, in the exceptional case, the court is informed of the need for a witness summons.[109]

4.95 It seems clear from this provision that, where a party continues to dispute an area of expert evidence agreed by the experts, that party must expect the court to have some contribution to make. There would seem to be a spectrum of possibility. It might be that the court simply expects to be informed of the objection and of its general nature. It might be,

---

[107] This is in order to avoid the inconvenience of the expert being delayed at court (the Experts Practice Direction, at para 8.1(3)).

[108] This is to ensure that minimum disruption is caused to professional schedules and that costs are minimised (ibid, at para 8.1(4)).

[109] Ibid, at para 8.2.

however, that the court will wish to give an indication whether the reasons for the continued objection are justified. Ultimately, it might be that the court refuses to permit what it regards as a disproportionate or unreasonable challenge, or sets strict boundaries within which any challenge to the otherwise agreed expert evidence is to be made.

4.96 In this respect, only time will tell. But there can be no question that the court is expected to take a more proactive role in setting the limits for any forensic challenge to otherwise agreed expert evidence. Sometimes, of course, expert evidence, and apparently unanimous agreement between experts, can be fundamentally and unforeseeably undermined by the forensic process. Fairness will require a delicate balance to be struck between the principle of proportionality and the need for rigour in the evaluation of expert evidence.

After the final hearing

4.97 Within ten business days of the Final Hearing, the solicitor instructing the expert shall inform that expert in writing of the outcome of the case and the use to which the expert's opinion was put.[110]

4.98 Where the court directs the preparation of a transcript, it may also direct that the solicitor instructing the expert shall send a copy to the expert within ten business days of receiving it.[111]

4.99 After a Final Hearing in the family proceedings court, the (lead) solicitor instructing the expert shall send the expert a copy of the court's written reasons for its decision within ten business days of their receipt.[112]

The Annex: sample letters of instruction

4.100 The Experts Practice Direction concludes with an Annex which contains two sample letters of instruction. The first contains sample questions to be put to a child mental health professional or paediatrician. The second contains sample questions for adult psychiatrists and applied psychologists. Both of these letters were drafted by the Family Justice Council.

---

[110] Ibid, at para 9.1.
[111] Ibid, at para 9.2.
[112] Ibid, at para 9.3.

CHAPTER FIVE

THE CASE MANAGEMENT COMPENDIUM

5.1 Identifying case management issues that require resolution is one thing. Being able to resolve them – and quickly – is quite another.

5.2 The Protocol[1] had contained among its appendices a seven page case management checklist. It was certainly comprehensive, but to the point of being overwhelming, and its existence did not stop many a case management issue escaping the early identification and resolution that was required.

5.3 The PLO Practice Direction[2] does not contain a separate case management checklist. The Draft Case Management Order doubles up to that end,[3] and the principal aim of this chapter is to complement it in that capacity.

5.4 By setting out what, at the date of writing, are the main legal principles governing their resolution, the hope is to provide a ready, accessible guide that will enable courts and practitioners to resolve quickly and easily the common case management issues that arise in these difficult cases.

5.5 The multi-faceted subject of expert evidence was dealt with in depth in the previous chapter. Within this, the following further core topics are addressed:

- allocation and transfer of proceedings;[4]
- parties;[5]
- unrepresented parties;[6]
- interim hearings, ICOs and residential assessments;[7]
- care plans;[8]
- threshold schedules and split hearings;[9]
- disclosure;[10]
- special measures;[11]

---

1 Practice Direction (Care Cases: Judicial Continuity and Judicial Case Management) [2003] 2 FLR 719.
2 Practice Direction: Guide to Case Management in Public Law Proceedings.
3 Ibid, at para 3.10.
4 At **5.7** et seq.
5 At **5.39** et seq.
6 At **5.58** et seq.
7 At **5.83** et seq.
8 At **5.107** et seq.
9 At **5.127** et seq.
10 At **5.155** et seq.
11 At **5.201** et seq.

- placement for adoption.[12]

5.6 It will doubtless be implicit from that list that, while the PLO Practice Direction has a potentially wider ambit, it is upon the case management issues in care and supervision proceedings, to which the Practice Direction directly applies, that this chapter focuses.

ALLOCATION AND TRANSFER OF PROCEEDINGS

5.7 At the time of writing, the procedural rules governing the allocation and transfer of public law children's (and other family) cases are in a state of transition. At one stage, it was intended that there would be a new statutory instrument, supplemented by a new practice direction, in force by April 2008 in time for the implementation of the Public Law Outline. That has not happened, though new rules on allocation, to be embodied in a new allocation and transfer of proceedings order and accompanying practice direction, are anticipated by the end of 2008 following consultation as to their content.[13]

5.8 At the time of writing, the rules governing allocation are set out in existing statutory instruments and directions, in particular:

- the Children (Allocation of Proceedings) Order 1991,[14] which lays down rules for determining the level of court to hear proceedings; and
- the Family Proceedings (Allocation to Judiciary) Directions 1999,[15] which allocate specific types of family proceedings to specific categories of judge.

5.9 Importantly, the former is 'complemented' (and to a large degree effectively replaced) by guidance contained in a document, issued in December 2006, that has become known in practice simply as the Draft President's Guidance on Allocation.[16]

5.10 Although described as 'draft guidance', and headed by a preamble indicating that it would be formally issued at a later date following any necessary amendment, that preamble also set out the encouragement of the President 'to implement the principles contained in the Guidance in your court centre so far as conditions permit'. With as yet no further document

---

12 At **5.244** et seq.

13 In October 2005, the Department for Constitutional Affairs (the predecessor of the Ministry of Justice) published a consultation paper, 'Focusing Judicial Resources Appropriately', seeking views on proposals for the future allocation of proceedings and in particular on managing growing demands on the High Court bench. Reform was planned following that consultation, but, in the event, the statutory instrument and practice direction have been delayed. A further consultation paper prepared jointly by HM Courts Service and the President of the Family Division was circulated amongst stakeholders on 27 March 2008, with a due closing date of 19 June 2008. It enclosed a draft new Allocation and Transfer of Proceedings Order and Practice Direction governing the allocation and transfer of proceedings between all three courts in the family jurisdiction. The covering letter (from Sally Field, Head of Family Division, HMCS) summarised the policy aims of the proposed reforms as being 'to ensure that cases are heard at the lowest most appropriate level commensurate with their complexity; to ease work pressures on the High Court and county court; to achieve a more rational distribution of cases between courts that have concurrent jurisdiction; to make best use of under-utilised family magistrates; and to reduce delays.'

14 SI 1991/1677, amended by statutory instrument on 14 occasions.

15 Approved by the Lord Chancellor under the Courts and Legal Services Act 1990, s 9, with the concurrence of the President of the Family Division, and amended variously in 2002, 2003, 2005 (twice) and 2007. Set out in amended form in the *Family Court Practice* (Jordans, 2008 ed), at p 2230.

16 The full name of the document is: 'Draft President's Guidance on the Distribution between Family Proceedings Courts, County Courts and High Court of Cases Concerning Children and Proceedings under Part IV of the Family Law Act 1996'.

having been published, courts are in practice largely following the Draft President's Guidance, which in many respects foreshadows the provisions set out in the draft allocation order and practice direction now subject to consultation.[17]

5.11 This discussion of the allocation and transfer of proceedings therefore summarises the provisions currently in force, drawing principally on the 1991 Order and the Draft President's Guidance. But what follows will of course need to be revisited when the new allocation order and practice direction finally come into force.

5.12 Before, however, considering the detail of the 1991 Order and the Draft President's Guidance, attention should be drawn to the references within the PLO Practice Direction and its related documents to allocation and transfer.

Allocation, transfer and the Public Law Outline

5.13 'Allocation' is not defined within the glossary to the PLO Practice Direction,[18] nor anywhere else within it. While the guideline documents, Form PLO5 ('Standard Directions Form (On Issue) Menu') and Form PLO6 ('Standard Directions Form (at First Appointment) Menu'), both use the word 'transferred' to mean the process of fixing the level and location of court, and 'allocated' to mean the process of identifying the specific judges responsible for case management and hearing the case, this distinction is not sustained consistently throughout the PLO Practice Direction itself.

5.14 There are a number of general provisions in the Practice Direction which impinge upon decisions about allocation. Part of the overriding objective of enabling the court to deal with cases justly is said to include ensuring that it is dealt with expeditiously,[19] in ways which are proportionate to the nature, importance and complexity of the issues,[20] and allotting to it an appropriate share of the court's resources.[21] Further on, it is important to note that judicial continuity is described as one of 'the main principles' underlying court case management in public law proceedings.[22] Indeed, one can readily foresee arguments that some or all of these principles ought to take precedence over provisions in the Draft President's Guidance or subsequent regulations.

5.15 The importance of identifying at an early stage the appropriate level of court for the case is recognised by the inclusion in the PLO Practice Direction's 'active case management' list of 'identifying the appropriate court to conduct the proceedings and transferring the proceedings as early as possible to that court'.[23]

---

17 The following aspects of the consultation paper are worthy of note. 'The criteria for hearing cases in the Family Division of the High Court should be pitched at a higher level . . . to ensure that High Court judges are deployed on cases that truly require their attention due to their knowledge and experience . . . [a]lso to enable the effective transfer of more complex cases down the levels of courts with the FPCs hearing more cases currently being heard in the county court' (para 6). To that end, the proposed new order provides that proceedings may not be heard in the High Court unless they are 'exceptionally complex, the outcome of the proceedings is important to the public in general, or there is another substantial reason', but this is supplemented by the detail of the draft practice direction, which repeats substantially (though not verbatim) the provisions of the Draft President's Guidance on Allocation. A further aim is to turn the power to transfer down into an obligation (para 12), whilst para 13 emphasises that one of the purposes of the proposed new order is to change 'the culture of mostly issuing private law Children Act and Part IV [Family Law Act 1996] cases in the county court'.

18 Found within the PLO Practice Direction at para 25.

19 The PLO Practice Direction, at para 2.1(1).

20 Ibid, at para 2.1(2).

21 Ibid, at para 2.1(5).

22 Ibid, at para 3.1(1).

23 Ibid, at para 3.15(2).

5.16 To that end, the Allocation Record and Timetable for the Child features as one of the documents included in the 'case management documentation'.[24] This document, as its name suggests, serves two purposes and is defined[25] as meaning a document containing:

(a) the local authority's proposal for allocation;

(b) the local authority's proposed Timetable for the Child;

(c) the court's allocation decisions and reasons; and

(d) the court's approved Timetable for the Child.

5.17 The local authority is responsible for updating the Allocation Record after each hearing.[26]

5.18 Although there is no standard prescribed form for the Allocation Record and Timetable for the Child, Form PLO4, a 'guideline' document', has been produced and it lists a number of factors which may provide the basis for allocation:

- existing orders or proceedings involving the family;
- mental health or incapacity problems;
- learning disabilities (parents and/or children);
- parallel criminal proceedings;
- immigration issues;
- placement order application made or proposed;
- interpreter being used;
- strong likelihood of conflicting expert evidence;
- judicial or courtroom availability or estimated length of hearing;[27]
- the nature of harm alleged (with a supplementary list identifying various types of serious harm and ancillary issues such as disclosure and public interest immunity); and
- 'other reasons', a portmanteau category including:
  - where the case involves a difficult point of law, issues of public policy or 'unusually complex or sensitive issues';
  - where a linked placement order application raises issues additional to those inherent in the care proceedings;
  - where a child is represented separately from the Guardian;
  - where a 'split hearing' is necessary and judicial continuity cannot otherwise be ensured; and
  - any international element.

---

24 Ibid, para 3.5(4).
25 Ibid, at para 25(4).
26 Ibid, at para 5.2.
27 Abbreviated on the form to 'ELH'.

5.19 The provenance of this list is unclear, as is whether there has been any cross-reference either to the Draft President's Guidance on Allocation or to the proposed new allocation order and practice direction.

5.20 Interestingly, Form PLO4 suggests that the applicant's allocation proposal should select one level of tribunal from the following list of six options:

- case manager and magistrates in the FPC;
- district judge (magistrates' court) in the FPC;
- district judge in the county court;
- circuit judge in the county court;
- DFJ/section 9 sitting as a Judge of the High Court;
- High Court Judge.

5.21 Under the Public Law Outline, the issue of allocation has to be considered at various stages of the process:

- As part of PLO Stage 1, the court issues the application on day 1. One of the objectives specified for the court on that day is 'to allocate proceedings',[28] and the allocation and/or transfer of the case forms part of the standard directions on issue. The Practice Direction, at para 11.3, further provides that the court will at this point consider allocation of the case and will transfer to the county court those cases which are obviously suitable for immediate transfer (such as one where there is evidence that a parent may be a protected party and require representation which currently cannot be obtained in the magistrates' court).
- Still within PLO Stage 1, the court, at the First Appointment (therefore by day 6) will, as part of its initial case management, 'confirm' allocation or, if appropriate, transfer the proceedings.[29]
- At PLO Stage 2, at the Case Management Conference, the court will 'confirm the allocation or the transfer of the case',[30] with provision made for this within the Draft Case Management Order.[31]

The 1991 Order

5.22 At the time of writing, the statutory instrument governing allocation remains the Children (Allocation of Proceedings) Order 1991,[32] 'complemented' by the Draft President's Guidance on Allocation of 2007. 'Complements' is the word used in the Draft President's Guidance itself to describe what it purports to do to the 1991 Order and other ancillary regulations, but this seems to be a euphemism for 'unofficially amends'.

[28] The PLO Practice Direction, at para 11.1(2).
[29] Ibid, at para 12.3(3).
[30] Ibid, at para 14.3(2).
[31] Ibid, at Annex C.
[32] Above.

5.23 The 1991 Order provides[33] that a magistrates' court may, on the application of a party or of its own motion, transfer[34] care proceedings 'when it considers it in the interests of the child to do so' having regard to:

(1) the 'no delay' principle set out in the Children Act 1989, s 1(2); and

(2) the following questions:
  - (a) whether the proceedings are exceptionally grave, important or complex, in particular:
    - (i) because of complicated or conflicting evidence about the risks involved to the child's physical or moral well-being or about other matters relating to the welfare of the child;
    - (ii) because of the number of parties;
    - (iii) because of a conflict with the law of another jurisdiction;
    - (iv) because of some novel and difficult point of law;
    - (v) because of some question of general public interest;
  - (b) whether it would be appropriate for those proceedings to be heard together with other family proceedings which are pending in another court; and
  - (c) whether transfer is likely significantly to accelerate the determination of the proceedings, where:
    - (i) no other method of doing so, including transfer to another magistrates' court, is appropriate; and
    - (ii) delay would seriously prejudice the interests of the child who is the subject of the proceedings.[35]

5.24 If the magistrates refuse to transfer, an application may be made to the county court.[36] The 1991 Order further provides[37] that the county court may transfer the case back,[38] where, having regard to the 'no delay' principle and the child's interests, it considers the criterion for the original transfer does not apply or no longer applies.[39]

5.25 Transfer from county court to High Court under the 1991 Order is permitted[40] where the county court, having regard to the 'no delay' principle, considers that the proceedings are appropriate for determination in the High Court and that such determination would be in the interests of the child.[41] Transfer back is permitted[42] on the same basis.[43] Applications under Part IV of the Children Act 1989 made at or transferred to county court level may only be made at or transferred to certain specified county courts, known as 'care centres'.[44] There is provision for the transfer from one FPC to another[45] and from one county court to another.[46]

---

33 Ibid, art 7(1).

34 The procedure for transfer from the family proceedings court to the county court is set out in the Family Proceedings Courts (Children Act 1989) Rules 1991 (SI 1991/1395), rr 6 and 14.

35 The 1991 Order (above), art 7(1)(a)–(c).

36 Ibid, art 9. The procedure is set out in the Family Proceedings Rules 1991 (SI 1991/1247), r 4.6(1)–(4).

37 Ibid, art 11(1).

38 The procedure for transfer back from the county court to the FPC is set out in the FPR, r 4.6(6) and (7).

39 This wording seems to require a change of circumstances before the case can be transferred back – it is not enough for the county court simply to disagree with the magistrates' reasons for transfer – though doubtless any enterprising circuit or district judge could conjure up a change of circumstance, if required.

40 Above, art 12(1).

41 The procedure for transfer to the High Court is set out in the FPR 1991, r 4.6(4).

42 The 1991 Order (above), art 13(1).

43 On an application to transfer back to the county court, the High Court will adapt the general directions procedure in the FPR 1991, r 4.14.

44 The 1991 Order (above), art 18(1) and (2). The courts falling into this category are listed in the Schedule to the 1991 Order.

45 Ibid, art 6. The procedure is set out in FPC(CA 1989)R 1991, r 6(1)–(4).

46 Ibid, art 10. The procedure is set out in FPR 1991, r 4.14.

The Draft President's Guidance on Allocation

5.26 The Draft President's Guidance on Allocation applies to all cases concerning children and proceedings under Part IV of the Family Law Act 1996. It states that it is 'designed to assist in deciding whether a case should be heard in the family proceedings court, the county court or the High Court'.[47] Part 1 deals with the choice between the FPC and the county court, Part 2 with the circumstances in which a High Court hearing is likely to be appropriate. The key elements of the Draft Guidance, insofar as it relates to public law cases, are as follows.

Family proceedings court or county court?

5.27 The decision whether to transfer a case from the FPC for hearing in the county court or vice versa must be tailored to the circumstances of the particular case within the context of local conditions and with particular regard to the question of delay.[48] There should be the fullest possible consultation between the courts in question to ensure that factors such as the availability and experience of magistrates and judges and present/anticipated pressures on listing are taken into account and to ensure that there is broad agreement between the courts that a proposed transfer is appropriate.[49]

5.28 The Draft Guidance identifies some general considerations applicable to all types of cases:

- It points out that delay in determining the appropriate hearing venue is almost always detrimental. The issue of allocation must be addressed speedily at the outset of every case. It must then be kept under effective review at all times because it should not be assumed that a case will necessarily remain in the court to which it has been allocated initially.[50]

- It recognises that, in the past, there have been indications that magistrates should confine themselves to hearing cases of no more than two or three days in length, and suggests that it is likely that the bulk of the work suitable for trial by lay magistrates in the FPC will continue to fall into this category. It adds, however, that with increased specialisation there may occasionally be cases of up to five days which it would be appropriate for them to hear. It is anticipated that it will rarely, if ever, be appropriate for lay magistrates to hear cases with a time estimate exceeding five days.[51]

- It describes as essential that the time estimate for a case includes all aspects of the procedure from the reading of the documents to the preparation and delivery of the magistrates' reasons.[52]

- It advises, in addition, that the volume of written evidence is taken into account not only in respect of the impact that it has on the time estimate but also as an independent factor in determining where a case should be tried. The existence of sizeable quantities of documentation of one type or another is likely to indicate that a case is unsuitable for trial in the FPC.[53]

---

47 Draft President's Guidance, at para 1.

48 Ibid, at para 5.

49 Ibid, at para 6, which adds that it is anticipated that in most areas arrangements will be made for consultation to take place between a judge in the county court and whichever is the most appropriate of a legal adviser/district judge (magistrates' court)/magistrate in the FPC in relation to the majority of individual cases. It also points out that, where this is not practical, a general approach should be agreed.

50 Ibid, at para 8.

51 Ibid, at para 10.

52 Ibid, at para 11.

53 Ibid, at para 13.

5.29 The Draft Guidance then makes a number of other general points on allocation:

- Where a case is likely to require judicial continuity over a period of time, the feasibility of providing such continuity (including possibly at short notice on occasions) should be taken into account.[54]

- The possibility should be borne in mind of transferring a single issue of particular difficulty or sensitivity from the FPC to the county court for determination rather than transferring the whole case.[55]

- Listing availability must always be ascertained before deciding where a case should be heard and may be determinative if the decision as to venue is finely balanced. However, there are some cases which, because of their complexity or the issues involved, require to be heard by a certain level of tribunal even if that means delay because of listing backlogs.[56]

- In all allocation/listing decisions, attention must be paid to the personal circumstances of the litigants which may make it particularly difficult for them, for reasons such as travelling arrangements and expenditure, to attend at certain courts.[57]

5.30 The Draft Guidance deals with private as well as public law children's cases, and its general philosophy is for as much of the former to be heard at FPC level as is practicable, the expectation being that in future the majority of straightforward private law disputes will be considered suitable for determination in the FPC, subject to pressures of work.[58] Plainly that philosophy has global implications for where public law children's cases should be heard.

5.31 So far as public law proceedings are concerned, the Draft Guidance reiterates art 7(1) of the 1991 Order. But, importantly, it adds that, in considering art 7(1)(a) (exceptional gravity, importance or complexity) and the issue of transfer generally, those of the factors set out in para 21 which are relevant to public law cases should be borne in mind.[59]

5.32 Paragraph 21 of the Draft Guidance lists a number of factors against and for trial in the FPC in private law children's cases. Of particular interest to public lawyers will be the following encompassed within the 'against' category:

- disputed allegation(s) of sexual abuse or of serious non-accidental injury or serious emotional or physical abuse or ill treatment of a child or disputed allegations of particularly serious domestic violence;

- a significant possibility of an intractable or prolonged dispute;

- cases which are relatively complex, for example because of:
  - the amount of evidential material involved;
  - the number of parties;
  - the characteristics of the parties (age, disposition, mental incapacity or mental illness etc);
  - particularly demanding conflicts in the evidence of lay witnesses;

---

54 Ibid, at para 14.
55 Ibid, at para 15. In practice, there have been mixed views about this option, which some judges feel offends against the principle of judicial continuity, now enshrined in the PLO Practice Direction, at para 3.1(1).
56 Ibid, at para 16.
57 Ibid, at para 18.
58 Ibid, at para 20.
59 Ibid, at para 27.

- disputed expert evidence with a degree of complexity – the Draft Guidance states that very few cases where there is a disagreement between two or more experts, other than social work witnesses, on material issues will be suitable for hearing in the FPC;
- the number of witnesses;
- sensitivity;
- novel or difficult points of law or issues which are likely to be of general public interest or of interest to the legal profession generally;
- unusual features such as cultural, religious or racial considerations if they do not come within the expertise of the local FPC;
- the active involvement of another jurisdiction;
- international considerations;

- cases in which a child may be invited to give evidence or requests to do so;
- cases where there is an issue as to whether part of the evidence should be withheld from a party or parties;
- cases in which there is real reason to suppose that the process or the outcome may have consequences for those involved which are unusually grave;
- contested applications to remove a child permanently or temporarily from the jurisdiction.

5.33 Given the broad ambit of that list, it is perhaps unsurprising to find the Draft Guidance adding that 'only straightforward public law cases will be suitable for hearing in the family proceedings court'.[60]

Hearing in the High Court?

5.34 Part 2 of the Draft Guidance deals with the circumstances in which a High Court hearing is likely to be appropriate. It emphasises that the resources of the High Court are limited and should be reserved for exceptional cases.[61]

5.35 It stipulates that, other than in exceptional circumstances, no case should be transferred to the High Court without prior consultation with the Family Division Liaison Judge for the Circuit. The Family Division Liaison Judge's views should be sought by the Designated Family Judge for the court in which the case is proceeding. The Family Division Liaison Judge will require a summary of the circumstances of the case and an explanation of the reasons why transfer is thought to be required.[62]

5.36 The Guidance points out that, as with cases in the FPC, it may be possible to transfer a single, particularly difficult or sensitive issue in a case to a High Court Judge for determination rather than transferring the whole case.[63]

5.37 The Draft Guidance states that a High Court hearing will not normally be justified merely because of any of the following:[64]

- intractable problems with regard to contact;

---

[60] Ibid.
[61] Ibid, at para 30.
[62] Ibid, at para 31.
[63] Ibid, at para 32. But note the comments at footnote 55.
[64] Ibid, at para 33.

- sexual abuse;
- injury to a child which is neither life-threatening nor permanently disabling;
- routine neglect, even if it spans many years and there is copious documentation;
- temporary or permanent removal to a Hague Convention country;
- standard human rights issues;
- uncertainty as to immigration status;
- the celebrity of the parties;
- the anticipated length of the hearing;
- the quantity of evidence, written and/or oral;
- the number of experts;
- the possible availability of a speedier hearing.

5.38 On the other hand, the Draft Guidance indicates that a High Court hearing is likely to be appropriate where:[65]

- there is alleged to be a risk that a child concerned in the proceedings will suffer serious physical or emotional harm in the light of:
  (i) the death of another child in the family, a parent or any other material person; or
  (ii) a grave crime committed by a parent or other material person, in particular where the essential factual framework is in dispute or there are issues over the causation of injuries or a material conflict of expert evidence;
- there is thought to be a risk to the life of any party to the proceedings;
- removal of the child is sought on a permanent or temporary basis to a country which is not a signatory to the Hague Convention;
- there is another foreign element which renders the case particularly complex;
- the identity of the child is unknown and particular difficulty is anticipated in establishing his or her parentage;
- a contested application is made under the Human Fertilisation and Embryology Act 1990;
- the issues for determination are particularly complex or novel by virtue of the means by which the child was conceived or the configuration of the child's family;
- the application concerns medical treatment for a child which involves a risk to the child's physical or emotional health which goes beyond the normal risks of routine medical treatment;

---

65 Ibid, at para 34.

- difficult issues are likely to arise by virtue of a need to withhold significant evidence or information from a party or parties to the case;
- an adoption order is sought in relation to a child who has been adopted abroad in a country whose adoption orders are not recognised here;
- the case is closely related to or arises from a recent or current High Court case;
- it is likely that the case will establish new principles, or alter existing principles.

PARTIES

5.39 The Public Law Outline requires active case management by the court, which includes identifying at an early stage who should be a party to the proceedings.[66]

Party status

5.40 The applicant in care proceedings is invariably the local authority.[67] Those whom the applicant believes to have parental responsibility for the child and the child him or herself are automatic respondents to the application.[68]

5.41 Notice of the proceedings must also be served on any local authority providing accommodation for the child, any person with whom the child is living at the time the application is issued, any party whom the applicant believes to be a party to pending relevant proceedings about the same child, every person whom the applicant believes to be a parent without parental responsibility, and if the child is living in a refuge certified under the Children Act 1989, s 51(1) or (2), the person providing the refuge.[69]

5.42 As these are specified proceedings, a Children's Guardian must be appointed for the child unless the court is satisfied that it is not necessary to do so in order to safeguard the child's interests.[70]

DNA testing

5.43 It may be necessary to use DNA testing to establish whether or not an individual is actually a parent or other birth relative of the child concerned. Where it is required, it should, as a matter of common sense, be directed as early as possible within the proceedings. In respect of such testing, the following guidance should be borne in mind:[71]

- Any order for DNA testing made by the family courts should be made, and specify that it was being made, pursuant to the Family Law Reform Act 1969 (the 1969 Act).
- The order should either identify the company undertaking the testing, or direct that the company be selected in accordance with the 1969 Act – only DNA experts on the accredited list should be instructed.

---

66 The PLO Practice Direction, at paras 3.14 and 3.15(8).
67 Although the NSPCC is also authorised to make applications, it has not taken up this role for some time.
68 FPC(CA 1989)R 1991, r 7(1); FPR 1991, r 4.7(1).
69 FPC(CA 1989)R 1991, r 4(3); FPR 1991, r 4.4(3).
70 See Children Act 1989, s 41(1); FPC(CA 1989)R 1991, r 10(1); FPR 1991, r 4.10(1).
71 See *Re F (Children) (DNA Evidence)* [2007] EWHC 3235 (Fam), [2008] 1 FLR 348.

- Taking samples from children should only be undertaken pursuant to the express order of the court; further samples might be taken only with court approval, following a written application to the judge. These requirements should be communicated to the identified DNA company in the letter of instruction.

- Save in cases where the issue was solely confined to paternity testing, all requests for DNA testing should be by letter of instruction, which should: (a) emphasise that the responsibilities of DNA experts were identical to those of any expert reporting in a family case and that their overriding obligation was to the court; (b) emphasise that if any test carried out in pursuance of their instructions cast any doubt on, or appeared relevant to the hypothesis set by their instructions, they should regard themselves as being under a duty to draw that to the attention of the court and the parties; (c) set out in clear terms precisely what relationships were to be analysed and, where available, the belief of the parties as to the extent of their relatedness; and (d) make it clear that if the DNA experts considered that there was any lack of clarity, or any ambiguity in their written instructions, or if they required further guidance, the DNA experts should revert to the solicitor instructing them, who should keep a note or memo of any such request.

- DNA experts preparing reports for court should bear in mind that they were addressing lay people; such reports should strive to interpret their analysis in clear language. Care should be taken to explain results within the context of identified conclusions, and particular care should be taken in the use of phrases such as 'this result provides good evidence'; such expressions should always be set within the parameters of current DNA knowledge and identify in plain terms the limitations as to the reliability of any test carried out. A 'likelihood ratio' by definition was a concept that had uncertainty inherent within it; the extent of the uncertainty would vary from test to test and the author of the report must identify and explain those parameters. Where any particular test and subsequent ratio of likelihood was regarded as in any way controversial within the mainstream of DNA expertise, the use of the test and the reasons for its use should be signalled to the court within the report.[72]

Acquiring party status

5.44 At the First Appointment, the court is required to consider giving directions:

- relating to 'the joining of a person who would not otherwise be a respondent under the Rules as a party to the proceedings';[73] and

- where any person to be joined as a party may be a protected party, relating to an investigation of that person's capacity to conduct the proceedings and the representation of that person and if appropriate invite the Official Solicitor to act for that person.[74]

---

72 A common form of order in practice for paternity testing is as follows: (1) pursuant to the Family Law Reform Act 1969, the local authority is permitted to arrange for DNA testing to ascertain whether such tests show that F is or is not thereby excluded from being the father of C, with such testing to be undertaken by [Cellmark Diagnostics] and with appropriate samples to be taken from F, from M and from C; (2) [Cellmark Diagnostics] shall by [insert date] file and serve a report setting out: (a) the results of the tests; (b) whether F is or is not thereby excluded from being the father of C; in relation to F, if not so excluded, the value, if any, of the results in determining whether he is the father of C; and the report shall be received by the court as evidence in the proceedings of the matters set out within it; (3) the costs of and arising out of such DNA testing shall be borne one quarter each between the local authority and the public funding certificates of M, F and C, the court certifying such division of cost to be fair and reasonable and that such expenses on the respective public funding certificates are properly and necessarily incurred.

73 The PLO Practice Direction, at para 12.3(6)(b).

74 Ibid, at para 12.3(6)(c).

5.45 This enables those who are not made respondents to an application to apply to be so, and for any person to apply that he or she or another person may be joined as or cease to be a party to the proceedings. Such a request may be made in Form C2.[75] If it is an application to be made a party, the court may grant it without a hearing or representations, or otherwise order that a date be fixed for consideration of the request or invite the parties to make written representations within a specified period of time. After the expiry of that period, the court will follow one of the courses set out above.[76] The court may also order that a person be joined as a party without application.[77]

5.46 A person who has parental responsibility must be granted any request to be joined as a party.[78] A father without parental responsibility will usually be joined unless there is a good reason for not doing so.[79]

5.47 Otherwise, party status may be accorded to a person (often a relative) who wishes to apply for a section 8 order subject to being granted leave. The test for granting leave is set out in the Children Act 1989, s 10(9), which provides that the court must consider the following matters:

- the nature of the proposed application for a section 8 order;
- the applicant's connection with the child;
- any risk there might be of the proposed application disrupting the child's life to such an extent that the child would be harmed by it;
- if the child is being looked after by a local authority, the local authority care plans for his or her future;
- the wishes and feelings of the child's parents.

5.48 In addressing those criteria, the welfare of the child is not the paramount consideration. While courts have, when considering such an application, applied the test 'is there a good, arguable case',[80] this test should not be substituted for that set out in s 10(9).[81] Parties applying in such circumstances should have an independent and relevant point to put forward,[82] especially if public funding is involved.

5.49 In cases where an individual not already a party is alleged to have caused significant harm to a child, he or she will usually be permitted to intervene in the proceedings for the purpose of defending the allegations (gaining intervener rather than full party status), although each case for intervention must be looked at on its own merits.[83] All applications will be subject to the overriding objective of the PLO Practice Direction.[84]

---

[75] FPC(CA 1989)R 1991, r 7(2); FPR 1991, r 4.7(2).

[76] FPC(CA 1989)R 1991, r 7(4); FPR 1991, r 4.7(3).

[77] FPC(CA 1989)R 1991, r 7(5); FPR 1991, r 4.7(5)

[78] FPC(CA 1989)R 1991, r 7(4); FPR 1991, r 4.7(4).

[79] *Re B (Care Proceedings: Notification of father without parental responsibility)* [1999] 2 FLR 408; *Re F (Care: Party status: Directions)* [1999] Fam Law 294; *Re P (Care Proceedings: Father's application to be joined as party)* [2001] 1 FLR 781.

[80] *Re G (Child Case: Parental Involvement)* [1996] 1 FLR 857.

[81] *Re J (Leave to issue Application for Residence Order)* [2003] 1 FLR 114.

[82] *North Yorkshire County Council v G* [1993] 2 FLR 732; *Re K (Care: Representation: Public Funding)* [2005] EWHC 167 (Fam), [2005] 2 FLR 422.

[83] *Re S (Care: Residence: Intervener)* [1997 1 FLR 497; *Re H (Care Proceedings: Intervener)* [2000] 1 FLR 775.

[84] The PLO Practice Direction, at para 2.1.

5.50 The PLO Practice Direction requires the parties other than the local authority to include in their case summaries the names, addresses, and contact details of any family or friends who it is suggested be approached in relation to long term care/contact or respite.[85]

5.51 This is undoubtedly with a view to enabling the court to do what is required of it by para 12.3(6)(d) of the Practice Direction, namely to consider giving directions relating to the identification of family and friends as such proposed carers. This complements the requirement upon the local authority to consider, wherever possible, potential alternative carers within the family in the pre-proceedings phase.[86] While this may lead to those identified becoming parties, it does not follow that they will need to be, nor that they will need representation at all stages of the case.

5.52 Notwithstanding the aims of the newly revised Volume 1 of the Children Act 1989 Guidance and Regulations, it will not always be the case that assessments of extended family members and friends will have taken place before proceedings are commenced, especially if the proceedings are started in an emergency. Also, the local authority assessments may not be positive. It is thus very important that, once care proceedings have started, wider family members who may be suitable to care for children should be identified and be put (or put themselves) forward at an early stage. This will avoid delay later in the proceedings, or an outright dismissal of their case if the court thinks the overall prospects of success do not justify further delay.[87] Where a local authority seeks a care order with a plan to place a child permanently outside the family, it has the burden of proving the case against a family placement.[88]

The Official Solicitor

5.53 The PLO Practice Direction requires the court at the First Appointment to consider giving directions where any person to be joined as a party may be a protected party,[89] and in any event to investigate as soon as possible any issue as to whether an adult party or intended party to the proceedings lacks capacity within the meaning of the Mental Capacity Act 2005 to conduct proceedings.[90] Such an adult will be a protected party and must have a representative to conduct the proceedings on his or her behalf.[91] This may be a litigation friend, next friend, or guardian ad litem. This role is often taken by the Official Solicitor.

5.54 The role of the Official Solicitor in family proceedings is now largely covered by Cafcass. On 2 April 2001 a *Practice Note*[92] was issued in relation to his continuing involvement in family proceedings. The Official Solicitor, in the absence of any other willing and suitable party, will act as next friend or guardian ad litem of an adult party under a disability. Medical evidence will usually be required before he can consent to act, and, if there is any difficulty in obtaining this, he should be consulted.

5.55 The Official Solicitor will also, in the absence of any other willing or suitable person, act as next friend or guardian ad litem of a child party whose welfare is not the subject of family proceedings.[93] The most common examples of this will be:

---

85 Ibid, at para 25(27).
86 See **2.29** et seq.
87 *G and B (Children)* [2007] EWCA Civ 358, [2007] 2 FLR 140.
88 *Re G (Care Proceedings: Placement for Adoption)* [2005] EWCA Civ 896, [2006] 1 FLR 47.
89 The PLO Practice Direction, at para 12.3(6)(c).
90 Ibid, at para 7.1.
91 Ibid.
92 *Practice Note (Official Solicitor: Appointment in Family Proceedings)* [2001] 2 FLR 155.
93 FPR 1991, rr 2.57, 9.2 and 9.5.

- when a child is also a parent of a child whose welfare is the subject of the proceedings (if a child respondent is already represented by a Cafcass officer in pending proceedings in which he or she is the subject, then the Official Solicitor will liaise with Cafcass to agree the most appropriate arrangements);

- where a child wishes to make an application in respect of another child (as long as the Official Solicitor has satisfied himself that the proposed proceedings would benefit the child applicant); or

- where a child witness may require intervener status (subject to the principles set out in *Re H (Care Proceedings: Intervener).*[94]

5.56 The Official Solicitor may also be invited to act or instruct counsel as 'a friend of the court'[95] if it appears to the court that such an invitation is more appropriately addressed to him rather than Cafcass Legal Services.

5.57 An order appointing the Official Solicitor should be expressed as being made subject to his consent,[96] and the *Practice Note*[97] suggests that a further directions appointment 28 days after the initial order would be helpful. How this will marry up with the PLO timetable remains to be seen.

UNREPRESENTED PARTIES

5.58 This section considers various issues arising in respect of parties who are not represented by lawyers.

5.59 Parents of children who are the subject of proceedings under Part IV and Part V of the Children Act 1989 are entitled to non-means tested public funding from the Legal Services Commission. Consequently, compared with private law proceedings, there are fewer public law cases in which parties appear without representation.

5.60 Occasionally some parents choose to appear without representation, even when able to get it free of charge. But more frequently the unrepresented litigant in care proceedings will be an intervener defending an allegation of child abuse or a family member joined as a respondent, where in both cases the cost of representation has simply proved too prohibitive.

5.61 A lack of representation places an enormous strain on the litigant in all children's cases. In addition to coming to terms with the strange world of courts and procedure, they have to deal with issues that are highly personal and important to their lives. Not infrequently, they show signs of strain. As Wall LJ recognised in the *O'Connell* case:[98]

> '[S]ometimes, as a consequence, [unrepresented litigants] are less coherent and less self-controlled than they would be in other circumstances. The corollary to this, in our view, is that any judge hearing a litigant in person is under a particular obligation to remain courteous and to ensure that the litigant in person has a full and fair hearing.'

---

94 Above.

95 Or 'amicus curiae' (as it was formerly known in more Latin-friendly times).

96 Amongst the specimen directions in the Form PLO6 is a direction for the Official Solicitor to act as a litigation friend on behalf of a protected adult or a non-subject child.

97 Above.

98 *In the Matter of the Children of Mr O'Connell, Mr Whelan and Mr Watson* [2005] EWCA Civ 759, [2005] 2 FLR 967 ('the *O'Connell* case'), at para [55].

The McKenzie friend procedure

5.62 In order to help litigants in person, a procedure has been developed whereby another adult is allowed to sit in court and provide certain types of assistance. Such an adult is known as a 'McKenzie friend' (named after the case in which the procedure was first developed).[99]

5.63 A McKenzie friend is defined in the PLO Practice Direction as 'any person permitted by the court to sit beside an unrepresented litigant in court by prompting, taking notes and giving advice to the litigant'.[100]

5.64 At the time that the PLO Practice Direction came into force, the applicable guidance on McKenzie friends was that issued by the President of the Family Division in 2005,[101] with its contents reinforced and supplemented by the principles set out by the Court of Appeal in the *O'Connell* case[102] and by the amendments to the Family Proceedings Rules 1991 and to the Family Proceedings Court (Children Act 1989) Rules 1991, which brought in respectively rules 10.20A and 23A.

The President's new Guidance on McKenzie friends

5.65 On 14 April 2008, however, the President issued new Guidance on McKenzie friends.[103] That new Guidance in large part replicates the prior position but also amplifies it in certain important respects. It provides a comprehensive and up-to-date guide to the McKenzie friend procedure.

5.66 The Guidance begins by recognising 'the growth of litigants in person in all levels of family court' and by making clear that it 'is to be regarded as a reminder that the attendance of a McKenzie friend will often be of advantage to the court in ensuring the litigant in person receives a fair hearing'.

5.67 The Guidance then sets out the following important principles:

- A litigant who is not legally represented has the right to have reasonable assistance from a lay person, sometimes called a McKenzie Friend ('MF'). This is the case even where the proceedings relate to a child and are being heard in private.
- A litigant in person wishing to have the help of a MF should be allowed such help unless the judge is satisfied that fairness and the interests of justice do not so require. The presumption in favour of permitting a MF is a strong one.
- A litigant in person intending to make a request for the assistance of a MF should be encouraged to make the application as soon as possible indicating who the MF will be.
- It will be most helpful to the litigant in person and to the court if the particular MF is in a position to advise the litigant in person throughout the proceedings.
- A favourable decision by the court, allowing the assistance of a MF, should be regarded as final and not as something which another party can ask the court to revisit later, save on the

---

[99] *McKenzie v McKenzie* [1971] P 33.
[100] At para 25(26).
[101] *President's Guidance of 13 May 2005* [2005] Fam Law 405.
[102] Above.
[103] Available at www.familylaw.co.uk.

ground of misconduct by the MF or on the ground that the MF's continuing presence will impede the efficient administration of justice.

- When considering any request for the assistance of a MF, the Human Rights Act 1998, Sch 1, Part 1, Art 6, is engaged; the court should consider the matter judicially, allowing the litigant reasonable opportunity to develop the argument in favour of the request.

- The litigant in person should not be required to justify his or her desire to have a MF; in the event of objection, it is for the objecting party to rebut the presumption in favour of allowing the MF to attend.

- Factors which should not outweigh the presumption in favour of allowing the assistance of a MF include:
  - the fact that proceedings are confidential and that the court papers contain sensitive information relating to the family's affairs;
  - the fact that the litigant in person appears to be capable of conducting the case without the assistance of a MF;
  - the fact that the litigant in person is unrepresented through choice;
  - the fact that the objecting party is not represented;
  - the fact that the hearing is a directions hearing or case management hearing;
  - the fact that a proposed MF belongs to an organisation that promotes a particular cause.

- The proposed MF should not be excluded from the courtroom or chambers while the application for assistance is made, and the MF should ordinarily be allowed to assist the litigant in person to make the application.

- The proposed MF should produce a short curriculum vitae or other statement setting out relevant experience and confirming that he/she has no interest in the case and understands the role of a MF and the duty of confidentiality.

- If a court decides in the exercise of its discretion to refuse to allow a MF to assist the litigant in person, the reasons for the decision should be explained carefully and fully to both the litigant in person and the would-be MF.

- The litigant may appeal that refusal, but the MF has no standing to do so.

- The court may refuse to allow a MF to act or continue to act in that capacity where the court forms the view that the assistance the MF has given, or may give, impedes the efficient administration of justice. However, the court should also consider whether a firm and unequivocal warning to the litigant and/or MF might suffice in the first instance.

- Where permission has been given for a litigant in person to receive assistance from a MF in care proceedings, the court should consider the attendance of the MF at any advocates' meetings directed by the court, and, with regard to cases commenced after 1 April 2008, consider directions in accordance with the PLO Practice Direction, para 13.2.

- The litigant in person is permitted to communicate any information, including filed evidence, relating to the proceedings to the MF for the purpose of obtaining advice or assistance in relation to the proceedings.

- Legal representatives should ensure that documents are served on the litigant in person in good time to seek assistance regarding their content from the MF in advance of any hearing or advocates' meeting.

- Listed under the heading 'what a McKenzie friend may do' are the following:
  - provide moral support for the litigant;
  - take notes;
  - help with case papers;
  - quietly give advice on points of law or procedure, issues that the litigant may wish to raise in court, and questions the litigant may wish to ask witnesses.

- Listed under the heading 'what a McKenzie friend may not do' are the following:
  - A MF has no right to act on behalf of a litigant in person. It is the right of the litigant who wishes to do so to have the assistance of a MF.
  - A MF is not entitled to address the court, nor examine any witnesses. A MF who does so becomes an advocate and requires the grant of a right of audience.
  - A MF may not act as the agent of the litigant in relation to the proceedings nor manage the litigant's case outside court, for example, by signing court documents.

- The Courts and Legal Services Act 1990, ss 27 and 28, govern exhaustively rights of audience and the right to conduct litigation. They provide the court with a discretionary power to grant lay individuals such rights.

- A court may grant an unqualified person a right of audience in exceptional circumstances and after careful consideration. If the litigant in person wishes the MF to be granted a right of audience or the right to conduct the litigation, an application must be made at the start of the hearing.

- Litigants in person should also be aware of the services provided by local Personal Support Units and Citizens' Advice Bureaux.[104]

5.68 The Guidance is of course predicated on the unrepresented litigant being aware of the McKenzie friend procedure. Although the PLO Practice Direction does not say so in terms, it would seem highly sensible for a court, faced with a litigant in person at the start of proceedings, to take the initiative and at that stage raise the question of representation and the possible appointment of a McKenzie friend, drawing attention to the President's new Guidance.

Unrepresented litigants and advocates' discussions

5.69 In the context of unrepresented litigants, particular issues arise under the PLO Practice Direction when it comes to dealing with advocates' discussions/meetings.

5.70 Advocates' discussions/meetings form an integral part of the whole PLO structure, and addressing the role within them of the litigant in person and any McKenzie friend appointed forms part of 'active case management'.

5.71 Paragraph 3.15(10) of the Practice Direction provides that 'active case management' includes 'directing discussion between advocates and litigants in person before the Case Management Conference and Issues Resolution Hearing', whilst para 13.2 adds the following:

> 'Where there is a litigant in person the court will consider the most effective way in which that person can be involved in the advocates' discussions and give directions as appropriate including directions relating to the part played by a McKenzie's friend.'

---

104 The Guidance indicates that the PSU at the Royal Courts of Justice in London can be contacted on 020 7947 7701, by email at cbps@bello.co.uk or at the enquiry desk, and that the CAB at the Royal Courts of Justice in London can be contacted on 020 7947 6564 or at the enquiry desk.

5.72 Although the case management checklist that is the Draft Case Management Order makes no specific reference to litigants in person, it will be incumbent upon the advocates for the other parties to have regard to the position of those who are unrepresented. Special care will be needed when dealing with litigants in person and McKenzie friends over such matters as the disclosure of confidential documents, the instruction of experts, special measures and the identification of key issues.

5.73 Whilst all advocates should have regard to the position of the litigant in person, in practice it may be sensible for one advocate – perhaps the representative for the Children's Guardian – to take particular responsibility for keeping the litigant in person fully informed and (provided no conflict of interest arises) giving guidance on procedure.

Litigants appearing in person – particular difficulties

5.74 The presence of litigants in person in care proceedings presents a number of challenges to the court.

5.75 First, given the complexity of the evidence, such a litigant may be at an acute disadvantage, especially as the other parties will usually be represented by experienced specialist advocates.

5.76 Secondly, the sheer volume of written material disclosed in such proceedings may present difficulties, both in terms of protecting confidentiality and in ensuring that the litigant in person has a grasp of the issues.

5.77 A further difficulty may arise when it is necessary for the litigant in person to cross-examine a witness, child or adult, who has made allegations of abuse, for none of the special measures set out in the Youth Justice and Criminal Evidence Act 1999 Act provides adequate protection for the witness in such circumstances.

5.78 In criminal proceedings, the Youth Justice and Criminal Evidence Act 1999, s 34, prohibits a person charged with sexual offences from cross-examining the complainant in person. In these circumstances, the court must invite the accused to arrange for a legal representative to act for him or her for the purpose of cross-examination. If the accused declines the invitation after due notice, the court must consider whether it is necessary in the interests of justice for the witness to be cross-examined by a legal representative on behalf of the accused, and if so must appoint a qualified representative for that purpose.[105]

5.79 There is at present no equivalent power in the civil (including family) jurisdiction, and in the absence of such a power there is no easy solution.

5.80 In the recent case of *H v L and R*,[106] a private law case involving an application for parental responsibility, the issue arose as to who should cross-examine a vulnerable adult witness who had alleged that the litigant in person father had sexually abused her.

5.81 With the father having a right to put his case under ECHR, Art 6, Roderic Wood J reviewed all the available options. It was inappropriate for the child's Guardian to ask questions on behalf of the father. CAFCASS Legal, the Official Solicitor and the Bar's Free Representation Unit all declined to act, for various reasons all accepted by the judge. Whilst it was open in theory for the court to cross-examine the witness, the judge expressed a sense of 'profound unease' at the thought of conducting such an exercise, and concluded that it should only be done in

---

105 Youth Justice and Criminal Evidence Act 1999, s 38.

106 [2006] EWHC 3099 (Fam), [2007] 2 FLR 162.

exceptional circumstances. In the end, and following the court's urgent request, the Attorney-General exceptionally agreed to provide an advocate, but the court explained that this was not to be a regular solution.[107]

5.82 At the end of his judgment, Roderic Wood J invited urgent attention to creating a new statutory provision for representation in such circumstances analogous to the existing framework in criminal cases under the 1999 Act, on the basis that there was no discernible difference between the two types of proceedings either in terms of policy or logic. But, until such provision is made, courts will have to resort to ad hoc solutions as best they can.

INTERIM HEARINGS, ICOS AND RESIDENTIAL ASSESSMENTS

5.83 The active case management required by the PLO Practice Direction will require the parties and the court to determine at an early stage whether there needs to be an urgent contested hearing. This will most frequently be where the court has to resolve whether or not there should be an interim care order, and will particularly occur where the prompt for proceedings (as it is often) has been a crisis in the family and where the local authority's proposed interim care plan is for removal.

Interim Hearings and ICOs

5.84 By the time of the First Appointment, the parties should have notified the court of the need for a contested hearing; and, in most cases, in line with the PLO, arrangements for contested interim hearings will be considered at it.[108] This approach will enable the parties and the court to identify the issues and evidence required for that contested hearing.[109]

5.85 An interim care or supervision order may be made in any proceedings where, on an application for a care or supervision order, the proceedings are adjourned.[110] Such an order must be made by the court, so a single justice will not suffice. A court shall not make an interim care or supervision order within care or supervision proceedings unless satisfied that there are reasonable grounds for believing that the circumstances with regard to the child are those required to satisfy the Children Act 1989, s 31(2).[111] Once that interim threshold is found crossed, the court then has to decide whether or not it is in the best interests of the child to make the

---

107 In an unreported care case heard in the High Court in 2007, allegations of sexual abuse were made by a girl and her three cousins, all vulnerable young adults, against the girl's father and their grandfather. The father, and various other parties, were all represented, but the grandfather did not qualify for public funding. Faced with the prospect of the grandfather cross-examining all four complainants in person, the trial judge explored several of the options considered in *H v L and R* (above). On this occasion, the Attorney-General was unable to assist. In the event, the then Chairman of the Family Law Bar Association, Anthony Kirk QC, agreed to represent the grandfather pro bono.

108 The Public Law Outline, Stage 1.

109 The Ministry of Justice's Care Proceedings Reforms website (www.justice.gov.uk/docs/faqs-care-proceedings-reforms.pdf) notes that when contested applications for interim care orders will be heard will depend on local resources. Some cases will be transferred on issue, with the first hearing in the county court, and some will be listed before a legal adviser in the FPC. In cases before the FPC, the FPC should endeavour to deal with the ICO application on the day of the First Appointment or the next working day. The website notes further that the court should have sufficient information on the issue of proceedings to determine the best way to proceed.

110 Children Act 1989, s 38(1), which provides that an ICO or ISO can also be made where a direction is given under Children Act 1989, s 37, for an investigation of the child's circumstances by the appropriate local authority.

111 Children Act 1989, s 38(2).

interim order sought on the basis of the care plan put forward by the local authority.[112] It is a mistake to confuse the threshold for an interim order with the question of what order, if any, should be made.[113]

5.86 Although the Court of Appeal (in a case that predated the Human Rights Act 1998) stated that an interim care order may be an impartial step to preserve the status quo pending the final hearing,[114] it is by no means a routine order, especially if the care plan pursuant to it is for the removal of the child.

5.87 A separation between child and parent in the interim should only be contemplated if the risk to the child's safety demands immediate separation.[115] Removal is a consideration separate from the existence of the interim threshold or the need for an interim order. When considering whether to remove a child at an interim stage the court had to consider whether there was an imminent risk of really serious harm; if there was not, the question of whether the parent was able to provide good enough long term care was a matter for the court to decide at a final hearing, and was not to be litigated at an interim hearing.[116] In determining such an application the court must bring into the balance the risk of short term emotional harm that is likely to occur as a result of removal, as against any harm that might result from the child remaining with his or her family.[117]

5.88 In any event, where the interim threshold under the Children Act 1989, s 38(2), is crossed, the paramountcy principle, the welfare checklist, the 'no order' principle and the proportionality principle all apply when the court is considering whether to make an interim care order, whether or not it is proposed that there should be any interim removal.

5.89 If an interim care or supervision order is made, then it will fall for renewal at the expiry of the time limit specified within it.[118] In many cases, the interim order will be renewed, in accordance with local protocols, without the need for any further evidence and in the absence of the parties. The order triggering this 'automatic renewal' procedure will ordinarily provide for the interim care (or supervision) order to be renewed with the written consent of all parties or in the absence of any written objection, and subject to confirmation that there has been no material change to the basis upon which the interim threshold was found crossed.

5.90 This procedure does not mean that a party cannot object to an interim care order being renewed and therefore insist on there being a hearing formally to consider the renewal. Nor does it mean that the local authority should not be considering over this period whether the child concerned should still be in their care.[119] But, in terms of the conduct of any renewal hearing, the following guidance should be borne in mind:

- An interim hearing was bound to be circumscribed in its ambit. Findings of fact on disputed issues should rarely be made at an interim stage and, when oral evidence was

---

112 The obligation upon the local authority to produce a care plan at the interim stages of the case is discussed at **5.109** et seq.

113 *Re K and H* [2006] EWCA Civ 1898, [2007 1 FLR 2043.

114 *Re G (Minors) (Interim Care Order)* [1993] 2 FLR 839.

115 *Re H (A Child) (Interim Care Order)* [2002] EWCA Civ, 1932, [2003] 1 FCR 350.

116 *Re L (Care Proceedings: Removal of Child)* [2008] 1 FLR 575.

117 *Re M (Interim Care Order: Removal)* [2005] EWCA Civ 1594, [2006] 1 FLR 1043.

118 The relevant time limits are set out within Children Act 1989, s 38(4) and (5). In broad terms, an interim order can be made for up to eight weeks in the first instance and up to four weeks thereafter.

119 ECHR jurisprudence has made clear that the positive duty to take measures to facilitate family reunification as soon as reasonably feasible begins to weigh on the responsible authorities with progressively increasing force as from the commencement of the period of care, subject always to being balanced against the duty to consider the best interests of the child, including the interest of the child not to have his or her de facto family situation changed again (see *KA v Finland (Application No 27751/95)* [2003] 1 FLR 696).

permitted, cross-examination should be restricted to the issues essential to establishing a holding position. The interim hearing was not a dress rehearsal for the full hearing.

- The court had the power to determine its own procedure and to control evidence and submissions. There was nothing improper in a judge, who had considered the papers and the reasons given by the previous judge for making an interim care order, limiting the scope of the oral hearing to (a) a consideration of whatever evidence might be relevant to such significant matters as might have changed since the last hearing, and (b) the impact that those changes might have on the s 38(2) grounds for the issue of the order for the next interim period. That was not to say that after the first interim order had been made no later application could be fully contested unless a change of circumstances was shown, but that the court, having the discretion to control its own procedure, could exercise that discretion in appropriate cases by concentrating upon changes in circumstances. The court had to make decisions tailored to the individual circumstances.[120]

Residential assessments

5.91 An interim hearing may also be required to determine whether or not there should be a residential assessment of the child and that child's parent or parents.

Purpose and ambit

5.92 The court's power to direct a residential assessment arises from the Children Act 1989, s 38(6), which provides that the court, upon making either an interim care or interim supervision order, may make such directions as it considers appropriate for the medical, psychiatric or other assessment of the child.

5.93 In *Re C (A Minor) (Interim Care Order: Residential Assessment)*[121] the House of Lords held that the phrase 'other assessment of the child' was not to be interpreted as limiting assessments to those types which were similar to medical or psychiatric examinations, nor was it to be construed as applying to assessments restricted to the child. As it is not possible to assess a young child apart from that child's environment, an assessment of the interaction between the child and those caring for him or her was an essential and legitimate aspect of it. The purpose of ordering a residential assessment should be to provide the court with the information necessary for it to make a decision as to whether a full care order should be made in respect of the child.

5.94 More recently, the House of Lords has once again considered the issue of residential assessments in the case of *Re G (Interim Care Order: Residential Assessment)*,[122] and the following principles should be noted:

- The purpose of the Children Act 1989, s 38(6), is to ensure that the court is in control of the evidence to be obtained about the child and put before the court, with the subsection enabling the court to obtain the information it needs for its ultimate decision and to control the information-gathering activities of others.

- The court has the power under s 38(6) to direct an examination or assessment of the child, including, where appropriate, the child's relationship with his or her parents, the risks that the parents may present to the child, and the ways in which those risks may be avoided or managed.

---

120 *Re B (Interim Care Orders: Renewal)* [2001] 2 FLR 1217.
121 [1997] 1 FLR 1.
122 [2005] UKHL 68, [2006] 1 FLR 601.

- The court only has power to direct an assessment where it is relevant to the questions which the court has to answer. Where the issue is how capable a parent is of meeting the child's needs, it is the present capacity with which the court is concerned. It cannot be a proper use of the court's powers under s 38(6), to seek to bring about change.[123]

- The principal focus of the assessment must be the child. Any services which were provided must be ancillary to the aim of obtaining the necessary information to make a decision. The court had no power under s 38(6) to ensure the provision of services beyond this either for the child or that child's family.

5.95 Baroness Hale also made plain that time was a factor to be considered:

> 'These conclusions are reinforced by the Act's emphasis on reaching decisions without delay. It cannot have been contemplated that the examination or assessment ordered under s 38(6) would take many months to complete. It would be surprising if it were to last more than 2 or 3 months at most.'[124]

5.96 Whilst the *Re G* decision undoubtedly checked the tide flowing in favour of a broader discretion under s 38(6), the potential relevance and importance of a residential assessment in a suitable case remains.

5.97 As the Court of Appeal emphasised in two cases decided in 2007,[125] sometimes a residential assessment can represent the only chance that parents have to demonstrate that they are able to provide good enough care to their child, and may make the difference between care within the family and outside adoption. Furthermore, the supervised setting ensures the child's safety, whilst at the same time allowing for the assessment of the parents' ability to care for him or her in all aspects of domestic and family life.

5.98 In the first case, *Re L and H*,[126] Wall LJ provided the following powerful rationale for the residential assessment taking place:

> 'As I see the case, it is manifestly in the interests of M to see if his parents are able to care for him, and it is the responsibility of the court to ensure that it has the best evidence on which to reach a conclusion about his welfare. It is also procedurally fair for his parents to be given the opportunity to demonstrate that they can overcome their manifest difficulties and care for him, and it would, in my judgment, be unfair were they to be denied that opportunity.'[127]

Funding

5.99 Because of their length[128] and the level of supervision entailed, it is inevitable that the cost of residential assessments will be high; and that factor, combined with the many demands upon local authority resources, has made the issue of the funding of residential assessments particularly contentious.

---

123 The House of Lords made clear that the capacity to change, to learn and to develop may well be part of the assessment of the parent's present capacity; also that, as a matter of current forecast, the investigation may look to the future to the extent of achieving an understanding of the present capacity of the parent to overcome any present deficiency. But what is impermissible is an assessment continuing over many months to follow the progress, if any, of the parent in improving his or her capacity to give proper care to the child, or in reducing the risk to the child which led to the interim care order being sought at the outset.

124 *Re G* (above), at para [68].

125 *Re L and H (Residential Assessment)* [2007] EWCA Civ 213, [2007] 1 FLR 1370; *Re K (Care Order)* [2007] EWCA Civ 697, [2007] 2 FLR 1066.

126 Above.

127 Ibid, at para [91].

128 Prior to the *Re G* decision, some units, such as the Cassel Hospital, provided a very thorough assessment in the most difficult cases. Often exceeding 6 months in length, such assessments did in certain cases allow families to be

5.100 The ability of the court to order a local authority to fund an appropriate residential assessment has long been recognised.[129] For a while, the blow was softened by the court's allied ability to apportion the costs incurred between the local authority and other publicly funded parties.[130] But, since October 2007, when the Legal Services Commission made changes to its funding guidance, that is no longer an option and the burden now falls squarely on the shoulders of the local authority.

5.101 In most cases where the issue of residential assessment arises, the question for the court is simply whether or not it should be directed. In some, the argument is as to the appropriate length of the assessment, with the local authority prepared to fund a shorter assessment than that sought by other parties. In both scenarios, the court is undoubtedly entitled to take into account the cost of the assessment and the fact that local authority resources are notoriously limited.[131] However, 'it is inappropriate for the court to require detailed evidence from senior officers of . . . reluctant local authorities and insist that they prove a so-called "money defence"'.[132]

5.102 In the recent case of *A Local Authority v M (Funding of Residential Assessments)*[133] a local authority was ordered to pay the entire cost of a residential assessment agreed to be in the child's best interests, notwithstanding that it had a deficit budget. In making the order, however, Bodey J noted that there was an urgent need for further consideration of the funding of necessary residential assessments. It was, he felt, unsatisfactory if not invidious that courts charged with taking serious and sensitive decisions about children should have to choose between (a) overburdening an already over-stretched local authority or (b) denying a residential assessment to a parent for whom it represented the only hope of avoiding the loss of his or her child to adoption. He thought that the case amply justified the Family Justice Council's opposition to the recent Funding Guidance amendments, in particular that which meant that the court could no longer direct a sharing of the costs of a residential assessment such as to achieve a contribution from the Legal Services Commission.

The impact of the PLO reforms

5.103 It will be interesting to see the nature and extent of the impact that the PLO and Experts Practice Directions will have on the issue of residential assessments. But, within this context, three consequences of these reforms appear to be likely:

(1) Early identification of the issues, proper case management and co-operation between the parties ought to ensure that any question of residential assessment should be raised and considered at an early stage of the case, with an early hearing date fixed to determine any contested application. It should now be far harder to argue for a residential assessment at the final hearing stage, when the application could have been made earlier in the process.

(2) Paragraphs 2.1(2) and 2.1(4) of the PLO Practice Direction provide, in amplification of the 'overriding objective', that 'dealing with a case justly includes, so far as is practicable . . . dealing with the case in ways which are proportionate to the nature, importance and complexity of the issues; [and] saving expense'. It can be foreseen that these objectives will

---

reunited in the face of enormous odds, but at considerable financial cost. Such lengthy 'assessments' are now very unlikely to be approved any longer by the courts as falling within the ambit of s 38(6).

129 See *Re M (Residential Assessment Directions)* [1998] 2 FLR 371.

130 See *Lambeth London Borough Council v S, C, V and J (by his Guardian); Legal Services Commission Intervening* [2005] EWHC 776, [2005] 2 FLR 1171; and *Sheffield City Council v V (LSC Intervening)* [2006] EWHC 1861 (Fam), [2007] 1 FLR 279, in which Bodey J gave guidance as to how to approach the task of apportionment.

131 See *R v Gloucestershire County Council and another, ex parte Barry* [1997] 2 WLR 459.

132 Per Baroness Hale in *Re G* (above), at para [70].

133 [2008] EWHC 162 (Fam).

be prayed in aid by some local authorities and relied on by some courts when the dispute is as to the length of a residential assessment to be directed, or as to whether a non-residential form of assessment would suffice to meet the justice of the case.

(3) Paragraph 2.1(5) of the PLO Practice Direction further provides that 'dealing with a case justly includes, so far as is practicable . . . allotting to it an appropriate share of the court's resources'. This provision will doubtless be used to reinforce the emphasis in recent case-law upon avoiding lengthy hearings to determine applications for residential assessments.[134]

Interim Care Orders at Final Hearings

5.104 As the name suggests, interim care orders are commonly made during the interim stages of the process. However, the court may also make interim care orders at listed final hearings, even where it has found the section 31 threshold criteria met.

5.105 There may of course be some obvious and compelling reason of procedural fairness which stops the final hearing going ahead. But there are also situations where the court decides that it is premature to make a final decision, and that the resultant delay is warranted to achieve the right outcome for the child concerned.[135] There are three main scenarios in which this can occur:

(1) The court determines that further assessment still needs to be carried out to provide the court with information necessary for its ultimate decision,[136] though, with the more proactive and front-loaded approaches of the PLO and Experts Practice Directions, this should now not happen nearly so frequently at the final hearing stage.

(2) The court decides that the care plan is inchoate or insufficiently clear, and seeks through the further adjournment to engineer a more complete and detailed care plan.

(3) The court wants the local authority more fundamentally to reconsider the aim and content of its care plan.

5.106 The significance of the care plan, and the court's duty to scrutinise it, will be implicit in all three scenarios, but especially in the second and third. The principles applicable where the court considers making interim care orders in those latter two situations are addressed in the following discussion of care plans.[137]

CARE PLANS

5.107 The importance of making plans for children in care has always been recognised as a crucial step in proceedings under Part IV of the Children Act 1989. Initially, it was a matter covered by guidance[138] and buttressed by a series of reported cases.[139] However, since the

---

134 See *Re G* (above), at para [70]; and *A Local Authority v M* (above).

135 As the final May 2003 report of the Lord Chancellor's Advisory Committee on Judicial Case Management in Public Law Children Act Cases (the Protocol [2003] 2 FLR 719 at p 806) recognised: 'The introduction of the Protocol should lead to better use of available resources and so reduction of unnecessary delay. However, it must be remembered and emphasised that PLCACs, by their very nature, sometimes call for flexibility and delay. The target in every case is to get the best possible outcome for the child concerned. There will always remain cases where there is a need for adapting or prolonging the procedure to fit changing circumstances or allow for constructive delay. The right answer cannot be sacrificed on the altar of speed and efficiency.'

136 See *Re G* (above).

137 See **5.114** et seq.

138 The Children Act 1989 Guidance and Regulations – Volume 3: Family Placements, chapter 2.

implementation of the Adoption and Children Act 2002, which inserted a new s 31A into the 1989 Act, the obligation to prepare a care plan has been statutory.

Preparing the care plan

5.108 Where an application is made on which a care order might be made with respect to a child, the appropriate local authority must, within such time as the court may direct, prepare a care plan for the future of the child.[140] For these purposes, the 'appropriate authority' is the local authority proposed to be designated in the order.[141] Such a plan is known as a 'section 31A plan',[142] and references to 'care plan' within the PLO Practice Direction are to a section 31A plan.[143]

5.109 It has been commonly thought that the duty upon a local authority to prepare a section 31A plan does not apply where at a hearing it only seeks an interim care order.[144] But a close scrutiny of the statute would suggest that the following actually represents the correct position:

- The court cannot make a final care order until it has considered a section 31A plan,[145] but can make an interim care order in those circumstances.[146]
- Where the court makes an interim care order at the same time as giving a direction under the Children Act 1989, s 37,[147] the requirement for a care plan clearly does not bite because the application being considered by the court is not 'an application . . . on which a care order might be made with respect to a child'.
- However, the position in care proceedings is different. Even though at any given interim hearing the local authority may only be seeking an interim care order, the court at all those interim hearings will nevertheless be considering 'an application . . . on which a care order might be made with respect to a child'. Accordingly, if the court has prior to that interim hearing directed a care plan for it, then the local authority is obliged to prepare one.
- This interpretation is reinforced by the Children Act 1989, s 31A(2), which provides that 'while the application [for a care order] is pending, the authority must keep any care plan prepared by them under review'.[148]

---

[139] See, for example, *Manchester CC v F: Note* [1993] 1 FLR 419; *Re J (Minors) (Care: Care Plan)* [1994] 1 FLR 253; *Re T (A Minor) (Care Order: Conditions)* [1994] 2 FLR 423.

[140] Children Act 1989, s 31A(1).

[141] Children Act 1989, s 31A(4). Children Act 1989, s 31(8), provides that the local authority designated in a care order must be: (a) the authority within whose area the child is ordinarily resident, or (b) when the child does not reside in the area of a local authority, the authority within whose area any circumstances arose in consequence of which the order is being made. Children Act 1989, s 31(8)(b), should be construed so as to read the word 'ordinarily' before the word 'reside' (*Northamptonshire CC v Islington LBC* [1999] 2 FLR 881). In determining the ordinary residence of a child under the Act, there shall be disregarded any period in which the child lives in any place while he is being accommodated by or on behalf of a local authority (s 105(6)(c)). A child who is placed with relatives by a local authority ceases to be 'provided with accommodation by or on behalf of a local authority' under s 105(6) (*Re H (Care Order: Appropriate Local Authority)* [2004] 1 FLR 534).

[142] Children Act 1989, s 31A(6).

[143] The PLO Practice Direction, at para 25(12).

[144] This, for example, is the view taken by the *Family Court Practice* (Jordans, 2008 ed), at p 640.

[145] Children Act 1989, s 31(3A).

[146] Children Act 1989, s 31A(5).

[147] This is a direction for an investigation by the local authority of the child's circumstances.

[148] Children Act 1989, s 31A(2), which adds that the care plan must be revised or a new plan prepared if the local authority thinks that some change to the existing plan is required.

5.110 What the Public Law Outline does is to provide the extra initial link that brings the requirement for the preparation of a care plan to bear for the first hearing in care proceedings. It does this:

- by stipulating that the 'care plan' is a 'checklist document' that must be prepared by the local authority for the proceedings;[149]
- by adding that 'pre-proceedings checklist compliance' is included within the 'standard directions' to be given by the court on issue (and therefore in advance of the First Appointment);[150] and
- by providing that the court's scrutiny of the care plan is one of the case management steps to be carried out by the court at the First Appointment.[151]

5.111 Accordingly, at the First Appointment the court should have a section 31A plan to consider, with the PLO stipulations in this regard fully consistent with the provisions of the Children Act 1989, s 31A, when properly construed.

5.112 A care plan must give any prescribed information and do so in the prescribed manner.[152] The Local Authority Circular of 12 August 1999[153] contains guidance as to the contents of the care plan, and provides that it should be structured in five sections as follows:

(1) *Overall aims* – aim of plan and timetable.

(2) *Child's needs* – the child's identified needs (including those arising from race, culture, religion or language, special educational, health or disability needs); the extent to which the wishes and views of the child have been obtained and acted upon; the reasons supporting this, or explanations of why these wishes or views have not been given absolute precedence; how those needs might be met; arrangements for, and the purpose of, contact in meeting the child's needs (specifying contact relationships), and proposals to restrict or terminate contact.

(3) *Views of others* – the extent to which the wishes and views of the child's parents and anyone else with a sufficient interest in the child (including representatives of other agencies) have been obtained and acted upon and the reasons supporting this or explanations of why these wishes and views have been discounted.

(4) *Placement details and timetable* – the proposed placement (type and details); the time that is likely to elapse before the proposed placement is made; the likely duration of placement in the accommodation; arrangements for health care (including consent to examination and treatment); arrangements for education; arrangements for reunification; other services to be provided to the child and/or the child's family either by the local authority or other agencies; support in the placement; specific detail of the parent's role in day-to-day arrangements.

(5) *Management and support by local authority* – who is to be responsible for implementing the plan (specific tasks and overall plan); dates of reviews; contingency plan, if placement

---

149 The PLO Practice Direction, at para 10.2.

150 The Public Law Outline, Stage 1. Directions to ensure compliance with the 'pre-proceedings checklist' is something also covered by the PLO Practice Direction, at para 11.4(1)(b).

151 The PLO Practice Direction, at para 12.3(5).

152 Children Act, s 31A(3).

153 LAC (99) 29, *Care Plans and Care Proceedings under the Children Act.*

breaks down; arrangements for input by parents, the child and others into the ongoing decision-making process; arrangements for notifying the responsible authority of disagreements or making representations.

5.113 The circular further provides that the plan should be signed by a senior local authority manager.

Scrutinising the care plan

5.114 The obligation upon the court to scrutinise the care plan at the First Appointment is replicated in identical terms for the Case Management Conference[154] and for the Issues Resolution Hearing.[155] Indeed, the provisions of the care plan are likely to feature prominently amongst the issues under consideration at the IRH.

5.115 Although not specifically on the face of Stage 4 of the Public Law Outline, the court's duty to scrutinise the care plan at final hearing will be implicit in the stated objective of the court determining the remaining issues.

5.116 This is of course an obligation long-recognised by the case-law, and one that has formed a central feature of care proceedings since the implementation of the Children Act 1989. In *Re J (Minors) (Care: Care Plan)*,[156] Wall J (as he then was) spelt out the duty of the court in this respect:

> '[T]he court [is required] carefully to scrutinise the care plan prepared by the local authority and to satisfy itself that the care plan is in the child's interests. Thus, if the court is not satisfied the care plan is in the best interests of the child, the court may refuse to make a care order.'[157]

5.117 The leading authority on the making of interim care orders at final hearings of care proceedings, by reason of the state of the care plan, remains that of the House of Lords in *Re S (Minors) (Care Order: Implementation of Care Plan); Re W (Minors) (Care Order: Adequacy of Care Plan)*.[158] The following principles should be noted:

- Interim care orders were not intended to be used as a means by which the court might continue to exercise a supervisory role over the local authority in cases in which it was in the best interests of a child that a care order should be made.

- Problems had arisen about how far courts should go in attempting to resolve uncertainties within care plans before making a care order. Where an uncertainty needed to be resolved before the court could decide whether it was in the best interests of the child to make a care order at all, the court should finally dispose of the matter only when the material facts were as clearly known as could be hoped.

- Some uncertainties relating to the details of the care plan were suitable for immediate resolution, in whole or in part, by the court in the course of disposing of the care order application; other uncertainties could and should be resolved before the court proceeded, during a limited period of 'planned and purposeful' delay.

---

[154] The PLO Practice Direction, at para 14.3(3).

[155] Although not expressly included in the steps to be taken by the court at the IRH, provided for by the Practice Direction, at para 15.3, the obligation for the court to scrutinise the care plan is listed in the PLO itself, Stage 3.

[156] [1994] 1 FLR 253.

[157] Ibid, at p 258.

[158] [2002] UKHL 10, [2002] 1 FLR 815. See also *C v Solihull Metropolitan Borough Council* [1993] 1 FLR 290; *Re J (Minors) (Care: Care Plan)* (above).

- Frequently the uncertainties involved in a care plan could only be worked out after the making of an order. Despite all the inevitable uncertainties, when deciding to make a care order the court should normally have before it a care plan which was sufficiently firm and particularised for all concerned to have a reasonably clear picture of the likely way ahead for the child in the foreseeable future.

- The degree of firmness to be expected, as well as the amount of detail in the plan, would vary from case to case, but, if the parents and the child's Guardian were to have a fair and adequate opportunity to make representations to the court on whether a care order should be made, the care plan must be appropriately specific.

- The court must always maintain a proper balance between the need to satisfy itself about the appropriateness of the care plan and the avoidance of over-zealous investigation into matters which were the responsibility of the local authority.

5.118 Those principles are particularly pertinent to the situation where the argument is that the care plan is inchoate or insufficiently specific.

5.119 But, in practice, there are cases where the court recognises that a care order may be inevitable but far more fundamentally disagrees with the aim and content of the care plan that it is being asked to approve.

5.120 As a matter of strict law, 'the only power of the court under Part IV is either to approve or refuse to approve the care plan . . .. [It] cannot dictate to the local authority what the care plan is to say'.[159] Thus, 'the court, if it seeks to alter the local authority's care plan, must achieve its objective by persuasion rather than by compulsion'.[160]

5.121 But, as the Court of Appeal's decision in *Re S and W (Care Proceedings)*[161] amply demonstrates, woe betide a local authority which misunderstands its relationship with the court and as a result does not take seriously any request by the court to rethink its care plan. As Wall LJ explains:

> 'It is, we think, worthwhile pausing for a moment to reflect on why a court is entitled to exercise a discretionary jurisdiction to adjourn in order to invite a local authority to reconsider. The answer, we think, is, like much of what we have already said, self-evident. Care proceedings are only quasi-adversarial. There is a powerful inquisitorial element. But above all, they are proceedings in which the court and the local authority should both be striving to achieve an order which is in the best interests of the child. There needs to be mutual respect and understanding for the different role and perspective which each has in the process. We repeat: the shared objective should be to achieve a result which is in the best interests of the child.'[162]

5.122 In an appropriate case, the court can properly require the local authority to reconsider its care plan more than once.[163] But, as Munby J recognised in *Re K (Care Proceedings: Care Plan)*,[164] there are limits to how far the court can go:

> 'How far the court can properly go down this road is a matter of some delicacy and difficulty. There are no fixed and immutable rules. It is impossible to define in the abstract or even to identify with any precision in the particular case the point to which the court can properly press matters but beyond

---

[159] Per Munby J in *Re L (Care Proceedings: Human Rights Claims)* [2003] EWHC 665 (Fam), [2003] 2 FLR 160, at para [11].
[160] Per Munby J in *Re K (Care Proceedings: Care Plan)* [2007] EWHC 393 (Fam), [2008] 1 FLR 1, at para [15].
[161] [2007] EWCA Civ 232, [2007] 2 FLR 275.
[162] Ibid, at para [35].
[163] See, for example, *Re X; Barnet London Borough Council v Y and X* [2006] 2 FLR 998, a decision of Munby J sitting as a county court judge.
[164] Above, at para [16].

which it cannot properly go. The issue is always one for fine judgment, reflecting sensitivity, realism and an appropriate degree of judicial understanding of what can and cannot sensibly be expected of the local authority.'

5.123 Indeed, the court may ultimately find itself in a situation where it has to choose the lesser of two evils.[165]

5.124 Where a court clearly believes a care order to be in the best interests of the child but has concerns about contact, the court should approve the care plan except in relation to contact. The question of contact could then be dealt with either by making a contact order there and then or by giving directions for future determination of that issue or by leaving it to one of the parties to make a suitable application. Refusing to approve the care plan and make a care order in these circumstances is not appropriate.[166]

5.125 Once a care order is made, the court has no power to monitor the administrative arrangements for the child.[167] There are two exceptions to this rule:

(1) The court has statutory powers under the Children Act 1989, s 34, to make orders for contact with children in care. This ostensibly wide discretion is, however, subject to the qualification that 'contact must not be allowed to destabilise or endanger the arrangements for the child and in many cases the plans for the child will be decisive of the contact application'.[168]

(2) Parents aggrieved by a local authority's implementation of a care order may, in certain circumstances, be able to bring a claim under the Human Rights Act 1998.[169] Such claims are most likely to arise if there is a change of care plan by the local authority very shortly after the care order is made.[170]

5.126 The possibility of post-care order proceedings reinforces the need for the care plan to be clear and comprehensive, and the allied importance of the court's duty to subject it to rigorous scrutiny.

THRESHOLD SCHEDULES AND SPLIT HEARINGS

5.127 Within this section the inter-related topics of threshold schedules and split hearings are addressed.

Threshold schedules

5.128 The Public Law Outline requires the local authority to prepare a Schedule of Proposed Findings, to be filed upon issuing the proceedings. It is one of the documents on the pre-proceedings checklist.[171]

---

165 See *Re S and D (Children: Powers of Court)* [1995] 2 FLR 456.
166 *Re K (Care Proceedings: Care Plan)* (above).
167 *Re S; Re W* (above).
168 Per Butler-Sloss LJ in *Re B (Minors) (Care: Contact: Local Authority's Plans)* [1993] 1 FLR 543, at p 551.
169 See *Re S; Re W* (above); *Re W (Removal into Care)* [2005] EWCA Civ 642, [2005] 2 FLR 1022; *Re C (Breach of Human Rights: Damages)* [2007] EWCA Civ 2, [2007] 1 FLR 1957.
170 See, for example, *Re M (Care: Challenging Decisions by Local Authority)* [2001] 2 FLR 1300; *Re C (Breach of Human Rights: Damages)* (above).
171 The PLO Practice Direction, at para 10.2.

5.129 The Schedule of Proposed Findings is defined within the PLO Practice Direction as meaning 'the schedule of findings of fact prepared by the local authority sufficient to satisfy the threshold criteria under section 31(2) of the 1989 Act and to inform the care plan'.[172]

5.130 Although it is likely that this document will be refined or even redrafted during the interim stages of the case, this requirement will at least ensure that the court, the local authority and all other parties focus on the key issues in the case at the earliest possible stage.

5.131 The PLO Practice Direction recognises that in some cases the circumstances are such that the safety and welfare of the child may be jeopardised if the start of the proceedings is delayed until all the checklist documents are made available to the court.[173] But it would be a rare case where the emergency is such that the local authority could not put forward at least an outline schedule at the outset.

5.132 There was certainly a time after the implementation of the Children Act 1989 when there was no requirement at all for the local authority to plead its case, which ended up being gleaned from the written and oral evidence provided. But gradually the practice changed. First it became common for a schedule of findings to be filed in time for the final hearing. It then became more usual for that schedule to be filed earlier and earlier in the proceedings, so that all were aware at an early stage of the likely issues, and, so far as the lay parties were concerned, of the case to be answered.

5.133 The practice of requiring the local authority to file a schedule of proposed findings was endorsed and rationalised by Hale LJ (as she then was) in *Re G (Care Proceedings: Threshold Conditions)*:[174]

> 'The local authority is not required to plead their case at the outset or indeed at all. It is now the practice in many courts to require the local authority before the final hearing to make a clear statement of the facts they wish the court to find and the basis upon which they allege that the threshold is crossed. In my view this should be routine, so that the parents can know the case they have to meet and have a fair opportunity to meet it.'

5.134 It was not, however, until the arrival of the Protocol in 2003 that the requirement for the filing of a schedule of findings was formalised. First, the local authority was required, upon issue of the proceedings, to set out a summary of all facts and matters relied upon, in particular those necessary to satisfy the threshold criteria; and then, during the process of preparing for the CMC, it was required to put its proposed threshold findings into schedule form. The Public Law Outline now requires that schedule to be prepared at the outset, although it is very clear that there is a continuing requirement for the court and all parties to identify the relevant issues in the case as it develops.

5.135 It is very important to note the distinction between on the one hand findings of fact and on the other findings that by their very nature mean that the threshold criteria have been met.

5.136 Findings as to primary facts – for example, that a child had been non-accidentally injured – may easily lead to the conclusion that that child was suffering significant harm pursuant to the Children Act 1989, s 31(2)(a), at the date that the local authority took protective measures. But such findings may not necessarily translate into a finding that a sibling, who has not been so injured, is 'likely to suffer' significant harm.

---

172 Ibid, at para 25(31).

173 Ibid, at para 10.3.

174 [2001] EWCA Civ 968, [2001] 2 FLR 1111, at para [12].

5.137 The ability of the court to use the proof of harm to one child to establish the likelihood of harm to another has been long recognised.[175] But the Children Act 1989, s 31, is specific to 'the child concerned': where more than one child is involved, it is necessary to consider each child separately even if in many cases a risk to one is a risk to all.[176]

5.138 In terms of likelihood of harm more generally in the threshold context, the following guidance of Wilson LJ in *AP v The Vale of Glamorgan Council, AS, CL and E-R*[177] should be borne in mind:[178]

> 'In any case where future risk is relied upon, it is . . . very important that a document should analyse and describe (if appropriate, separately in relation to each child, if more than one) how that risk is alleged to arise from the alleged primary facts. Undoubtedly in some cases the reasons may indeed be "obvious" and may be shortly stated; and we do not suggest that an elaborate document is necessarily required. The document may form part of the document which also describes the alleged primary facts, but it should at any rate be a separate and clearly headed part of it. There must be clarity in the distinction between what are the contentions of fact and the contentions of risk.'

5.139 It is the receipt of further evidence (especially expert evidence) after the commencement of proceedings that makes it likely that the local authority will have to refine or redraft its original findings/threshold schedule as the case progresses, and at least until the IRH.

5.140 If other material becomes available after the commencement of proceedings which is relevant to and capable of satisfying the threshold criteria, then the local authority ought to consider whether it should be put before the court and for the court to make findings on it, even if such material did not represent the basis upon which the local authority initially intervened. The threshold has to have been crossed by the date on which the local authority first intervened to protect the child, but, in establishing that the threshold had been crossed at that date, the local authority is entitled to rely upon information acquired after the date of intervention, and even on later events, if those later events were capable of proving the state of affairs at the date of intervention.[179]

5.141 It is a matter for the court to decide whether all the issues of fact raised need to be determined, whether or not the parties are in agreement.[180] In such circumstances, the court will now have to bear in mind the overriding objective of the PLO Practice Direction (namely the need to deal with the case justly, having regard to the welfare issues involved) and doubtless, as part of that overriding objective, the principle of proportionality.[181]

5.142 As a matter of good practice, any schedule of findings sought should be both precise and concise, and should plead facts to be found rather than (as too many do) 'local authority concerns' or reported speech. Findings schedules should also be available in electronic form in all cases.[182] In some cases, they may also usefully take the format of a Scott Schedule.[183]

---

175 See *Re CB and JB (Care Proceedings: Guidelines)* [1998] 2 FLR 211, at pp 221–222.

176 *AP v The Vale of Glamorgan Council, AS, CL and E-R* [2007] EWCA Civ 1265, per Wilson LJ at para [35].

177 Ibid.

178 Ibid, at para [51].

179 See *Re G (Care Proceedings: Threshold Conditions)* (above); *Re A (Children: Split Hearing)* [2006] EWCA Civ 714, [2007] 1 FLR 905.

180 In *Re G (A minor) (Care Order: Threshold Conditions)* [1994] 2 FLR 69, Wall J (as he then was) held that the agreement of the parties as to the threshold being made out did not deprive the court of the duty to satisfy itself that the criteria were made out, and that it should not take the lowest common denominator as the basis of the order. See also *Stockport Metropolitan Borough Council v D* [1995] 1 FLR 873; *Re B (Agreed Findings of Fact)* [1998] 2 FLR 968; *Re M (Threshold Criteria: Parental Concessions)* [1999] 2 FLR 728; *Re D (Child: Threshold Criteria)* [2001] 1 FLR 274.

181 The PLO Practice Direction, at para 2.1.

182 See *Merton London Borough Council v K; Re K (Care: Representation: Public Funding)* [2005] EWHC 167 (Fam), [2005] 2 FLR 422.

183 Ibid.

Split hearings

5.143 Some cases, particularly those where serious allegations are made and need to be determined, are best dealt with by means of a split hearing. Per Bracewell J in *Re S (Care Proceedings: Split Hearing)*:[184]

> 'Courts and practitioners need to be alert to identify those cases which are suited to a split hearing. In general, they are likely to be cases in which there is a clear and stark issue, such as sexual or physical abuse. Local authorities and guardians ad litem can and should give assistance to the court in identifying such cases in order to prevent delay and the ill-focused use of scarce expert resources.'

5.144 Split hearings usually involve the court considering the case in two stages. The first involves the establishment of the primary facts, which may often include an assessment as to whether the threshold criteria are satisfied. The second entails a resolution of the 'welfare' issues and a determination of the outcome. In some (albeit rare) split hearing cases, it may be necessary for there to be three stages – fact-finding, threshold determination and outcome hearing – or for the threshold decision to be made within the confines of the outcome hearing.[185]

5.145 Consequently, where the court is contemplating a split hearing, it is essential that the issues to be resolved in the first limb of the hearing are clearly defined and that the consequences of any such findings are fully understood by the parties.[186]

5.146 Thus, if the court is dealing with a single-issue case in which the facts found will determine the threshold criteria under the Children Act 1989, s 31(2), the directions to be given by the court and which set up the first limb of that hearing must:

- identify precisely the purpose of the hearing, namely to decide whether or not the threshold criteria are established; and

- identify with as much precision as possible the facts upon which the local authority relies and which it asserts will, if proved, establish the criteria.[187]

5.147 Alternatively, if the purpose of the first limb is not to decide whether or not the threshold criteria are satisfied, but to resolve an issue of fact which will affect the manner in which subsequent assessments of the parties are to be made, then the issues which the court is being asked to resolve and the facts which it is being invited to find must equally be clearly spelled out.[188]

5.148 In both scenarios, this is best achieved by an order of the court which sets up the first limb of the hearing, which order should identify clearly the issues which are to be addressed at it.[189]

5.149 It follows that, while in many cases they may end up meaning the same thing, the label 'threshold hearing' must be used with great care and in particular must not be confused with 'fact-finding hearing'.[190]

---

[184] [1996] 2 FLR 773.

[185] See *AP v The Vale of Glamorgan Council* (above).

[186] See *Re A (Children: Split Hearing)* [2006] EWCA Civ 714, [2007] 1 FLR 905.

[187] Ibid. In a suitable case, this can be achieved by express reference to a threshold schedule filed.

[188] Ibid.

[189] Ibid.

[190] See *AP v The Vale of Glamorgan Council* (above).

5.150 Any findings made at a fact-finding or threshold hearing must be clearly set out on the face of or appended to the order made at its conclusion.[191]

5.151 Where there is a split hearing, the same judge or magistrates should hear the case throughout, if at all possible.[192]

5.152 Not only should courts be alert to those cases potentially suitable for split hearings and carefully weigh the advantages and disadvantages of such a course,[193] but they should not delay in doing so.

5.153 Somewhat surprisingly, the PLO Practice Direction, like the Protocol before it, does not address how split hearings fit into the process. In fact, the phrase is never mentioned. But, as a matter of general approach, early identification of cases suitable for split hearings should be the objective. Indeed, this would seem to be the view of Cafcass, whose new Reporting to Court Policy[194] lists the question of whether there is a need for a finding of fact hearing as an area to address in the checklist for the Children's Guardian providing verbal analysis at the First Appointment.[195]

5.154 Whilst most split hearings will be of the nature contemplated above, it should be noted that other forms of split hearing can occur in practice. Given the desirability of achieving as much certainty for the child sooner rather than later, there is nothing wrong in the court determining, in advance of the local authority final care plan, that a particular individual was not going to be in a position to care for the child safely within the timescale that the child needed.[196]

DISCLOSURE

5.155 The issue of disclosure arises in care and supervision proceedings in a number of ways, and is here addressed under five separate sub-headings:

(1) disclosure into the proceedings by the local authority;

(2) disclosure into the proceedings from third parties;

(3) disclosure out of the proceedings;

(4) the withholding of evidence from parties;

(5) the PLO Practice Direction – further provisions on disclosure.

---

191 *Re M and MC (Care: Issues of Fact: Drawing of Orders)* [2002] EWCA Civ 499, [2003] 1 FLR 461.

192 *Re G (Care Proceedings: Split Hearing)* [2001] 1 FLR 872.

193 Having a split hearing can lengthen the overall process. But, equally, they can lead to an early resolution of proceedings if the threshold is not found crossed, or, in those cases where the threshold criteria are found met, it can assist subsequent assessments to have a clear factual basis established sooner rather than later.

194 Set out in Appendix 6 to this book.

195 The Cafcass Reporting to Court Policy, at its Appendix 3. For its part, the MOJ Care Proceedings Reforms website comments: 'There will be no changes to finding of fact hearings. Most of the cases where finding of fact hearings are required will be timetabled around the CMC so that a finding of fact hearing is directed and an adjourned CMC can consider the outcome for further directions'.

196 *North Yorkshire County Council v B* [2007] Fam Law 895.

Disclosure into the proceedings by the local authority

5.156 Whilst the issue of disclosure arises at various points during the PLO Practice Direction, what in this context is most striking is the requirement for early, upfront disclosure by the local authority – a requirement which ought to assist the court and all parties to identify at an early stage the key issues in the case.

5.157 The stipulated requirement for pre-proceedings checklist compliance obliges the local authority to disclose a number of documents from its files upon the issue of proceedings. These comprise the following:

- previous court orders and judgments/reasons;[197]
- any relevant assessment materials – to include initial[198] and core[199] assessments, reports provided pursuant to the Children Act 1989, s 7 or s 37, assessments of relatives and friends, and any other assessment materials (such as a genogram);[200]
- other relevant reports and records – to include single, joint or inter-agency materials (for example, health & education/Home Office and immigration documents), records of discussions with the family, and key local authority minutes and records for the child (including strategy discussion records);[201]
- any pre-existing care plans (for example, a child in need plan, a looked after child plan and a child protection plan);
- the social work chronology;[202]
- letters before proceedings.[203]

5.158 In recent years it has become commonplace for there to be substantial disclosure from local authority files, and indeed from the police and other agencies, but historically this has usually taken place once the proceedings have been issued, and sometimes in the later and advanced stages of the case.

5.159 Over a series of reported judgments, the higher courts have given guidance on the procedure to be adopted when considering what documents should be disclosed to which individuals and to the court.

---

197 Where leave is required to disclose such previous orders/judgments preventing their filing at the outset, the MOJ Care Proceedings Reforms website indicates that local authorities should alert the court to the fact that there have been previous orders and summarise what happened in these cases and why they are relevant.

198 'Initial assessment' means the assessment undertaken by the local authority in accordance with *The Framework for the Assessment of Children in Need and their Families* (Department of Health, 2000) (the PLO Practice Direction, at para 25(20)).

199 'Core assessment' means the assessment undertaken by the local authority in accordance with *The Framework for the Assessment of Children in Need and their Families* (Department of Health, 2000) (the PLO Practice Direction, at para 25(13)).

200 'Genogram' means a family tree, setting out in diagrammatic form the family's background (the PLO Practice Direction, at para 25(18)).

201 'Strategy discussion record' means a note of the strategy discussion within the meaning of 'Working Together to Safeguard Children' (2006) (the PLO Practice Direction, at para 25(37)).

202 Ibid, at para 25(34).

203 Meaning any letter from the local authority containing written notification to the parents and others with parental responsibility for the child of the local authority's plan to apply to court for a care or supervision order (ibid, at para 25(23)).

5.160 So far as the local authority is concerned, it is under a duty to:

(a) consider what documents it possesses; and

(b) to disclose such documents as it considers may be relevant, not only in support of its own case, but which may modify or cast doubt upon it.[204]

5.161 If the local authority wishes to claim public interest immunity in respect of any documents that it holds, then a letter should be written to the other parties' legal advisers and to the Children's Guardian drawing general attention to the existence of the documents and inviting an application to the court if disclosure is required. Any invitation to initiate costly, intrusive and pointless fishing expeditions should, however, be avoided. There should (subject to public interest immunity) be a presumption in favour of disclosure of potentially helpful information.[205]

5.162 It is a matter for the court to decide whether the public interest in confidentiality outweighs the public interest that a party to proceedings should obtain information relevant to his or her case.[206]

5.163 In the case of *Re R (Care: Disclosure: Nature of proceedings)*[207] Charles J emphasised that all cases decided before *R v Chief Constable of West Midlands Police ex parte Wiley; R v Chief Constable of Nottinghamshire Police ex parte Sunderland*[208] should be viewed with care, and stressed in particular that general statements to the effect that social work records are covered by public interest immunity in principle should be consigned to history.

5.164 The confidentiality of documents and records should be considered individually on the basis of their contents, and the case for non-disclosure should be compelling for it to succeed.[209] Indeed, the PLO requirement for disclosure at the start of the process takes this presumption to its logical conclusion.

5.165 Nevertheless, experience suggests that some element of disclosure from the local authority will continue to take place at later stages of the proceedings, either because documents are overlooked (especially if the proceedings start as an emergency), or if matters which do not appear relevant at the start of the case later become so.

5.166 The Children's Guardian is entitled to examine and copy certain social work records pursuant to the Children Act 1989, s 42.[210]

Disclosure into the proceedings from third parties

5.167 The PLO pre-proceedings checklist provides for the disclosure of joint and inter-agency materials.

5.168 This may include police evidence, which, if it is going to form part of the local authority's case, should be disclosed at the earliest possible stage, subject to any objection on behalf of the police.

---

204 See *Re C (Expert evidence: Disclosure: Practice)* [1995] 1 FLR 204; *Re R (Care: Disclosure: Nature of proceedings)* [2002] 1 FLR 755.

205 Ibid.

206 *Re M (A Minor) (Disclosure of Material)* [1990] 2 FLR 36.

207 Above.

208 [1995] 1 AC 274.

209 *Re R* (above).

210 *Re R (Care Proceedings: Disclosure)* [2000] 2 FLR 751.

5.169 Most local authorities will operate a working protocol with the police authority that covers the disclosure of documents to the local authority and into care proceedings. If, however, there remains any difficulty relating to the disclosure of police evidence, any party who wishes to obtain further disclosure from the police may make an application within the proceedings, directed at the appropriate Chief Constable, for a witness summons to include the production of documents.[211]

5.170 Generally, there is an understanding that documents already disclosed to the local authority and upon which it relies will have to be disclosed to all the parties, but there are occasions when the police are still conducting their enquiries and wish to withhold information for a short period (particularly, for example, when they wish to interview or re-interview a relevant party). If there is a compelling case for such, and the non-disclosure is strictly time-limited, such non-disclosure may be permitted.[212]

5.171 Otherwise, and where disclosure from the police is not thought likely to be contentious, it is common for the parties to insert a direction as to disclosure into the order, giving permission to the Chief Constable to apply to vary or discharge the direction within a specified period of time if he or she so wishes.

5.172 The same point arises with medical and other records. Hospitals and GP practices are regularly asked for disclosure of their records relating to a particular patient and, as the records usually relate to a party to the proceedings or a relevant child, there is usually no difficulty, subject to the payment of copying charges.

5.173 If such disclosure is contentious, then an application can be made within the care proceedings, with the relevant health authority as respondent. The applicant must show that the records are relevant, and that disclosure is necessary for the fair disposal of the proceedings.[213] It will then be a matter for the court to weigh up the public interest in the confidentiality of the records as against the public interest that justice should be done.

Disclosure out of the proceedings

5.174 The disclosure of information arising out of family proceedings to third parties is currently governed:

- in the High Court and county court, by Family Proceedings Rules 1991, r 10.20A;
- in the family proceedings court, by Family Proceedings Court (Children Act 1989) Rules 1991, r 23A, which is almost in identical terms.

5.175 The proceedings to which r 10.20A applies are those which:

(a) relate to the exercise of the inherent jurisdiction of the High Court with respect to minors;

(b) are brought under the Children Act 1989; or

---

211 *Re M (Child Abuse: Video Evidence)* [1995] 2 FLR 571. For examples of working protocols and standard request forms, see www.dca.gov.uk/family/metpol-protocol.pdf; www.dca.gov.uk/family/metpol-northerncircuit.pdf; www.dca.gov.uk/family/metpol-expmem.pdf.

212 *Re B (A Minor) (Disclosure of Evidence)* [1993] 1 FLR 191.

213 *Re R (Care: Disclosure: Nature of Proceedings)* (above).

(c) otherwise relate wholly or mainly to the maintenance or upbringing of a minor.[214]

5.176 For the purposes of the law relating to contempt of court, information relating to the proceedings (whether or not contained in a document filed with the court) may be communicated:

(a) where the court gives permission; or

(b) to a party, a legal representative of a party, a professional legal adviser, a Cafcass officer or a Welsh family proceedings officer, the welfare officer, the Legal Services Commission, an expert whose instruction has been authorised by the court, and a professional acting in furtherance of the protection of children.[215]

5.177 The latter is an important inclusion, as 'professional acting in furtherance of the protection of children' includes:

(a) an officer of a local authority exercising child protection functions;

(b) a police officer who is:
  (i) exercising powers under the Children Act 1989, s 46; or
  (ii) serving in a child protection unit or a paedophile unit of a police force;

(c) any professional person attending a child protection conference or review in relation to a child who is the subject of the proceedings to which the information relates; or

(d) an officer of the NSPCC.[216]

5.178 The phrase 'acting in furtherance of the protection of children' should be given a broad interpretation.[217] Such an interpretation means that the police can be given information from the proceedings as long as they are acting in a child protection capacity, although they will need leave to use the documents for the purpose of a criminal investigation.[218]

5.179 Both sets of rules provide a table setting out who is permitted to disclose information to whom, and for what purpose.[219]

5.180 A party may communicate any information relating to the proceedings:

- to a lay adviser[220] or McKenzie friend[221] for the purpose of obtaining advice or assistance in relation to the proceedings;

- to their spouse, civil partner, cohabitant[222] or close family member for the purpose of confidential discussions which will enable them to receive support;

---

214 FPR 1991, r 10.20A(1)(a), (b) and (c). The only material difference between FPR 1991, r 10.20A, and FPC(CA 1989)R 1991, r 23A, is here: there is no equivalent definition within the FPC rules as they relate exclusively to Children Act 1989 proceedings.

215 FPC(CA 1989)R 1991, r 23A(1)(a) and (c); FPR 1991, r 10.20A(2)(a)–(c).

216 The National Society for the Prevention of Cruelty to Children.

217 *A Local Authority v D (Chief Constable of Thames Valley Police Intervening)* [2006] EWHC 1465, [2006] 2 FLR 1053.

218 Ibid.

219 FPC(CA 1989) R 1991, r 23A(2); FPR 1991, r 10.20A(3).

220 Meaning a non-professional person who gives lay advice on behalf of an organisation in the lay advice sector.

221 Meaning any person permitted by the court to sit beside an unrepresented litigant to assist that litigant by prompting, taking notes and giving him or her advice. See **5.62** et seq.

222 Meaning 'one of two persons who are neither married to each other nor civil partners of each other but are living together as husband and wife or as if they were civil partners'.

- to a health care professional or a person or body providing counselling services for children or families to enable them or their child to obtain counselling or health care;

- to various individuals or bodies with the purpose of making or responding to an appeal under Child Support Act 1991, s 20, and to an adoption panel[223] to enable the adoption panel to discharge its functions.

5.181 The table also allows disclosure in a variety of other circumstances for a variety of purposes, including disclosure to a mediator for the purpose of mediation in relation to the proceedings, to a person conducting an approved research project,[224] to those considering complaints against legal representatives or advisers,[225] accreditation bodies[226] or those assessing quality assurance systems.[227] In some instances, only a party may be able to disclose the information; in others, information may also be disclosed by legal representatives, legal advisers, or any person lawfully in receipt of information. These provisions are obviously designed to avoid individuals having to make costly and time-consuming applications to the court in situations where disclosure should normally be ordered, but it is absolutely vital that those considering disclosure should check with the detail of the table before doing so.

5.182 Finally, a party may disclose the text or summary of the whole or part of a judgment given in the proceedings to:

(a) an elected representative[228] or peer to enable that individual to give advice, investigate any complaint or raise any question of policy or procedure;

(b) the General Medical Council for the purpose of making a complaint thereto; and

(c) to a police officer for the purpose of a criminal investigation – a significant development from the old rules as, although courts did routinely allow for such disclosure, it was by no means automatic.

5.183 Those individuals or bodies to whom information may be communicated set out in the table may only communicate that information:

- for the purpose or purposes for which they received it; or

- of professional development or training providing that any communication does not, or is not likely to identify any person involved in the proceedings without that person's consent.[229]

5.184 The enactment of these rules has obviated the need for many of the orders for disclosure which used to be routinely made. Nonetheless, there are still occasions when disclosure is requested which can only be granted with the leave of the court.

---

223 Which is defined as 'a panel established in accordance with regulation 3 of the Adoption Agencies Regulations 2005 or regulation 3 of the Adoption Agencies (Wales) Regulations 2005'.

224 'Approved research project' means a project of research: (a) approved in writing by a Secretary of State after consultation with the President of the Family Division, (b) approved in writing by the President of the Family Division, or (c) conducted under Children Act 1989, s 83, or Criminal Justice and Courts Services Act 2000, s 13.

225 This would mean disclosure to the Law Society, the General Council of the Bar, the Institute of Legal Executives or the Legal Services Ombudsman.

226 Meaning the Law Society, Resolution or the Legal Services Commission.

227 Which means the Law Society, the LSC or the General Council of the Bar.

228 A member of the House of Commons, a member of the National Assembly for Wales, or an English or Welsh MEP.

229 FPC(CA 1989)R 1991, r 23(A)(3); FPR 1991, r 10.20A(4).

5.185 In those circumstances, it is a matter for the court to weigh up the competing factors, which will vary in importance from case to case depending on the relevant facts and the purpose and identity of the individual or body seeking disclosure.

5.186 Many, if not most, applications for disclosure following care proceedings (or findings made within them) will come from the police. The factors to be taken into account by the court in dealing with those applications were set out by the Court of Appeal in *Re EC (A minor) (Care Proceedings: Disclosure)*,[230] and remain applicable today. The importance of each of the various factors that follow will inevitably vary very much from case to case:[231]

(1) The welfare and interests of the child or children concerned in the care proceedings. If the child is likely to be adversely affected by the order in any serious way, this will be a very important factor.

(2) The welfare and interests of other children generally.

(3) The maintenance of confidentiality in children cases.

(4) The importance of encouraging frankness in children's cases. This is a very important factor and is likely to be of particular importance in a case to which the Children Act 1989, s 98(2), applies. The underlying purpose of s 98 is to encourage people to tell the truth in cases concerning children, and the incentive is that any admission will not be admissible in evidence in a criminal trial. However, the added incentive of guaranteed confidentiality is not given by the words of the section and cannot be given.

(5) The public interest in the administration of justice. Barriers should not be erected between one branch of the judicature and another because this may be inimical to the overall interests of justice.

(6) The public interest in the prosecution of serious crime and the punishment of offenders, including the public interest in convicting those who have been guilty of violent or sexual offences against children. There is a strong public interest in making available material to the police which is relevant to a criminal trial. In many cases, this is likely to be a very important factor.

(7) The gravity of the alleged offence and the relevance of the evidence to it. If the evidence has little or no bearing on the investigation or the trial, this will militate against a disclosure order.

(8) The desirability of co-operation between various agencies concerned with the welfare of children, including the social services departments, the police service, medical practitioners, health visitors, schools, etc. This is particularly important in cases concerning children.

(9) In a case to which s 98(2) applies, the terms of the section itself, namely that the witness was not excused from answering incriminating questions, and that any statement of admission would not be admissible against him or her in criminal proceedings. Fairness to the person who has incriminated him/herself and any others affected by the incriminating statement and any danger of oppression would also be relevant considerations.

(10) Any other material disclosure which has taken place.

---

230 [1996] 2 FLR 725.

231 Ibid, at p 733.

5.187 Whilst the public interest in protecting the confidentiality of proceedings and encouraging frankness within them is extremely important, in practice in police applications this usually has to give way to the public interest in the desirability of co-operation between various agencies concerned with the welfare of children, and in the administration of justice and prosecution of serious crime.

5.188 It is not inevitable that the police will be given disclosure of evidence from the proceedings in addition to the judgment, although a perusal of the authorities and experience suggest that applications by the police will often succeed. As a matter of law, however, there is no presumption in favour of disclosure, and the court is more likely to refuse an application where there has been a frank acknowledgement of responsibility by an abusing parent.[232]

5.189 Applications by professional bodies such as the General Medical Council[233] and the UK Council of Nurses[234] for disclosure of information relating to relevant professionals have succeeded in circumstances where it was clearly important that the public might need to be protected.

5.190 In *Re Z (Children) (Disclosure: Criminal proceedings)*,[235] Munby J held that it would be exceptional for a family court to withhold from a defendant's criminal lawyer material which might assist in the preparation of a defence.

The withholding of evidence from parties

5.191 There may be some occasions where the police wish the local authority to withhold evidence from a party to the proceedings for a limited period of time to enable them to carry out further investigations. There may also be other occasions where the court may be asked to direct that evidence not be disclosed to a party. Before the passing of the Human Rights Act 1998, the only interests capable of denying a litigant access to documents were the interests of children involved in the litigation.[236] This, however, is no longer the case.

5.192 In *Re B (Disclosure to other parties)*,[237] Munby J held that, whilst an entitlement to a fair trial under ECHR, Art 6, was absolute, this did not mean an absolute and unqualified right to see all the documents. The interests of anyone else who was involved in the case, whether as victim, party or witness, and who could demonstrate that their Art 8 rights were sufficiently engaged, could have the effect of denying a party access to documents. Non-disclosure must be limited to what the situation imperatively demanded and was justified only when the case was compelling or strictly necessary, with the court being rigorous in its examination of the feared harm and any difficulty caused to the litigant, counterbalanced by procedures designed to ensure a fair trial. In that case, he upheld a mother's application that certain documents relating to two of her children should not be disclosed to the father of one of her other children.

5.193 The court's starting point is in favour of disclosure of all information relevant to its decision, but, when contemplating non-disclosure, the issue will come down to striking a fair balance between the various interests involved.[238]

---

232 See *Re AB (Care Proceedings: Disclosure of Medical Evidence to Police)* [2002] EWHC 2198 (Fam), [2003] 1 FLR 579; *Re M (Care Proceedings: Disclosure: Human Rights)* [2001] 2 FLR 1316.

233 *A County Council v W and others (Disclosure)* [1997] 1 FLR 574.

234 *Re L (Care Proceedings: Disclosure to Third Party)* [2000] 1 FLR 913.

235 [2003] EWHC 61 (Fam), [2003] 1 FLR 1194.

236 *Re D (Adoption Reports: Confidentiality)* [1995] 2 FLR 687.

237 [2001] 2 FLR 1017.

238 *Re X (Adoption: Confidential Procedure)* [2002] EWCA Civ 828, [2002] 2 FLR 476.

The PLO Practice Direction – further provisions on disclosure

5.194 There are two further provisions in the PLO Practice Direction dealing with the issue of disclosure which merit mention.

5.195 The first is that found at para 3.15(13), which has doubtless been introduced to avoid the parties and the court being swamped with documents which in the end do not prove to be necessary and which can tend to obscure the key issues in the case. It provides that 'active case management' includes:

- controlling the nature and extent of the documents which are to be disclosed to the parties and presented to the court; and
- controlling whether and, if so, in what manner the documents disclosed are to be presented to the court.

5.196 Secondly there appears within Stage 4 of the PLO Table the sentence 'Disclose documents as required after hearing', a phrase which is not further defined.

5.197 Whilst presumably this latter provision is intended principally to cover specific applications or orders for disclosure of documents out of the proceedings (such as to the police), it may also be an allusion to the other not uncommon scenario of one party to the proceedings wanting to reveal information within them, possibly to the media.

5.198 Save for the important exceptions permitted by the Family Proceedings Rules 1991, r 10.20A, and the Family Proceedings Court (Children Act 1989) Rules 1991, r 23A, there is a statutory prohibition in the Administration of Justice Act 1960, s 12, against the publication of information relating to proceedings brought under the Children Act 1989. While this section prevents the publication of a court judgment and imposes restrictions upon discussion of the facts and evidence in the case, it does not prevent publication of the names of the parties, the child or the witnesses.[239] The prohibition in the Administration of Justice Act 1960, s 12, continues indefinitely, unless the court gives permission for the information to be published.[240]

5.199 The Children Act 1989, s 97(2), contains a further statutory prohibition against the publication of any material intended or likely to identify any child as being involved in proceedings in which any power under that Act or the Adoption and Children Act 2002 may be exercised by the court in relation to that or any other child. That prohibition, however, ceases when the proceedings come to an end, although, if the court then concludes that the welfare and ECHR, Art 8, rights of the child require a continued prohibition on publicity identifying him or her as having been the subject of them, then it can grant an injunction to that effect.[241]

5.200 Whether the court is exercising the so-called disclosure or restraint jurisdictions, it has to apply the principles explained by Lord Steyn in *Re S (A Child) (Identification: Restrictions on Publication)*,[242] and by Sir Mark Potter P in *A Local Authority v W, L,W, T and R*.[243] This involves

---

239 *Re B (A Child) (Disclosure)* [2004] EWHC 411 (Fam), [2004] 2 FLR 142. The prohibition extends also to proceedings under the inherent jurisdiction of the High Court and to proceedings which otherwise relate wholly or mainly to the maintenance of a minor.

240 For an example of a case in which publicity was permitted, see *Re Webster; Norfolk CC v Webster and others* [2006] EWHC 2733 (Fam), [2007] 1 FLR 1146.

241 *Clayton v Clayton* [2006] EWCA Civ 878, [2007] 1 FLR 11.

242 [2004] UKHL 47, [2005] 1 FLR 591, at para [17].

243 [2005] EWHC 1564 (Fam), [2006] 1 FLR 1, at para [53].

the court undertaking a 'parallel analysis' of those of the ECHR rights as are engaged (which will usually be Arts 6, 8 and 10), leading to an 'ultimate balancing test' reflecting the Convention principle of proportionality.[244]

SPECIAL MEASURES

5.201 'Special measures' is a term which has become familiar to English criminal lawyers as meaning steps to assist vulnerable and intimidated witnesses to give evidence. It has been used informally in family cases in recent years, but now makes a formal appearance for the first time.

5.202 Whilst the term 'special measures' is not defined in the PLO Practice Direction it appears at various points:

(1) Para 7 identifies that seeking advice on special measures is a step that the representative of an adult party who lacks capacity may wish to take when deciding what approach to take about that party giving evidence.[245]

(2) Within the 'Further Hearings' section of the draft Case Management Order,[246] the following are mentioned:
   - 21. special measures and security;
   - 22. attendance at court;
   - 23. use of technology and special requirements, particularised as: (a) video link, (b) conference telephone link, (c) hearing assistance, (d) DDA requirements, and (e) translation directions.

(3) Para 14.3 of the PLO Practice Direction, which contains a list of steps to be taken at the CMC, includes[247] '[identifying] any special measures such as the need for access for the disabled or provision for vulnerable witnesses'.[248]

5.203 Given these references, it is surprising that the phrase 'special measures' is not defined in the PLO Practice Direction. Nor does it appear in the Family Proceedings Rules 1991, the Family Proceedings Courts (Children Act 1989) Rules 1991 or the Civil Procedure Rules.[249]

---

244 In this context, reference should also be made to the President's *Practice Direction (Applications for Reporting Restriction Orders)* of 18 March 2005 [2005] 2 FLR 120, and the *Practice Note (Official Solicitor: CAFCASS: Applications for Reporting Restriction Orders)* of the same date [2005] 2 FLR 111.

245 The PLO Practice Direction, at para 7.3, provides: 'Where the adult is a protected party, his or her representative should be involved in any instruction of an expert, including the instruction of an expert to assess whether the adult, although a protected party, is competent to give evidence. The instruction of an expert is a significant step in the proceedings. The representative will wish to consider (and ask the expert to consider), if the protected party is competent to give evidence, their best interests in this regard. The representative may wish to seek advice about 'special measures'. The representative may put forward an argument on behalf of the protected party that the protected party should not give evidence.'

246 Annex C to the PLO Practice Direction. Intended to be used both when drawing up orders and as a case management checklist (ibid, at para 3.10). The 'Further Hearings' section is at paras 20–23.

247 Ibid, at para 14.3(7).

248 In this context, it should be noted that the 'Local Authority Case Summary', which must be prepared for each case management hearing, is required to include 'a summary of any concerns the local authority may have about the mental capacity of an adult to care for the child or the capacity of the adult to prepare for the proceedings' (ibid, at para 25(24)(e)). This would appear to require the local authority to identify any difficulties in participating in the proceedings which are likely to be experienced by those adults who may care for the child, but, as drafted, this obligation on the local authority does not extend to any other adults who may be witnesses but not parties.

249 The only provision in the CPR dealing with this topic is r 32.3, which simply provides that 'the court may allow a witness to give evidence through a video link or by other means'.

The approach of the criminal courts

5.204 Inevitably, therefore, the family court will be directed to the much more detailed provisions about 'special measures' in criminal cases, in particular the statutory scheme set out in Part II, chapter 1, of the Youth Justice and Criminal Evidence Act 1999 ('the 1999 Act'), which provides for the court to give 'special measures directions' in cases of vulnerable and intimidated witnesses. Indeed, it is this provision that introduces the phrase 'special measures' as a term of art into the English legal system.

5.205 Whilst this is not the place for a detailed analysis of the criminal law provisions,[250] a short discussion of them is necessary, because, in the absence of any other clear guidance, it can be anticipated that the family courts will be inclined to apply those provisions in public children law cases (and, where appropriate, in private law cases in due course).

5.206 The 1999 Act distinguishes between vulnerable and intimidated witnesses. Whilst family courts are more likely to encounter cases involving vulnerable witnesses, examples of intimidated witnesses are by no means unknown.

5.207 The 1999 Act, at s 16(1) and (2), defines a vulnerable witness (that is to say, a witness in criminal proceedings who is eligible for assistance on grounds of age or incapacity) as:

(a) one who is under the age of 17 at the time of the hearing; or

(b) one whom the court considers that the quality of the evidence given by the witness is likely to be diminished by reason of any of the following circumstances:
   - that the witness suffers from mental disorder within the meaning of the Mental Health Act 1983;
   - that the witness otherwise has a significant impairment of intelligence and social functioning;
   - that the witness has a physical disability;
   - that the witness is suffering from a physical disorder.

In determining whether a witness falls into any of these categories, the court must consider any views expressed by the witness.[251]

5.208 An intimidated witness is defined by the 1999 Act, at s 17(1). A witness is eligible for assistance by virtue of that provision on the ground of fear or distress about testifying, if the court is satisfied that the quality of evidence given by the witness is likely to be diminished by reason of fear or distress on the part of the witness in connection with testifying in the proceedings.

5.209 The ancillary provisions of s 17 are set out in terms referable to criminal proceedings, although are clearly capable of being applied by analogy to family cases.

5.210 Thus s 17(2) provides that, in determining whether a witness comes within subsection (1), the court must take into account in particular:

(a) the nature and alleged circumstances of the offence;

(b) the age of the witness;

---

[250] For which see *Archbold* (2008 ed), at para 8-52 et seq, and *Achieving Best Evidence in Criminal Proceedings: Guidance for Vulnerable or Intimidated Witnesses including Children* (Home Office Communication Directorate, 2002).

[251] Youth Justice and Criminal Evidence Act 1999, s 16(4).

(c) such of the following as appear to the court to be relevant:
   (i) the social and cultural background and ethnic origin of the witness;
   (ii) the domestic and employment circumstances of the witness; and
   (iii) any religious beliefs or political opinions of the witness;

(d) any behaviour towards the witness on the part of the accused, members of the family or associates of the accused, or any other person likely to be an accused or a witness in the proceedings.

Again, in determining if a witness's evidence is likely to be diminished by reason of fear or distress about testifying, the court must consider any views expressed by the witness.[252]

5.211 There is, in addition, a special provision for complainants in sexual cases. A witness who is such a complainant is eligible for assistance unless he or she informs the court of his or her 'wish not to be so eligible'.[253]

5.212 Importantly, s 16(5) provides:

> '[R]eferences in [the provisions for both vulnerable and intimidated witnesses] to a witness's evidence are to its quality in terms of completeness, coherence and accuracy; and for this purpose 'coherence' refers to a witness's ability in giving evidence to give answers which address the questions put to the witness and can be understood both individually and collectively.'

5.213 The 1999 Act then proceeds to outline the special measures potentially available to the two categories of witness. These provisions are subject to four general qualifications:

(1) The special measures may not be taken unless the court has been notified by the Secretary of State that relevant arrangements may be made available for implementing any such measure.[254]

(2) The Secretary of State may by statutory instrument amend, add to or remove the provisions for special measures.[255]

(3) The question whether a special measure direction should be given may be raised by any party, or by the court of its own motion.[256]

(4) The court retains an inherent jurisdiction to make any order about giving evidence, even when the witness is not 'eligible' within the meaning of the 1999 Act.[257]

5.214 The special measures provided in the 1999 Act are the following:

- screening the witness from the accused;[258]
- evidence via live link;[259]
- evidence given in private;[260]

---

252 Ibid, s 17(3).
253 Ibid, s 17(4).
254 Ibid, s 18(2).
255 Ibid, s 18(5).
256 Ibid, s 19(1).
257 Ibid, s 19(6).
258 Ibid, s 23.
259 Ibid, s 24.
260 Ibid, s 25.

- removal of wigs and gowns;[261]
- video recordings to stand as evidence-in-chief;[262]
- video recording of cross-examination and re-examination;[263]
- examination of a witness through an intermediary;[264] and
- aids to communication.[265]

5.215 The provisions for video recording of cross-examination and re-examination, which may in due course be brought in for criminal trial by jury, and the removal of wigs and gowns have no real resonance for care proceedings. All the other provisions, however, need to be considered.

Video recordings as evidence

5.216 A special measure direction in criminal proceedings may provide for a video recording of an interview of the witness to be admitted as evidence in chief of the witness.[266] The criminal procedure also gives the court power to refuse to admit the recording or part of it in the interests of justice: in considering whether or not to do so, it must consider whether any prejudice to the accused which might result from admitting the recording is outweighed by the 'desirability' of showing it.[267] The statute also provides that, notwithstanding a previous special measures direction, the court may refuse to admit the recording if the witness is unavailable for cross-examination.[268]

5.217 In care proceedings, all such recordings are admissible as relevant hearsay evidence, even if the witness is unavailable for cross-examination. It is a matter for the court to determine what weight to attach to the recording. In practice, if an adult witness fails to attend for cross-examination, it is unlikely that the court will make findings on the basis of such recordings unless corroborated elsewhere.

The child and video evidence in care proceedings

5.218 The position is different if the witness is a child. The long-established practice in care proceedings, recently reiterated by the Court of Appeal in *LM v Medway Council, RM and YM*,[269] is that it is undesirable that a child should give evidence. Particular justification is required before that course is taken and in practice cases in which children give evidence are likely to be rare. Per Smith LJ:[270]

> 'In considering whether to make an order [for the child to give evidence], the judge will have to balance the need for the evidence in the circumstances of the case against what he assesses to be the potential for harm to the child. In assessing the need for oral evidence in the context of care proceedings, the judge should, in my view, take account of the importance of the evidence to the process of his decision about the child's future. It may be that the child's future cannot be

---

261 Ibid, s 26.
262 Ibid, s 27.
263 Ibid, s 28 (not yet in force).
264 Ibid, s 29.
265 Ibid, s 30.
266 Ibid, s 27(1).
267 Ibid, s 27(2) and (3).
268 Ibid, s 27(4).
269 [2007] EWCA Civ 9, [2007] 1 FLR 1698.
270 Ibid, at para [45].

satisfactorily determined without that evidence. In assessing the risk of harm or oppression, the judge should take heed of current research into the effect on children of giving evidence and should not rely only upon his impression of the child, although that will of course be relevant.'

5.219 Per Wilson LJ in the same case:[271]

> 'The welfare of the child is the paramount consideration in the substantive inquiry and is always relevant to, although not paramount in, its procedural determinations such as a direction for oral evidence. So the effect on the child of receiving questions on matters of supreme sensitivity from lawyers obliged to seek to advance their respective cases, including in some cases questions suggesting that things which the child knows to have happened to him did not happen to him and that he is mistaken or even lying about them, needs carefully and imaginatively to be gauged.'

5.220 The lack of the facility for the parties to ask questions of the child is factored into the assessment of the weight to be attached to the evidence in the interview.[272]

5.221 Given that clear approach, the family court is often presented with (and only has by way of evidence from the child) a video recording of an interview in which the child makes allegations of abuse. The video recording is admitted as a form of hearsay evidence and it is for the court to decide its weight and credibility. The court can also receive expert evidence to explain and interpret the video, but evidence of a diagnosis of sexual abuse calls for a very high level of expertise from someone with clinical experience as, or akin to, a child psychologist or psychiatrist.[273]

5.222 In *Re N (Child Abuse)*,[274] Ward LJ gave some guidance on the matters which the expert explaining and interpreting the video might usefully cover. These include:[275]

> 'such things as the nuances of emotion and behaviour, the gestures and the body movements, the use or non-use of language and its imagery, the vocal inflections and intonations, the pace and pressure of the interview, the child's intellectual and verbal abilities, or lack of them, and any signs or the absence of signs of fantasising.'

Additional evidence

5.223 There will, however, be cases where the subject of the video recording (whether adult or older child) does give evidence beyond that contained in the video recording.

---

271 Ibid, at para [58], where Wilson LJ commented that the remarks in this context of Coleridge J in *B v Torbay Council* [2007] 1 FLR 203, at para [17], 'should be treated with great caution'. In considering that in the instant case the judge was correct to require the child to be cross-examined, Wilson LJ, at para [61], commented that it '[did] not reflect the straightforward situation in which a parent who has been accused by a child denies the accusation and aspires to cross-examine her or him'.

272 Ibid, per Wilson LJ, at para [56].

273 *Re N (Child Abuse: Evidence)* [1996] 2 FLR 214, in which the Court of Appeal also made the point that, in receiving that evidence, it was important to separate out the admissible from the inadmissible, indicating that it was for the judge alone to decide whether the child should be believed and that evidence from an expert should be couched in terms of inconsistency or consistency of a fact with sexual abuse. Such dicta about inadmissibility, however, have to be viewed in light of the subsequent decision of the Court of Appeal in *Re M and R (Child Abuse: Evidence)* [1996] 2 FLR 195. The Civil Evidence Act 1972, s 3, had brought to an end the rule that expert evidence on an issue in the case, in particular the ultimate issue, was not admissible. Thereafter expert evidence in a case dealing with issues, including the ultimate issue, was admissible, subject to the overriding requirement of relevance, which, together with questions of weight, was a matter for the judge.

274 Above.

275 Ibid, at p 221. Experts in this field will nowadays quite commonly use a technique to assess credibility called Criterion Based Content Analysis (CBCA), in which the interview is analysed for the presence of a number of specific CBCA criteria (five or more are usually taken as being typical of a credible account). There is, however, some controversy about this approach.

5.224 The criminal provisions provide that, when a recording is admitted as evidence in chief under the Youth Justice and Criminal Evidence Act 1999, s 27, the witness may not give other evidence in chief as to any matter which in the opinion of the court has been dealt with adequately in the recording. Further evidence in chief may be given, with the court's permission, as to any other matter which is dealt with in the recording, but it seems that no further evidence in chief may be given about matters not covered at all in the recording.

5.225 A more flexible approach, however, is adopted in care proceedings where the recording is admitted as relevant hearsay evidence. The party relying on the recording may not adduce other evidence from the interviewee that is not set out in an appropriate written statement without the leave of the court.[276] In practice, such leave is frequently sought and almost invariably given, provided that the matters then adduced have been disclosed to the other parties.

5.226 This more flexible approach is necessary given that the enquiry in care proceedings will often range more widely than the relatively narrow issue of specific alleged offences. Indeed, in an appropriate case, it is fairly common for such witnesses to be asked further questions by the advocate who called them, although the court will usually not allow the questions to range over all the matters covered in the video-recorded interview. Before giving oral evidence, the interviewee should be given an opportunity to watch the video of the interview and at the start of the oral evidence asked to confirm the accuracy of what was said. It follows that a witness giving evidence in chief in these circumstances is then liable to be cross-examined.

Evidence by live link and behind screens

5.227 A 'live link' is defined by the 1999 Act, s 24(8), as a live television link or other arrangement whereby a witness, while absent from the courtroom or other place where the proceedings are being held, is able to see and hear a person there and to be seen and heard by the judge and advocates.

5.228 Larger court centres now usually provide arrangements for a link whereby the witness sits in a separate room in the court building.[277]

5.229 The 1999 Act has recently been amended so as to enable the court to arrange for a vulnerable defendant to give evidence via live link.[278]

5.230 However, despite technological advances, there remain difficulties. It is all too common for the picture or sound to be of inadequate quality. In addition, many lawyers feel that the process of giving evidence via live link is not achieving its desired aim. Far from making it easier for the witness, it often seems to make it more confusing and disorienting. Sitting alone (or with one supporter) in a room, being asked questions by strangers sitting in another room full of other people, can be a strange and unsettling experience, particularly if the picture and sound are defective.

5.231 Where a live link is unavailable, or inappropriate for other reasons, a witness may give evidence from behind a screen. This enables the witness to be hidden from view from the accused, or the lay parties in care proceedings, but seen by the judge and advocates.

5.232 The disadvantage of screens is that, despite being unable to see the lay parties, the witness may have feelings of vulnerability, anxiety or fear simply from being in the same room. For this

---

276 FPC(CA 1989)R 1991, r 17(3); FPR 1991, r 4.17 (3).

277 With the growth in video conferencing facilities, other arrangements are increasingly being used, for example between the court and barristers' chambers.

278 Youth Justice and Criminal Evidence Act 1999, s 33A–33C, inserted by the Police and Justice Act 2006, s 47.

reason, live link has become more fashionable. Nevertheless, screens have an advantage in that they enable normal face-to-face communication between the witness and the judge and advocates.[279]

Intermediaries and other aids to communication

5.233 The 1999 Act, s 29, provides for the examination of a witness through an intermediary. The function of an intermediary is defined as being:[280]

> 'to communicate (a) to the witness, questions put to the witness, and (b) to any person asking such questions, the answers given by the witness in reply to them, and to explain such questions and answers so far as necessary to enable them to be understood by the witness or person in question.'

5.234 The examination through an intermediary must take place in circumstances in which the tribunal and advocates are able to see and hear the examination of the witness and to communicate with the intermediary.[281] Provision is made for a formal declaration to be made by the intermediary.[282] A video interview in which the witness is questioned through an intermediary may be admitted under the 1999 Act, s 27, provided that the intermediary made the formal declaration before the interview and the court gives prior approval of the intermediary.

5.235 Under the criminal law, the provisions as to intermediaries are only applicable in cases of vulnerable (as opposed to intimidated) witnesses and, at present, only available in certain pilot areas.[283]

5.236 In addition, the 1999 Act, s 30, provides that a special measures direction may provide for a vulnerable witness, while giving evidence, to be provided with such device as the court considers appropriate with a view to enabling questions or answers to be communicated to or by the witness despite any disability or disorder or other impairment which the witness has or from which that witness suffers.

5.237 Any party wishing to call a witness whose evidence may require an intermediary must prepare the application with care. The precise reason for the intermediary must be identified and where appropriate expert evidence obtained.

5.238 If the criminal rules are to be applied by analogy,[284] the terms of the 1999 Act, s 16, must be borne in mind. It is only if the quality of a witness's evidence (in the sense of its completeness,

---

279 One possible solution would be for the witness to give evidence in court, or in a specially adapted room, in the presence of the judge/tribunal and the advocates, with the lay parties and any solicitors' representatives observing the process via a live link. It would be necessary for the advocates to keep in contact with those instructing them, but this could be arranged either by short adjournments of by computer or even text message link. This proposal would be entirely in keeping with the PLO Practice Direction, at para 23, to the effect that 'where the facilities are available to the court and the parties, the court will consider making full use of technology including electronic information exchange and video and telephone conferencing'. Such an arrangement would enable better communication between the witness and the court without the witness coming into the presence of the lay parties.

280 Youth Justice and Criminal Evidence Act 1999, s 29(2).

281 Ibid, s 29(3).

282 Ibid, s 29(5), and Criminal Procedure Rules, r 29.9.

283 It is intended to roll out the scheme to cover the whole country. There are already a number of registered intermediaries, selected for their skills in assisting communication. They may be trained speech and language therapists, psychologists or other professionals. Others are now being recruited by the Office of Criminal Justice Reform. It should be noted that these provisions are in addition to the long-established use of interpreters at common law. Clearly they are buttressed by ECHR, Art 6. For further guidance on the use and function of intermediaries, see *Achieving Best Evidence* (above), at para 5.78 et seq.

284 In a recent unreported care case in the High Court, the court had to consider an application for a witness to give evidence through an intermediary. Although refusing the application on the facts of the case, the trial judge held that

coherence and accuracy) is likely to be diminished by reason of his or her mental disorder or significant impairment of intelligence and social function, or physical disability or disorder that any special measure, including an intermediary, can be authorised in criminal proceedings.

5.239 It seems likely that the circumstances in which an intermediary will be used in criminal proceedings are relatively limited by the terms of these provisions, in particular by the use of the word 'significant' in s 16(2). Some impairment or abnormality in intelligence or social functioning will be insufficient unless it can be characterised as 'significant'. Furthermore such impairment, even of a 'significant' level, will only warrant the use of an intermediary where it is likely to lead to a diminution in the 'completeness, coherence or accuracy' of the evidence within the meaning of s 16(5).

5.240 There are strong reasons for limiting the circumstances in which an intermediary will be used. It is highly probable that the process of cross-examination, that lies at the heart of the forensic process, will be impeded by their use. Whereas an interpreter merely translates the words verbatim into another language, there is a danger that an intermediary will re-interpret the words of the question in an attempt to communicate it to the witness. The evidence is not merely what the witness wants to say; it is also what he or she says in response to questions, which may be critical and challenging. How he or she responds to such questions forms a crucial part in the court's assessment of the evidence. If the questioner is prevented from putting their client's case in a way which he or she chooses, then a risk of injustice arises.

Procedure for making decisions about special measures

5.241 Where the issue of special measures arises, the procedure to be adopted in criminal cases (and likely to be adopted in public law children's cases until specific provision for them is made) is as follows:[285]

(1) The court must determine whether the witness is eligible for assistance under either s 16 and/or s 17.

(2) The court must determine whether any of the special measures available in relation to the witness, or any combination of them, would in the court's opinion be likely to improve the quality of evidence given by the witness.[286]

(3) If so, the court must determine which of the measures (or combination of them) would in its opinion be likely to maximise so far as practicable the quality of such evidence.[287]

(4) The court must then give a direction providing for the measure or measures so determined to apply to the witness's evidence.[288] Such a direction must specify particulars of the provision made in the direction in respect of each special measure which is to apply to the witness's evidence.[289]

---

the court had the power to permit the examination of a witness to be conducted in this way, and that the principles justifying the use of intermediaries in criminal proceedings also applied in care proceedings.

285 These provisions are supported by detailed regulations set out in the Criminal Procedure Rules 2005, Part 29 (see *Archbold* (2008 ed), at para 8-56 et seq).

286 Youth Justice and Criminal Evidence Act 1999, s 19(2)(a).

287 Ibid, s 19(2)(b)(i).

288 Ibid, s 19(2)(b)(ii).

289 Ibid, s 19(4).

(5) Once made, a special measures direction may be discharged or varied, either on the application of a party (if there has been a material change of circumstances) or by the court of its own motion.[290]

5.242 There are special provisions for child witnesses set out in the 1999 Act, s 21. In simple terms, it is obligatory for the court to make a special measures direction in the case of a child witness, so that any video recording is admissible under s 27 and for any other evidence to be given via a live link under s 24. This rule is subject to three limitations:[291]

(1) The direction may only be given if the specific measure is available.

(2) A video recording should only be admitted if the court is of the opinion, having regard to all the circumstances, that it should be admitted in the interests of justice.

(3) The rule does not apply to the extent that the court is satisfied that compliance with it would not be likely to maximise the quality of the witness's evidence so far as practicable.[292]

5.243 In making a decision about the use of special measures in public law children's cases, the family court will also of course have to give effect to the PLO Practice Direction's overriding objective of dealing with cases justly, having regard to the welfare issues involved. Indeed, all five of the specific aspects of the overriding objective particularised in para 2.1 of the Practice Direction are likely to arise. Most obviously, the court will have to have regard to the necessity of ensuring that the parties are on an equal footing, that a party whose case turns on the evidence of a vulnerable witness is not at a disadvantage. Equally, however, all parties must be able to challenge the evidence of such witnesses in a way that enables the court to make an accurate assessment of its relevance and reliability.

PLACEMENT FOR ADOPTION

5.244 The Adoption and Children Act 2002 introduced fundamental changes to the process of placing children for adoption. It was designed to simplify the process, to enable a crucial element of the decision-making process to be undertaken at an earlier stage, to shift the emphasis to a concentration on the welfare of the child, and to avoid delay.[293]

5.245 Thus, once a local authority is satisfied that a child who is subject to a care order, or ongoing care proceedings, ought to be placed for adoption, it must apply for a placement order,[294] which authorises it to place the child with any prospective adopters who may be chosen by the authority.[295] Indeed, in the absence of parental consent to placement, the local authority cannot place the child for adoption without first obtaining a placement order.[296] The question of dispensing with parental consent, which had long been the contentious issue in adoption

---

[290] Ibid, s 20(2).

[291] Youth Justice and Criminal Evidence Act 1999, s 21(4).

[292] This limitation does not apply to a child witness who falls into the category of being 'in need of special protection' (that is if the offence falls into one of the categories listed in s 35(3) (sexual offences, kidnapping etc, child cruelty, and assault) (ibid, s 21(5). In certain circumstances, the provisions relating to child witnesses are extended to witnesses who are over 17 at the time of the hearing but were under 17 when a relevant recording was made (see s 22 for the full provisions). For judicial comment on the special measures for children, see *R(D) v Camberwell Green Youth Court* [2005] 2 Cr App R 1.

[293] *Re F (a child)* [2008] EWCA Civ 439, per Wall LJ, at para [72].

[294] Adoption and Children Act 2002, s 22(2).

[295] Ibid, s 21(1).

[296] Ibid, s 18.

proceedings, is now considered much earlier in the process, at the point when the court is considering whether or not to make a placement order,[297] applying the revised test based on welfare.[298]

5.246 Once a placement order has been made (on the basis that parental consent has been given or dispensed with) the natural parent's rights are severely curtailed. He or she is prevented from opposing the subsequent adoption application except with the court's leave.[299] Leave is also required before a parent can apply to revoke a placement order.[300] Furthermore, after a placement order has been made, the local authority's statutory obligation under the Children Act 1989[301] to allow contact between the child and that child's parents ceases,[302] although the parents and others[303] may apply to the court for a contact order. Thus, in the context of permanency, the making of a placement order is ultimately more important than the making of a care order since it puts the child firmly on the road to permanent separation from the natural family.

5.247 However, a local authority, in its capacity as an adoption agency, cannot apply for a placement order until it is satisfied that the child ought to be placed for adoption, and this cannot happen until there has been complete compliance with the requirements of the Adoption Agencies Regulations 2005.[304]

5.248 These include:

(a) a requirement to open a case record for the child to hold information concerning the adoption process;[305]

(b) a requirement to provide counselling and information for, and ascertain the wishes and feelings of, the child[306] and the parent or guardian;[307]

(c) a requirement to obtain information about the child[308] and his or her family;[309]

(d) a requirement to prepare a written report ('the permanence report') for the adoption panel.[310]

---

297 Ibid, s 21(3).

298 Ibid, s 52.

299 Ibid, s 47(3) and (5). Leave can only be given if: (1) there has been a change in circumstances since the placement order was made (s 47(7)) 'which is material, and of a nature and degree which is sufficient to open the door to a consideration by the court of the exercise of its discretion to give the parents leave to defend'; and (2) the court then, in the exercise of its discretion, decides that permission should be given, having regard to the paramount consideration of the child's welfare throughout his life (see *Re P (Adoption: Leave Provisions)* [2007] EWCA Civ 616, [2007] 2 FLR 1069).

300 Adoption and Children Act 2002, s 24(2) and (3). It should be noted that, although, as in the case of applications for leave to oppose an adoption order after the making of a placement order, the decision whether to grant leave is a two stage process, the court is not obliged at the second stage to give paramount consideration to the child's welfare: notwithstanding that, on establishment of a change in circumstances, the welfare of the child and the prospect of success should both be weighed in the exercise of the court's discretion (see *M v Warwickshire CC* [2007] EWCA Civ 1084, [2008] 1 FLR 1093).

301 Children Act 1989, s 34(1).

302 Adoption and Children Act 2002, s 26(1).

303 Ibid, s 26(3).

304 *Re P-B (Placement Order)* [2006] EWCA Civ 1016, [2007] 1 FLR 1106.

305 Adoption Agency Regulations 2005 (SI 2005/389), reg 12.

306 Ibid, reg 13.

307 Ibid, reg 14.

308 Ibid, reg 15.

309 Ibid, reg 16.

310 Ibid, reg 17.

5.249 The adoption panel, which is independent of the local authority,[311] must consider the case of every child referred by an adoption agency (the local authority) and make a recommendation to the agency as to whether the child should be placed for adoption.[312] The recommendation is not binding on the agency, but the agency decision-maker (a senior officer in the local authority) must take the recommendation into account when coming to a decision about whether the child should be so placed.[313]

5.250 All these requirements must be met in order for the local authority to come to a decision that the child ought to be adopted. But, provided that they have been met, and the local authority is satisfied that the child ought to be adopted, it must issue the application for a placement order.

5.251 In many cases this process will take place alongside the care proceedings. Indeed, in *Re T (Children: Placement Order)*,[314] Hughes LJ made the following observation:

> 'Plainly a placement order can be, and perhaps usually should be, made at the same time as a care order is made on a plan for adoption which the judge approves, even though at that stage a good deal of investigation and preparation is needed before the child can actually be placed, and it is not known whether a suitable family will be found or not.'[315]

5.252 In an appropriate case, the court will permit a placement application made at a late stage in the course of care proceedings to be listed and determined at the same hearing.[316]

5.253 In *Re R (Care Plan for Adoption: Best Interest)*[317] (a decision prior to the coming into force of the Adoption and Children Act 2002), Hedley J held that, in scrutinising a care plan for adoption before making a final care order, the court had to be satisfied not only that adoption was in the best interests of the child, but also that the local authority was capable of delivering on its care plan, and that, in general terms, in order to establish this, the local authority would have to have held a best interests panel and to have ratified the panel's decision.

5.254 As a corollary of the above principles, local authorities now ought not to file care plans for adoption without prior panel consideration and decision-maker approval, and courts ought not to endorse those plans without that process having been undertaken.

5.255 There is, however, nothing wrong in the court determining, in advance of the local authority final care plan, that a particular individual was not going to be in a position to care for the child safely within the timescale that the child needed.[318] Indeed, in those cases where the local authority has failed procedurally to get its act in order, but where the evidence as to parental caring capacity is complete, it would be far more sensible for the court to resolve that issue as planned rather than adjourn off the entirety of its disposal/outcome decisions.

---

311 Ibid, reg 3.

312 Ibid, reg 18.

313 Ibid, reg 19.

314 [2008] EWCA Civ 542.

315 Ibid, at para [17].

316 *Re P-B (Placement Order)* (above). In that case, the adoption panel had met and approved the care plan on the first day of the final care hearing, the local authority had issued the application for a placement order two days later, the judge agreed to list the application immediately, to be disposed of as part of the continuing care hearing, and went on to grant both the care and placement orders. The Court of Appeal, in dismissing the parents' appeal, noted that the local authority had clearly signalled its intention to pursue adoption and to make a placement order application if and as soon as the panel approved placement for adoption: in those circumstances, it was hard to identify what benefit would have resulted to the parents from the adjournment of the application, and correspondingly hard to identify a prejudice to them in hearing it immediately.

317 [2006] 1 FLR 483.

318 *North Yorkshire County Council v B* [2007] Fam Law 895.

5.256 In order to avoid delays in placing the child, the local authority as adoption agency will usually be keen to start the search for prospective adopters as soon as possible. The first step will be to look at its own list of potential adopters and other lists held locally or nationally. For some children, wider advertisement will be needed. Whilst there is no legal obligation upon the local authority to obtain the court's permission to advertise, good professional practice as recognised by the specialist publications requires either parental consent or a court endorsement for the presentation of a particular child as being available for adoption.[319]

5.257 Permission to advertise a child for adoption will not be granted by the court until the local authority has concluded, after complete compliance with the requirements of the Adoption Agencies Regulations, that the child ought to be placed for adoption. Where the court has yet to hold a final hearing in care proceedings and is yet to endorse the plan for adoption, it is unlikely to give permission to advertise the child for adoption unless the plan is unopposed or there is some exceptional feature justifying advertising at that stage.[320]

5.258 Given the various complexities of the placement for adoption process, it might have been expected that the PLO reforms would have included detailed guidance on how a plan and application for placement for adoption should be addressed in the context of care proceedings.

5.259 Thus it was not surprising that early publicity about the PLO reforms indicated that a new practice direction on placement for adoption would be issued alongside the PLO for implementation in April 2008.

5.260 The more assiduous case management anticipated under the PLO Practice Direction makes it likely that courts will be even keener to ensure that there is no delay in the proceedings as a result of failures to comply with adoption procedure, hence the need to ensure that the two processes are mutually compliant.

5.261 Indeed, this much has been stressed by the President of the Family Division:

> '[T]he procedures to be followed, before the local authority becomes satisfied that in its view adoption is the right outcome for the child, are necessarily rigorous and time-consuming. The court will therefore be concerned to avoid any delay and wherever possible to determine any placement order application along with the section 31 Children Act proceedings.'[321]

5.262 In the event, there is no new practice direction for placement applications, although the President has indicated that in due course one may be needed to clarify the procedural steps to be taken to ensure that the placement order application is listed and heard within the overall timetable for the child.[322]

5.263 In the meantime, local authorities and other parties will have to ensure that, alongside the requirements of the PLO Practice Direction, they bear in mind the provisions of the Adoption and Children Act 2002, its supporting regulations and guidance, and the case-law that has already emerged since the Act came into force at the very end of 2005.

---

319 *Re K (Adoption: Permission to Advertise)* [2007] EWHC 544 Fam, [2007] 2 FLR 326, per McFarlane J, at para [22].
320 Ibid, at para [37].
321 Inaugural Resolution Annual Lecture, 6 March 2008.
322 Ibid. The President also indicated that the DCSF would be writing to Directors of Social Services, setting out the expectations in this regard and the nature and timing of the social work steps necessary to be taken in the adoption proceedings, and that the letter would be circulated to practitioners, judges and magistrates for their information.

APPENDIX 1

PRACTICE DIRECTION: GUIDE TO CASE MANAGEMENT IN PUBLIC LAW PROCEEDINGS ('THE PLO PRACTICE DIRECTION', INCORPORATING THE PUBLIC LAW OUTLINE)

Foreword

The Protocol for Judicial Case Management in Public Law Children Act Cases came into operation in November 2003, distilling good practice and focusing on a new approach to case management. While the Protocol has become well-established as the framework for case management and has encouraged parties and the courts to tackle the causes of delay in resolving cases for children, both the Thematic Review published by the Judicial Review Team (JRT) in December 2005 and the Government Child Care Proceedings Review of May 2006 identified areas where it has not achieved its objective and in which practice needs improvement.

Analysis of the causes of delay has revealed a number of exacerbating features. For example, many cases have proved unwieldy through having been brought to court before local authority pre-proceedings work is complete. In others, lack of robust judicial case management has led to widespread failure to identify early, and concentrate upon resolving, the determinative issues in the case. It is also clear that children can suffer because parents and families are insufficiently engaged in the process both pre-proceedings and during the progress of the case. Acting on those findings, the JRT, in consultation with their colleagues and the other key agencies in the Family Justice System have formulated the streamlined and simplified case management procedures which are set out in the Public Law Outline (PLO), and supported by a detailed Practice Direction.

At the same time, the Department for Children, Schools and Families and Welsh Assembly Government have revised their statutory guidance for local authorities (The Children Act 1989 Guidance and Regulations) in liaison with the JRT so as to ensure that the PLO and the Guidance complement each other and the best use is made of resources. In all cases where it is safe and practicable to do so, courts will expect local authorities to have completed procedures and involved families in accordance with the pre-proceedings stage of the PLO.

The PLO has been tested in various centres across England and Wales, and the family magistrates and judiciary trying care cases have been trained to identify and remain focussed on the key issues in the case with the aim of making the best decisions within the timetable for the child.

I have been much encouraged throughout the process, in particular at the seminars and other training events organised or overseen by the trainers of the Judicial Studies Board, to see the enthusiasm with which judges and magistrates have applied themselves to mastering the details of the PLO, accepting the need for careful and decisive case management within its structure, identifying the essential issues, setting the timetable for their disposal, and eliminating unnecessary evidence or hearings in respect of non-determinative matters.

Particular thanks are due to those who have drafted the provisions of the PLO and its supporting documentation and to those who have devised and delivered the necessary training. Please may I urge all of you to put it into practice with your customary dedication.

Sir Mark Potter
President of the Family Division
April 2008

The Practice Direction below is made by the President of the Family Division under the powers delegated to him by the Lord Chief Justice under Schedule 2, Part 1, paragraph 2(2) of the Constitutional Reform Act 2005, and is approved by the Lord Chancellor.

PRACTICE DIRECTION: GUIDE TO CASE MANAGEMENT IN PUBLIC LAW PROCEEDINGS

Scope

1.1 This Practice Direction applies to care and supervision proceedings. In so far as practicable, it is to be applied to all other Public Law Proceedings.

1.2 This Practice Direction will come into effect on 1st April 2008. It does not apply to applications issued before 1st April 2008 but the court may direct in any individual case that the Case Management Tools and Case Management Documentation referred to in the Direction will apply either wholly or partly to those applications. This is subject to the overriding objective below and to the proviso that such a direction will neither cause further delay nor involve repetition of steps already taken or decisions already made in the case.

1.3 This Practice Direction is to be read with the Rules and is subject to them.

1.4 A Glossary of terms is at paragraph 25.

The overriding objective

2.1 This Practice Direction has the overriding objective of enabling the court to deal with cases justly, having regard to the welfare issues involved.

Dealing with a case justly includes, so far as is practicable –

(1) ensuring that it is dealt with expeditiously and fairly;
(2) dealing with the case in ways which are proportionate to the nature, importance and complexity of the issues;
(3) ensuring that the parties are on an equal footing;
(4) saving expense; and
(5) allotting to it an appropriate share of the court's resources, while taking into account the need to allot resources to other cases.

Application by the court of the overriding objective

2.2 The court must seek to give effect to the overriding objective when it –

(1) exercises the case management powers referred to in this Practice Direction; or
(2) interprets any provision of this Practice Direction.

Duty of the parties

2.3 The parties are required to help the court further the overriding objective.

Court case management

The Main Principles

3.1 The main principles underlying court case management in Public Law Proceedings are –

(1) judicial continuity: each case will be allocated to one or not more than two case management judges (in the case of magistrates' courts, case managers), who will be responsible for every case management stage in the proceedings through to the Final Hearing and, in relation to the High Court or county court, one of whom may be – and where possible should be – the judge who will conduct the Final Hearing;
(2) main case management tools: each case will be managed by the court by using the appropriate main case management tools;
(3) active case management: each case will be actively case managed by the court with a view at all times to furthering the overriding objective;
(4) consistency: each case will, so far as compatible with the overriding objective, be managed in a consistent way and using the standardised steps provided for in this Direction.

The Main Case Management Tools

The Timetable for the Child

3.2 The court will set an appropriate Timetable for the Child who is the subject of the proceedings.

3.3 The Timetable for the Child will be set by the court to take account of all significant steps in the child's life that are likely to take place during the proceedings. Those steps include not only legal steps but also social, care, health and education steps.

3.4 Examples of the dates the court will record and take into account when setting the Timetable for the Child are the dates of –

(1) any formal review by the Local Authority of the case of a looked after child (within the meaning of section 22(1) of the 1989 Act);
(2) the child taking up a place at a new school;
(3) any review by the Local Authority of any statement of the child's special educational needs;
(4) an assessment by a paediatrician or other specialist;
(5) the outcome of any review of Local Authority plans for the child, for example, any plans for permanence through adoption, Special Guardianship or placement with parents or relatives;
(6) a change or proposed change of the child's placement.

Case Management Documentation

3.5 The case management documents include the –

(1) Application form;
(2) Supplementary Form PLO1;
(3) Schedule of Proposed Findings;
(4) Allocation Record and the Timetable for the Child;
(5) Case Analysis and Recommendations provided by Cafcass or Cafcass Cymru;
(6) Local Authority Case Summary;
(7) Other Parties' Case Summaries;

(8) Draft Case Management Orders.

3.6 The court will encourage the use of those case management documents which are not prescribed by the Rules.

The Case Management Record

3.7 The court's filing system for the case will be known as the Case Management Record and will include the following main documents –

(1) the Supplementary Form PLO1 which will be the index of documents on the Record;
(2) in care and supervision proceedings, any Letter Before Proceedings and any related subsequent correspondence confirming the Local Authority's position to parents and others with parental responsibility for the child;
(3) the Case Management Documentation;
(4) Standard Directions on Issue and on First Appointment;
(5) the Draft Case Management Orders approved by the court.

3.8 Parties or their legal representatives will be expected to retain their own record containing copies of the documents on the court's Case Management Record.

The First Appointment

3.9 The purpose of the First Appointment is to confirm allocation of the case and give initial case management directions.

The Draft Case Management Order

3.10 The draft form of a Case Management Order is a special form of order containing terms of general application to be used as appropriate for each case. The form of order is not only to be used for drawing up orders in the form prescribed by the Rules at the end of a hearing. The form is also to be used as a case management checklist. The form contains standard provisions designed to help parties, their legal representatives and the court –

(1) identify the relevant issues and the procedural directions which may be required;
(2) monitor changes to the relevant issues and compliance with the court's directions;
(3) focus on what the proceedings are intended to achieve.

Advocates Discussion/Meeting

3.11 The court will consider directing advocates to have discussions before the Case Management Conference and the Issues Resolution Hearing. Advocates may well find that the best way to have these discussions is to meet. Such discussion is intended to facilitate agreement and to narrow the issues for the court to consider. Advocates and litigants in person may take part in the Advocates' meeting or discussions.

The Case Management Conference

3.12 In each case there will be a Case Management Conference to enable the case management judge or case manager, with the co-operation of the parties, actively to manage the case and, at the earliest practicable opportunity to –

(1) identify the relevant and key issues; and

(2) give full case management directions including confirming the Timetable for the Child.

The Issues Resolution Hearing

3.13 In each case there will be an Issues Resolution Hearing before the Final Hearing to –

(1) identify any remaining key issues; and
(2) as far as possible, resolve or narrow those issues.

Active Case Management

3.14 The court must further the overriding objective by actively managing cases.

3.15 Active case management includes –

(1) identifying the Timetable for the Child;
(2) identifying the appropriate court to conduct the proceedings and transferring the proceedings as early as possible to that court;
(3) encouraging the parties to co-operate with each other in the conduct of the proceedings;
(4) retaining the Case Management Record;
(5) identifying all facts and matters that are in issue at the earliest stage in the proceedings and at each hearing;
(6) deciding promptly which issues need full investigation and hearing and which do not;
(7) deciding the order in which issues are to be resolved;
(8) identifying at an early stage who should be a party to the proceedings;
(9) considering whether the likely benefits of taking a particular step justify any delay which will result and the cost of taking it;
(10) directing discussion between advocates and litigants in person before the Case Management Conference and Issues Resolution Hearing;
(11) requiring the use of the Draft Case Management Order and directing advocates and litigants in person to prepare or adjust the draft order where appropriate;
(12) standardising, simplifying and regulating –

    (a) the use of Case Management Documentation and forms;
    (b) the court's orders and directions;

(13) controlling –

    (a) the use and cost of experts;
    (b) the nature and extent of the documents which are to be disclosed to the parties and presented to the court;
    (c) whether and, if so, in what manner the documents disclosed are to be presented to the court;
    (d) the progress of the case;

(14) where it is demonstrated to be in the interests of the child, encouraging the parties to use an alternative dispute resolution procedure if the court considers such a procedure to be appropriate and facilitating the use of such procedure;
(15) helping the parties to reach agreement in relation to the whole or part of the case;
(16) fixing the dates for all appointments and hearings;
(17) dealing with as many aspects of the case as it can on the same occasion;
(18) where possible dealing with additional issues which may arise from time to time in the case without requiring the parties to attend at court;
(19) making use of technology; and
(20) giving directions to ensure that the case proceeds quickly and efficiently.

The Expectations

4.1 The expectations are that proceedings should be –

(1) conducted using the Case Management Tools and Case Management Documentation referred to in this Practice Direction in accordance with the Table contained in paragraph 9 below and known as the Public Law Outline;
(2) finally determined within the timetable fixed by the court in accordance with the Timetable for the Child – the target times in the Public Law Outline being adhered to and being taken as the maximum permissible time for the taking of the step referred to in the Outline.

4.2 However, there may be cases where the court considers that the child's welfare requires a different approach from the one contained in the Public Law Outline. In those cases, the court will –

(1) determine the appropriate case management directions and timetable; and
(2) record on the face of the order the reasons for departing from the approach in the Public Law Outline.

How the parties should help court case management

Main Methods of Helping

Good Case Preparation

5.1 The applicant should prepare the case before proceedings are issued. In care and supervision proceedings the Local Authority should use the Pre-proceedings Checklist.

The Allocation Record and The Timetable for the Child

5.2 The applicant must prepare and file the Allocation Record and the Timetable for the Child. The Allocation Record must contain the applicant's allocation proposal and a record of the court's allocation decision and reasons. The Timetable for the Child will be part of the Allocation Record. The applicant should provide information to update the Timetable regularly. The applicant is to be responsible for updating the Allocation Record including the Timetable after each hearing.

Case Management Documentation

5.3 The parties must use the Case Management Documentation.

Co-operation

5.4 The parties and their representatives should co-operate with the court in case management, including the fixing of timetables to avoid unacceptable delay, and in the crystallisation and resolution of the issues on which the case turns.

Directions

5.5 The parties or their legal representatives will –

(1) monitor compliance with the court's directions; and

(2) tell the court or court officer about any failure to comply with a direction of the court or any other delay in the proceedings.

The Case Management Record

5.6 The parties or their legal representatives are expected to retain a record containing copies of the documents on the court's Case Management Record.

The Draft Case Management Order

5.7 Parties should start to consider the content of the Draft Case Management Order at the earliest opportunity either before or in the course of completing applications to the court or the response to the application. They should in any event consider the Draft Case Management Order after the First Appointment.

5.8 There should be ongoing consideration of the Draft Case Management Orders throughout the proceedings. The Draft Case Management Orders should serve as an *aide memoire* to everyone involved in the proceedings of –

(1) the Timetable for the Child;
(2) the case management decisions;
(3) the identified issues.

5.9 Only one Draft Case Management Order should be filed with the court for each of the Case Management Conference and the Issues Resolution Hearing. It is the responsibility of the advocate for the applicant, which in care and supervision proceedings will ordinarily be the Local Authority, to prepare those drafts and be responsible for obtaining comments from the advocates and the parties.

5.10 In paragraphs 5.3, 5.7 and 5.9 "parties" includes parties' legal representatives.

Ethnicity, Language, Religion and Culture

6 At each case management stage of the proceedings, particularly at the First Appointment and Case Management Conference, the court will consider giving directions regarding the obtaining of evidence about the ethnicity, language, religion and culture of the child and other significant persons involved in the proceedings. The court will subsequently consider the implications of this evidence for the child in the context of the issues in the case.

Adults who may be protected parties

7.1 The court will investigate as soon as possible any issue as to whether an adult party or intended party to the proceedings lacks capacity (within the meaning of the Mental Capacity Act 2005) to conduct the proceedings. An adult who lacks capacity to conduct the proceedings is a protected party and must have a representative (a litigation friend, next friend or guardian ad litem) to conduct the proceedings on his or her behalf.

7.2 Any issue as to the capacity of an adult to conduct the proceedings must be determined before the court gives any directions relevant to that adult's role within the proceedings.

7.3 Where the adult is a protected party, his or her representative should be involved in any instruction of an expert, including the instruction of an expert to assess whether the adult, although a protected party, is competent to give evidence. The instruction of an expert is a significant step in the proceedings. The representative will wish to consider (and ask the expert to consider), if the protected party is competent to give evidence, their best interests in this regard. The representative may wish to seek advice about 'special measures'. The representative may put forward an argument on behalf of the protected party that the protected party should not give evidence.

7.4 If at any time during the proceedings, there is reason to believe that a party may lack capacity to conduct the proceedings, then the court must be notified and directions sought to ensure that this issue is investigated without delay.

Child likely to lack capacity to conduct the proceedings when he reaches 18

8 Where it appears that a child is –

(1) a party to the proceedings and not the subject of them;
(2) nearing his or her 18th birthday; and
(3) considered likely to lack capacity to conduct the proceedings when he reaches 18,

the court will consider giving directions relating to the investigation of a child's capacity in this respect.

Outline of the process and how to use the main Case Management Tools

9.1 The Public Law Outline set out in the Table below contains an outline of –

(1) the order of the different stages of the process;
(2) the purposes of the main case management hearings and matters to be considered at them;
(3) the latest timescales within which the main stages of the process should take place.

9.2 In the Public Law Outline –

(1) "CMC" means the Case Management Conference;
(2) "FA" means the First Appointment;
(3) "IRH" means the Issues Resolution Hearing;
(4) "OS" means the Official Solicitor.

Public Law Outline

<table>
<tr><th colspan="2">PRE-PROCEEDINGS</th></tr>
<tr><th colspan="2">PRE-PROCEEDINGS CHECKLIST</th></tr>
<tr><td colspan="2">The Checklist Documents:</td></tr>
<tr><td>Documents to be disclosed from the LA's files:
• Previous court orders & judgments/reasons
• Any relevant Assessment Materials
  • Initial and core assessments
  • Section 7 & 37 reports
  • Relatives & friends materials (e.g. a genogram)
• Other relevant Reports & Records
  • Single, joint or inter-agency materials (e.g. health & education/Home Office & Immigration documents)
  • records of discussions with the family
  • Key LA minutes & records for the child (including Strategy Discussion Record)</td><td>• Pre-existing care plans (e.g. child in need plan, looked after child plan & child protection plan)
• Social Work Chronology
• Letters Before Proceedings
Documents to be prepared for the proceedings:
• Schedule of Proposed Findings
• Initial Social Work Statement
• Care Plan
• Allocation Record & Timetable for the Child</td></tr>
</table>

<table>
<tr><th colspan="2">STAGE 1 – ISSUE AND THE FIRST APPOINTMENT</th></tr>
<tr><th>ISSUE</th><th>FIRST APPOINTMENT</th></tr>
<tr><td>On DAY 1 and by DAY 3</td><td>By DAY 6</td></tr>
<tr><td>Objectives: To ensure compliance with pre-proceedings checklist; to allocate proceedings; to obtain the information necessary for initial case management at the FA</td><td>Objectives: To confirm allocation; to give initial case management directions</td></tr>
<tr><td>On Day 1:
• The LA files:
• Application Form
• Supplementary Form PLO1
• Checklist documents

• Court officer issues application
• Court nominates case manager(s)
• Court gives standard directions on issue including:
• Pre-proceedings checklist compliance
• Allocate and/or transfer
• Appoint children's guardian
• Appoint solicitor for the child
• Case Analysis for FA
• Invite OS to act for protected persons (non subject children & incapacitated adults)
• List FA by Day 6
• Make arrangements for contested hearing (if necessary)

By Day 3
• Allocation of a children's guardian expected
• LA serves the Application Form, Supplementary Form PLO1 and the Checklist Documents on parties</td><td>• Parties notify LA & court of need for a contested hearing
• Court makes arrangements for a contested hearing
• Initial case management by Court including:
• Confirm Timetable for the Child
• Confirm allocation or transfer
• Identify additional parties & representation (including allocation of children's guardian)
• Identify "Early Final Hearing" cases
• Scrutinise Care Plan

• Court gives standard directions on FA including:
• Case Analysis and Recommendations for Stages 2 & 3
• LA Case Summary
• Other Parties' Case Summaries
• Parties' initial witness statements
• For the Advocates' Meeting
• List CMC or (if appropriate) an Early Final Hearing
• Upon transfer</td></tr>
</table>

STAGE 2 – CASE MANAGEMENT CONFERENCE	
ADVOCATES' MEETING	**CMC**
No later than 2 days before CMC	**No later than day 45**
Objectives: To prepare the Draft Case Management Order; to identify experts and draft questions for them	**Objectives:** To identify issue(s); to give full case management directions
• Consider all other parties' Case Summaries and Case Analysis and Recommendations • Identify proposed experts and draft questions in accordance with Experts Practice Direction • Draft Case Management Order • Notify court of need for a contested hearing • File Draft Case Management Order with the case manager/case management judge by 11am one working day before the CMC	• Detailed case management by the court • Scrutinise compliance with directions • Confirm Timetable for the Child • Identify key issue(s) • Confirm allocation or transfer • Consider case management directions in the Draft Case Management Order • Scrutinise Care Plan • Check compliance with Experts Practice Direction • Court issues Case Management Order • Court lists IRH and, where necessary, a warned period for Final Hearing

<table>
<tr><th colspan="2">STAGE 3 – ISSUES RESOLUTION HEARING</th></tr>
<tr><th>ADVOCATES' MEETING</th><th>IRH</th></tr>
<tr><td>Between 2 and 7 days before the IRH</td><td>Between 16 & 25 weeks</td></tr>
<tr><td>Objective: To prepare or update the Draft Case Management Order</td><td>Objectives: To resolve and narrow issue(s); to identify any remaining key issues</td></tr>
<tr><td>
• Consider all other parties' Case Summaries and Case Analysis and Recommendations
• Draft Case Management Order
• Notify court of need for a contested hearing/time for oral evidence to be given
• File Draft Case Management Order with the case manager/case management judge by 11am one working day before the IRH
</td><td>
• Identification by the court of the key issue(s) (if any) to be determined

• Final case management by the court:
  • Scrutinise compliance with directions
  • Consider case management directions in the Draft Case Management Order
  • Scrutinise Care Plan
  • Give directions for Hearing documents:
    • Threshold agreement or facts/issues remaining to be determined
    • Final Evidence & Care Plan
    • Case Analysis and Recommendations
    • Witness templates
    • Skeleton arguments
    • Judicial reading list/reading time/judgment writing time
    • Time estimate
    • Bundles Practice Direction compliance
    • List or confirm Hearing
• Court issues Case Management Order
</td></tr>
</table>

<table>
<tr><th colspan="2">STAGE 4</th></tr>
<tr><th colspan="2">HEARING</th></tr>
<tr><td colspan="2">In accordance with the Timetable for the Child</td></tr>
<tr><td colspan="2">Objective: To determine remaining issues</td></tr>
<tr><td>• All file & serve updated case management documents & bundle
• Draft final order(s) in approved form</td><td>• Judgment/Reasons
• Disclose documents as required after hearing</td></tr>
</table>

Starting the Proceedings

10.1 The applicant, which in care and supervision proceedings will ordinarily be the Local Authority, must file the Supplementary Form PLO1 with the application form. The applicant must also file an Allocation Record and Timetable for the Child which includes the applicant's allocation proposal.

Pre-proceedings Checklist

10.2 The documents which the court will expect to see attached to the application form for a care or supervision order are set out in the Pre-proceedings Checklist in the Public Law Outline. The Pre-proceedings Checklist should be used at the earliest opportunity as a guide to what documents the court will expect to see at the start of the proceedings and should be filed with the application form. The Pre-proceedings Checklist will promote good case preparation.

Compliance with Pre-proceedings Checklist

10.3 It is recognised that in some cases the circumstances are such that the safety and welfare of the child may be jeopardised if the start of proceedings is delayed until all of the documents appropriate to the case and referred to in the Pre-proceedings Checklist are available. The court recognises that the preparation may need to be varied to suit the circumstances of the case. The court is likely to make directions relating to the preparation of any missing documentation at the start of the proceedings and at the First Appointment. The court also recognises that some documents on the Pre-proceedings Checklist may not exist and may never exist, for example, the Section 37 report, and that in urgent proceedings no Letter Before Proceedings may have been sent.

What the Court will do at the Issue of Proceedings

Objectives

11.1 The objectives at this stage are for the court –

(1) in care and supervision proceedings, to ensure compliance with the Pre-proceedings Checklist;
(2) to allocate proceedings;
(3) to obtain the information necessary to enable initial case management at the First Appointment.

11.2 The steps which the court will take once proceedings have been issued include those set out in paragraphs 11.3 to 11.5 below.

Allocation

11.3 The court will consider allocation of the case and transfer those cases to the county court which are obviously suitable for immediate transfer. An example of a case of this kind is where there is evidence that a parent may be a protected party and require representation which currently cannot be obtained in the magistrates' court.

Other Steps to be taken by the Court

Directions

11.4 The court will –

(1) consider giving directions –

  (a) appropriate to the case including Standard Directions On Issue;
  (b) in care and supervision proceedings, relating to the preparation and filing of documents on the Pre-proceedings Checklist which are not yet available;
  (c) relating to representation of any protected party and where appropriate invite the Official Solicitor to act for a protected party or any child who is a party to, but is not the subject of, the proceedings and where appropriate invite the Official Solicitor to act as his or her guardian ad litem;

(2) appoint a children's guardian in specified proceedings (in relation to care and supervision proceedings the court will expect that Cafcass or Cafcass Cymru will have received notice from the Local Authority that proceedings were going to be started);
(3) appoint a solicitor for the child under section 41(3) of the 1989 Act where appropriate;
(4) request the children's guardian or if appropriate another officer of the service or Welsh family proceedings officer to prepare a Case Analysis and Recommendations for the First Appointment;
(5) make arrangements for a contested hearing, if necessary.

Setting a date for the First Appointment

11.5 The court will set a date for the First Appointment normally no later than 6 days from the date of issue of the proceedings and in any event in line with the draft Timetable for the Child

Case Managers in the Magistrates' Courts

11.6 In the magistrates' courts, the justices' clerk may nominate one but not more than two case managers.

The First Appointment

Objectives

12.1 The First Appointment is the first hearing in the proceedings. The main objectives of the First Appointment are to –

(1) confirm allocation; and
(2) give initial case management directions having regard to the Public Law Outline.

12.2 The steps which the court will take at the First Appointment include those set out in paragraphs 12.3 to 12.6 below.

Steps to be taken by the Court

12.3 The court will –

(1) confirm the Timetable for the Child;

(2) make arrangements for any contested interim hearing such as an application for an interim care order;
(3) confirm the allocation of the case or, if appropriate, transfer the case;
(4) request the children's guardian or if appropriate another officer of the service or Welsh family proceedings officer to prepare a Case Analysis and Recommendations for the Case Management Conference or Issues Resolution Hearing;
(5) scrutinise the Care Plan;
(6) consider giving directions relating to –
    (a) those matters in the Public Law Outline which remain to be considered;
    (b) the joining of a person who would not otherwise be a respondent under the Rules as a party to the proceedings;
    (c) where any person to be joined as a party may be a protected party, an investigation of that person's capacity to conduct the proceedings and the representation of that person and if appropriate invite the Official Solicitor to act for that person;
    (d) the identification of family and friends as proposed carers and any overseas, immigration, jurisdiction and paternity issues;
    (e) in Public Law Proceedings other than care and supervision proceedings, the documents to be filed with the court;
    (f) evidence to be obtained as to whether a parent who is a protected party is competent to make his or her own statement.

Early Final Hearing Cases

12.4 Cases which are suitable for an Early Final Hearing are likely to be those cases where the child has no parents, guardians, relatives who want to care for the child, or other carers. Examples are those cases where the child is an abandoned baby or where a child has been brought into this country and abandoned. The court will –

(1) identify at the First Appointment whether the case is one which is suitable for an Early Final Hearing; and
(2) set a date for that Final Hearing.

Setting a date for the Case Management Conference

12.5 The court will set a date for the Case Management Conference normally no later than 45 days from the date of issue of the proceedings and in any event in line with the Timetable for the Child.

Advocates' Meeting/discussion and the Draft Case Management Order

12.6 The court will consider directing a discussion between the parties' advocates and any litigant in person and the preparation of a Draft Case Management Order as outlined below.

Experts

12.7 A party who wishes to instruct an expert should comply with the Experts Practice Direction. Where the parties are agreed on any matter relating to experts or expert evidence, the draft agreement must be submitted for the court's approval as early as possible in the proceedings.

Advocates' Meeting/discussion and the Draft Case Management Order

13.1 The main objective of the Advocates' Meeting or discussion is to prepare the Draft Case Management Order.

13.2 Where there is a litigant in person the court will consider the most effective way in which that person can be involved in the advocates' discussions and give directions as appropriate including directions relating to the part to be played by any McKenzie Friend.

13.3 Timing of the discussions is of the utmost importance. The need for discussions outside the "court room door" of matters, which could have been discussed at an earlier time, is to be avoided. Discussions are to take place no later than 2 days before the Case Management Conference or the Issues Resolution Hearing whichever is appropriate. The discussions may take place earlier than 2 days before those hearings, for example, up to 7 days before them.

13.4 Following discussion the advocates should prepare or adjust the Draft Case Management Order. In practice the intention is that the advocate for the applicant, which in care and supervision proceedings will ordinarily be the Local Authority, should take the lead in preparing and adjusting the Draft Case Management Order following discussion with the other advocates.

13.5 Where it is not possible for the advocates to agree the terms of the Draft Case Management Order, the advocates should specify on the Draft Case Management Order, or on a separate document if more practicable –

(1) those provisions on which they agree; and
(2) those provisions on which they disagree.

13.6 Unless the court directs otherwise, the Draft Case Management Order must be filed with the court no later than 11am on the day before the Case Management Conference or the Issues Resolution Hearing whichever may be appropriate.

13.7 At the Advocates' Meeting or discussion before the Case Management Conference, the advocates should also try to agree the questions to be put to any proposed expert (whether jointly instructed or not) if not previously agreed. Under the Experts Practice Direction the questions on which the proposed expert is to give an opinion are a crucial component of the expert directions which the court is required to consider at the Case Management Conference.

Case Management Conference

Objectives

14.1 The Case Management Conference is the main hearing at which the court manages the case. The main objectives of the Conference are to –

(1) identify key issues; and
(2) give full case management directions.

14.2 The steps which the court will take at the Case Management Conference include those steps set out in paragraphs 14.3 to 14.5 below.

Steps to be taken by the Court

14.3 The court will –

(1) review and confirm the Timetable for the Child;
(2) confirm the allocation or the transfer of the case;
(3) scrutinise the Care Plan;
(4) identify the key issues;
(5) identify the remaining case management issues;
(6) resolve remaining case management issues by reference to the Draft Case Management Order;
(7) identify any special measures such as the need for access for the disabled or provision for vulnerable witnesses;
(8) scrutinise the Case Management Record to check whether directions have been complied with and if not, consider making further directions as appropriate;
(9) where expert evidence is required, check whether the parties have complied with the Experts Practice Direction, in particular section 4 (Preparation for the relevant hearing) and consider giving directions as appropriate.

Case Management Order

14.4 The court will issue the approved Case Management Order. Parties or their legal representatives will be expected to submit in electronic form the final approved Draft Case Management Order on the conclusion of, and the same day as, the Case Management Conference

Setting a date for the Issues Resolution Hearing/Final Hearing

14.5 The court will set –

(1) a date for the Issues Resolution Hearing normally at any time between 16 and 25 weeks from the date of issue of the proceedings and in any event in line with the Timetable for the Child; and
(2) if necessary, specify a period within which the Final Hearing of the application is to take place unless a date has already been set.

The Issues Resolution Hearing

Objectives

15.1 The objectives of this hearing are to –

(1) resolve and narrow issues; and
(2) identify key remaining issues requiring resolution.

15.2 The Issues Resolution Hearing is likely to be the hearing before the Final Hearing. Final case management directions and other preparations for the Final Hearing will be made at this hearing.

Steps to be taken by the Court

15.3 The court will –

(1) identify the key issues (if any) to be determined;
(2) review and confirm the Timetable for the Child;
(3) consider giving case management directions relating to –

(a) any outstanding matter contained in the Draft Case Management Order;
(b) the preparation and filing of final evidence including the filing of witness templates;
(c) skeleton arguments;
(d) preparation and filing of bundles in accordance with the Bundles Practice Direction;
(e) any agreement relating to the satisfaction of the threshold criteria under section 31 of the 1989 Act or facts and issues remaining to be determined in relation to it or to any welfare question which arises;
(f) time estimates;
(g) the judicial reading list and likely reading time and judgment writing time;

(4) issue the Case Management Order.

15.4 For the avoidance of doubt the purpose of an Issues Resolution Hearing is to –

(1) identify key issues which are not agreed;
(2) examine if those key issues can be agreed; and
(3) where those issues cannot be agreed, examine the most proportionate method of resolving those issues.

15.5 The expectation is that the method of resolving the key issues which cannot be agreed will be at a hearing (ordinarily the Final Hearing) where there is an opportunity for the relevant oral evidence to be heard and challenged.

Attendance at the Case Management Conference and the Issues Resolution Hearing

16 An advocate who has conduct of the Final Hearing should ordinarily attend the Case Management Conference and the Issues Resolution Hearing. Where the attendance of this advocate is not possible, then an advocate who is familiar with the issues in the proceedings should attend.

Flexible Powers of the Court

17.1 Attention is drawn to the flexible powers of the court either following the issue of the application in that court, the transfer of the case to that court or at any other stage in the proceedings.

17.2 The court may give directions without a hearing including setting a date for the Final Hearing or a period within which the Final Hearing will take place. The steps, which the court will ordinarily take at the various stages of the proceedings provided for in the Public Law Outline, may be taken by the court at another stage in the proceedings if the circumstances of the case merit this approach.

17.3 The flexible powers of the court include the ability for the court to cancel or repeat a particular hearing. For example, if the issue on which the case turns can with reasonable practicability be crystallised and resolved by having an Early Final Hearing, then in the fulfilment of the overriding objective, such a flexible approach must be taken to secure compliance with section 1(2) of the 1989 Act.

Alternative Dispute Resolution

18.1 The court will encourage the parties to use an alternative dispute resolution procedure and facilitate the use of such a procedure where it is –

(1) readily available;
(2) demonstrated to be in the interests of the child; and
(3) reasonably practicable and safe.

18.2 At any stage in the proceedings, the parties can ask the court for advice about alternative dispute resolution.

18.3 At any stage in the proceedings the court itself will consider whether alternative dispute resolution is appropriate. If so, the court may direct that a hearing or proceedings be adjourned for such specified period as it considers appropriate –

(1) to enable the parties to obtain information and advice about alternative dispute resolution; and
(2) where the parties agree, to enable alternative dispute resolution to take place.

18.4 It is expressly recognised that no party can or should be obliged to enter into any form of alternative dispute resolution if they are unwilling to do so.

Co-operation

19.1 Throughout the proceedings the parties and their representatives should co-operate wherever reasonably practicable to help towards securing the welfare of the child as the paramount consideration.

19.2 At each court appearance the court will ask the parties and their legal representatives –

(1) what steps they have taken to achieve co-operation and the extent to which they have been successful;
(2) if appropriate the reason why co-operation could not be achieved; and
(3) the steps needed to resolve any issues necessary to achieve co-operation.

Agreed Directions

20.1 The parties, their advisers and the children's guardian, are encouraged to try to agree directions for the management of the proceedings.

20.2 To obtain the court's approval the agreed directions must –

(1) set out a Timetable for the Child by reference to calendar dates for the taking of steps for the preparation of the case;
(2) include a date when it is proposed that the next hearing will take place.

Variation of case management timetable

21 It is emphasised that a party or the children's guardian must apply to the court at the earliest opportunity if they wish to vary by extending the dates set by the court for –

(1) a directions appointment;
(2) a First Appointment;
(3) a Case Management Conference;
(4) an Issues Resolution Hearing;
(5) the Final Hearing;
(6) the period within which the Final Hearing of the application is to take place; or
(7) any discussion between advocates or for the filing of the Draft Case Management Orders.

Who performs the functions of the Court

22.1 Where this Practice Direction provides for the Court to perform case management functions, then except where any Rule, Practice Direction, any other enactment or the Family Proceedings (Allocation to Judiciary) Directions ([1999] 2 FLR 799) provides otherwise, the functions may be performed –

(1) in relation to proceedings in the High Court or in a district registry, by any judge or district judge of that Court including a district judge of the principal registry;
(2) in relation to proceedings in the county court, by any judge or district judge including a district judge of the principal registry when the principal registry is treated as if it were a county court; and
(3) in relation to proceedings in a magistrates' court by –
    (a) any family proceedings court constituted in accordance with sections 66 and 67 of the 1980 Act;
    (b) a single justice; or
    (c) a justices' clerk.

22.2 The case management functions to be exercised by a justices' clerk may be exercised by an assistant justices' clerk provided that person has been specifically authorised by a justices' clerk to exercise case management functions. Any reference in this Practice Direction to a justices' clerk is to be taken to include an assistant justices' clerk so authorised. The justices' clerk may in particular appoint one but not more than two assistant justices' clerks as case managers for each case.

22.3 In proceedings in a magistrates' court, where a party considers that there are likely to be issues arising at a hearing (including the First Appointment, Case Management Conference and Issues Resolution Hearing) which need to be decided by a family proceedings court, rather than a justices' clerk, then that party should give the court written notice of that need at least 2 days before the hearing.

22.4 Family proceedings courts may consider making arrangements to ensure a court constituted in accordance with s 66 of the 1980 Act is available at the same time as Issues Resolution Hearings are being heard by a justices' clerk. Any delay as a result of the justices' clerk considering for whatever reason that it is inappropriate for a justices' clerk to perform a case management function on a particular matter and the justices' clerk's referring of that matter to the court should then be minimal.

Technology

23 Where the facilities are available to the court and the parties, the court will consider making full use of technology including electronic information exchange and video or telephone conferencing.

Other Practice Directions

24.1 This Practice Direction must be read with the Bundles Practice Direction.

24.2 The Bundles Practice Direction is applied to Public Law Proceedings in the High Court and county court with the following adjustments –

(1) add "except the First Appointment, Case Management Conference, and Issues Resolution Hearing referred to in the Practice Direction: Guide to Case Management in Public Law Proceedings where there are no contested applications being heard at those hearings" to paragraph 2.2 ;

(2) the reference to –

  (a) the "Protocol for Judicial Case Management in Public law Children Act Cases [2003] 2 FLR 719" in paragraph 6.1;

  (b) the "Practice Direction: Care Cases: Judicial Continuity and Judicial Case Management" in paragraph 15; and

  (c) "the Public Law Protocol" in paragraph 15

shall be read as if it were a reference to this Practice Direction.

24.3 This Practice Direction replaces Practice Direction: Care Cases: Judicial Continuity and Judicial Case Management appended to the Protocol for Judicial Case Management in Public Law Children Act Cases [2003] 2 FLR 719.

Glossary

25 In this Practice Direction –

(1) "the 1989 Act" means the Children Act 1989;

(2) "the 1980 Act" means the Magistrates' Courts Act 1980;

(3) "advocate" means a person exercising a right of audience as a representative of, or on behalf of, a party;

(4) "Allocation Record and the Timetable for the Child" means a document containing –

  (a) the Local Authority's proposal for allocation;

  (b) the Local Authority's proposed Timetable for the Child;

  (c) the court's allocation decisions and reasons; and

  (d) the court's approved Timetable for the Child;

(5) "alternative dispute resolution" means the methods of resolving a dispute other than through the normal court process;

(6) "assistant justices' clerk" has the meaning assigned to it by section 27(5) of the Courts Act 2003;

(7) "the Bundles Practice Direction" means the Practice Direction Family Proceedings: Court Bundles (Universal Practice to be Applied in all Courts other than Family Proceedings Court) of 27 July 2006;

(8) "Case Analysis and Recommendations" means a written or oral outline of the case from the child's perspective prepared by the children's guardian or other officer of the service or Welsh family proceedings officer at different stages of the proceedings requested by the court, to provide –

  (a) an analysis of the issues that need to be resolved in the case including –

    (i) any harm or risk of harm;

    (ii) the child's own views;

    (iii) the family context including advice relating to ethnicity, language, religion and culture of the child and other significant persons;

    (iv) the Local Authority work and proposed care plan;

    (v) advice about the court process including the Timetable for the Child; and

    (vi) identification of work that remains to be done for the child in the short and longer term; and

  (b) recommendations for outcomes, in order to safeguard and promote the best interests of the child in the proceedings;

(9) "Case Management Documentation" includes the documents referred to in paragraph 3.5;

(10) "Case Management Record" means the court's filing system for the case which includes the documents referred to at paragraph 3.7;

(11) "case manager" means the justices' clerk or assistant justices' clerk who manages the case in the magistrates' courts;

(12) "Care Plan" means a "section 31A plan" referred to in section 31A of the 1989 Act;

(13) "Core Assessment" means the assessment undertaken by the Local Authority in accordance with The Framework for the Assessment of Children in Need and their Families (Department of Health, 2000);

(14) "court" means the High Court, county court or the magistrates' court;

(15) "court officer" means –

(a) in the High Court or a county court, a member of court staff; and
(b) in a magistrates' court, the designated officer;

(16) "Draft Case Management Order" means the draft case management document in the form of an order set out at Annex C to this Practice Direction;

(17) "Experts Practice Direction" means the Practice Direction on Experts in Family Proceedings relating to Children which is to come into force on the same date as this Practice Direction;

(18) "genogram" means a family tree, setting out in diagrammatic form the family's background;

(19) "hearing" includes a directions appointment;

(20) "Initial Assessment" means the assessment undertaken by the Local Authority in accordance with The Framework for the Assessment of Children in Need and their Families (Department of Health, 2000);

(21) "Initial Social Work Statement" means a statement prepared by the Local Authority strictly limited to the following evidence –

(a) the precipitating incident(s) and background circumstances relevant to the grounds and reasons for making the application including a brief description of any referral and assessment processes that have already occurred;
(b) any facts and matters that are within the social worker's personal knowledge limited to the findings sought by the Local Authority;
(c) any emergency steps and previous court orders that are relevant to the application;
(d) any decisions made by the Local Authority that are relevant to the application;
(e) information relevant to the ethnicity, language, religion, culture, gender and vulnerability of the child and other significant persons in the form of a 'family profile' together with a narrative description and details of the social care and other services that are relevant to the same;
(f) where the Local Authority is applying for an interim order: the Local Authority's initial proposals for the child (which are also to be set out in the Care Plan) including placement, contact with parents and other significant persons and the social care services that are proposed;
(g) the Local Authority's initial proposals for the further assessment of the parties during the proceedings including twin track /concurrent planning (where more than one permanence option for the child is being explored by the Local Authority);

(22) "legal representative" means a barrister or solicitor, solicitor's employee or other authorised litigator (as defined in the Courts and Legal Services Act 1990) who has been instructed to act for a party in relation to the proceedings;

(23) "Letter Before Proceedings" means any letter from the Local Authority containing written notification to the parents and others with parental responsibility for the child of the Local Authority's plan to apply to court for a care or supervision order;

(24) "Local Authority Case Summary" means a summary for each case management hearing in the form set out at Annex B to this Practice Direction which must include the following information –

(a) the applications which have been issued in the current proceedings;
(b) any previous proceedings in relation to the child[ren] and any orders made in previous proceedings or in the current proceedings to which the child[ren] is/are subject;
(c) the present living arrangements for the child[ren] and arrangements for contact between the child[ren] and parent(s) or other relevant adult or child;
(d) a very brief summary of the incident(s) or circumstances giving rise to the application and of the background to the proceedings;
(e) a summary of any concerns the Local Authority may have about the mental capacity of an adult to care for the child or the capacity of the adult to prepare for the proceedings;
(f) the Key Issues in the case;
(g) any agreements that there are as to the Key Issues or the findings of fact sought by the Local Authority;
(h) whether an application for placement for adoption is among the range of options that will have to be considered;
(i) any current or proposed proceedings (e.g. criminal proceedings, other family proceedings, disciplinary, immigration or mental capacity/health determinations) which are relevant to the determination of the application(s)
(j) the issues and directions which the court will need to consider at the Case Management Conference/Issues Resolution Hearing, including any interim orders sought;
(k) any steps which have not been taken or directions not complied with, an explanation of the reasons and he effect, if any, on the Timetable for the Child;
(l) a recommended reading list and suggested reading time;
(m) any additional information relevant to the Timetable for the Child or for the conduct of the hearing or the proceedings;
(n) the contact details of all advocates, their solicitors (where appropriate) and other significant persons e.g. the Local Authority key worker or team manager and the children's guardian;

(25) "justices' clerk" has the meaning assigned to it by section 27(1) of the Courts Act 2003;
(26) "McKenzie Friend" means any person permitted by the court to sit beside an unrepresented litigant in court to assist the litigant by prompting, taking notes and giving advice to the litigant;
(27) "Other Parties' Case Summaries" means summaries by parties other than the Local Authority containing –

(a) the party's proposals for the long term future of the child (to include placement and contact);
(b) the party's reply to the Local Authority's Schedule of Proposed Findings;
(c) any proposal for assessment / expert evidence; and
(d) the names, addresses and contact details of any family or friends who it is suggested be approached in relation to long term care/contact or respite;

(28) "Pre-proceedings Checklist" means the checklist of documents set out in the Public Law Outline;
(29) "Public Law Proceedings" means proceedings for –

(a) a residence order under section 8 of the 1989 Act with respect to a child who is the subject of a care order;
(b) a secure accommodation order under section 25 of the 1989 Act;

(c) a care order under section 31(1)(a) of the 1989 Act of the discharge of such an order under section 39(1) of the 1989 Act;
(d) an order giving permission to change a child's surname or remove a child from the United Kingdom under section 33(7) of the 1989 Act;
(e) a supervision order under section 31(1)(b) of the 1989 Act, the discharge or variation of such an order under section 39(2) of that Act, or the extension or further extension of such an order under paragraph 6(3) of Schedule 3 to that Act;
(f) an order making provision for contact under section 34(2) to (4) of the 1989 Act or an order varying or discharging such an order under section 34(9) of that Act;
(g) an education supervision order, the extension of an education supervision order under paragraph 15(2) of Schedule 3 to the 1989 Act, or the discharge of such an order under paragraph 17(1) of Schedule 3 to that Act;
(h) an order varying directions made with an interim care order or interim supervision order under section 38(8)(b) of the 1989 Act;
(i) an order under section 39(3) of the 1989 Act varying a supervision order in so far as it affects a person with whom the child is living but who is not entitled to apply for the order to be discharged;
(j) an order under section 39(3A) of the 1989 Act varying or discharging an interim care order in so far as it imposes an exclusion requirement on a person who is not entitle to apply for the order to be discharged;
(k) an order under section 39(3B) of the 1989 Act varying or discharging an interim care order in so far as it confers a power of arrest attached to an exclusion requirement;
(l) the substitution of a supervision order for a care order under section 39(4) of the 1989 Act;
(m) a child assessment order or the variation or discharge of such an order under section 43(12) of the 1989 Act;
(n) an order permitting the Local Authority to arrange for any child in its care to live outside England and Wales under paragraph 19(1) of Schedule 2 to the 1989 Act;
(o) a contribution order, or the variation or revocation of such an order under paragraph 23(8), of Schedule 2 to the 1989 Act;

(30) "Rules" means rules of court governing the practice and procedure to be followed in Public Law Proceedings;
(31) "Schedule of Proposed Findings" means the schedule of findings of fact prepared by the Local Authority sufficient to satisfy the threshold criteria under section 31(2) of the 1989 Act and to inform the Care Plan;
(32) "Section 7 report" means any report under section 7 of the 1989 Act;
(33) "Section 37 report" means any report by the Local Authority to the court as a result of a direction under section 37 of the 1989 Act;
(34) "Social Work Chronology" means a schedule containing –

(a) a succinct summary of the significant dates and events in the child's life in chronological order – a running record to be updated during the proceedings;
(b) information under the following headings –
(i) serial number;
(ii) date;
(iii) event-detail;
(iv) witness or document reference (where applicable);

(35) "specified proceedings" has the meaning assigned to it by section 41(6) of the 1989 Act;
(36) "Standard Directions on Issue and on First Appointment" includes the directions set out in the Public Law Outline, Stage 1;
(37) "Strategy Discussion Record" means a note of the strategy discussion within the meaning of "Working Together to Safeguard Children" (2006);

(38) "Supplementary Form PLO1" means the form set out at Annex A to this Practice Direction which is to be filed with the application form and then used as the Index to the Court's Case Management Record;

(39) "Timetable for the Child" means the timetable set by the court which is appropriate for the child who is the subject of the proceedings and forms part of the Allocation Record.

Annex A:
Supplementary Form PLO1

ANNEX A

SUPPLEMENTARY FORM PLO 1

Application for a care order or supervision order: Supplementary Form

PART 1 - Pre-proceedings checklist

This checklist must be completed and filed by the local authority with any application for a care order or supervision order to specify the pre-proceedings documents filed with the application [Column (a)] and to identify those which are not applicable [N/A]. If any relevant document is not filed with the application, the reason and any expected date of filing must be stated [Column (d)]. Columns (b) and (c) are for use by the court to record any pre-proceedings documents filed subsequently.
All documents filed with the application must be clearly marked with their description and numbered consecutively in the following sequence

	Category	Document	N/A	(a) Filed on issue	(b) Filed by FA	(c) Filed by CMC	(d) Reason not filed/ expected date of filing
	Documents prepared for the proceedings						
1	Schedule of Proposed Findings						
2	Initial Social Work Statement						
3	Care Plan						
4	Allocation Record and Timetable for the Child						
	Documents held by the local authority						
5	Previous proceedings	Orders					
		Judgment/reasons					
6	Any relevant assessment materials	Initial/core assessment					
		Section 7 & 37 reports					
		Relatives and friends materials (e.g. a genogram)					
7	Other relevant reports and records	Single, joint or inter-agency materials					
		Records of discussions with the family					
		Key LA minutes and records for the child, (inc. Strategy Discussion Record)					
8	Pre-existing care plans (e.g. child in need plan, looked after child plan & child protection plan)						
9	Social Work Chronology						
10	Letters Before Proceedings						
11	Other relevant pre-proceedings documents (specify)						

PART 2 - Record of case management documents filed

This Part is for use by the court to record case management documents filed with the court for Stages 1, 2 and 3

		Filed for FA	**Filed for CMC**	**Filed for IRH**	**Notes**
1	Local Authority Case Summary				
2	Other Parties' Case Summaries				M
					F
					Other
3	Parties' initial witness statements				M
					F
					Other
4	CAFCASS/ CAFCASS CYMRU Case Analysis and Recommendations				
5	Draft Case Management order for CMC/IRH				
6	Other case management documents (specify)				

Annex B:
The Local Authority's Case Summary

ANNEX B

The Local Authority's Case Summary

Applications and previous proceedings

1. The applications that have been issued in these proceedings are:

Applicant	Order Sought	Date	Bundle ref.

2. The child[ren] is/are subject to the following orders previously made in these/other proceedings:

Order	in favour of	Court	Date of order	Case no.	Bundle ref.

Arrangements for the child[ren]

3. The present arrangements for the child[ren] is/are

(a) Living arrangements:

Child	Living with:

(b) contact arrangements:

Child	Having contact with:	Frequency

Summary of precipitating events and background

4. The following is a brief summary of the incident(s) or circumstances giving rise to the application and of the background to the proceedings:

Mental Capacity

5. The local authority has no/ the following concerns about the mental capacity of the mother/ father/ *[other adult]* to care for the child or to prepare for the proceedings:

Key issues and findings

1. The Key Issues in the case are:

a)	
b)	
c)	
d)	

2. With reference to the above Key Issues the following are agreed:

a)	
b)	
c)	
d)	

3. In addition, the following findings of fact sought by the local authority are agreed on the following basis:

Finding sought	Basis of agreement

Related applications/proceedings

4. This is / is not a case where an application for placement for adoption is among the range of options that will have to be considered.

5. The following current or proposed proceedings (eg criminal proceedings, other family proceedings, disciplinary, immigration or mental capacity/health determinations) are relevant to the determination of the application(s):

Proceedings	Parties	Court/Body	Stage reached	Comments.

Issues and directions for CMC/IRH

6. At the Case Management Conference/Issues Resolution Hearing the following issues, directions and interim orders will need to be considered by the court:

a)	
b)	
c)	
d)	
e)	
f)	

Compliance

7. The following steps have not been taken for the reasons explained and the effect on the timetable is as follows:

Key Date	Step to be taken	Reason for non-compliance	Expected date of compliance/ Effect on timetable

Recommended reading list and reading time

8. The following are the key documents to be read in preparation for the hearing:

Document	Author	Status/role	Date	Bundle page

9. The suggested reading time required for the hearing is:

Additional information

10. The following additional information is relevant to the timetable for the child(ren) or for the conduct of the hearing or of the proceedings

Contact details: advocates, solicitors and key professionals

Party	Status	Name	Tel:	Email:
Applicant Local Authority	Advocate Solicitor Key worker/team manager			
Respondents: (1) Mother (2) Father (3) Other party	 (1) Advocate Solicitor (2) Advocate Solicitor (3) Advocate Solicitor			
Child(ren)	Advocate Solicitor Guardian:			

Annex C: Draft Case Management Order

ANNEX C

Draft Case Management Order Case No

Child(ren) No

[ ] Family Proceedings / County Court

The High Court sitting at [ ]

The Principal Registry of the Family Division

PART 1 – Preliminary

The child[ren] is / are:

Name	**Boy/Girl**	**Date of Birth**
(1) (2) (3)		

Date of this Order:

Ordered by:

Sitting in private/public

at the Case Management Conference / Issues Resolution Hearing

or at the [contested] hearing of an application [made without notice] by

for

or [other]

The court heard the advocates for the following parties:

Party	**Status**	**Counsel/solicitor/Advocate**
Applicant	Local Authority	
Respondents: **(1) X** **(2) Y** **(3) Z**	 Mother Father Other	
Child(ren)	Guardian:	

And the following parties in person:

Party	**Status**

The court has heard and read the evidence set out on the Record of Hearing [Form C22]

This order is made on the basis of the information recorded in Part 3 about the timetable for the child(ren), the key issues and any agreements and decisions made

---

PART 2 - Order

The Court Orders that:

Orders relating to the child

1 *Record of Prescribed Forms of Order which are to be issued separately [C23 to C49]*
e.g. Interim care order / interim supervision order / interim residence order / contact order

Joinder of parties/parentage issues

2 Party status

3 Paternity / Maternity and tracing / involvement of absent parent / previous carers

Appointment of Children's Guardian / Children's Solicitor / Official Solicitor

4. Appointment of children's guardian / solicitor for the child

5. Appointment of Official Solicitor as guardian ad litem / litigation friend for a non-subject child or protected party

Transfer / Allocation to Case Manager / Case Management Judge

6. Transfer

7. Allocation

Evidence to be filed

8. Evidence
    a. local authority
    b. parents
    c. [other]
    d. children's guardian

9. Assessments
    a. Core and initial
    b. Parenting (inc residential)
    c. Friends and Family
    d. [other, inc specialist]

10. Care planning

Other documents

11. LA's Schedule of Proposed Findings

12. LA Case Summary, Other Parties' Case Summaries and the Case Analysis and Recommendations

13. Disclosure of documents (whether to be filed and/or served)
    a. Key LA minutes and records not disclosed as pre-proceedings documents
    b. Health records (inc GP, HV, clinic and hospital)
    c. Education records (inc SEN)
    d. Police records (inc DV logs)
    e. Contact notes

Expert evidence

14. Identification of expert

15. Identification of Key Issue(s) to be addressed

16. Permission to instruct
    a. Responsibility for instruction (joint/sole)
    b. Letter of instruction
    c. Timetable
    d. Filing and service of report (paper/electronic)
    e. Questions to expert
    f. Permission to examine/observe child
    g. Funding
    h. Arrangements for expert to give oral evidence (in person or by video/audio-link)

17. Experts' meeting
    a. Responsibility to arrange and chair
    b. Questions
    c. Schedule of agreements and disagreements

Advocates' Meeting

18. Meeting

19. Draft Case Management Order and experts proposals

Further Hearings

20. The next hearing is at [ ][a.m.][p.m.] on [ ]

    at [ ] and is:

    [The Issues Resolution Hearing]

    [An Early Final Hearing]

    [A Fact Finding Hearing at which the findings set out in the local authority's schedule of findings are to be determined]

    [The Final Hearing at which]

    [Other (specify the AIM of the hearing)]

21. Special Measures and Security

22. Attendance at court

23. Use of Technology and Special requirements
    a. videolink
    b. conference telephone link
    c. hearing assistance
    d. DDA requirements
    e. translation directions

Other applications

24. Directions in other concurrent applications (e.g. for Residence/Contact)

25. Directions in Placement for Adoption Applications

Bundles for hearings

26. Bundles Practice Direction requirements
    a. Agreed or revised Threshold / Schedule of Findings
    b. Witness Template
    c. Skeleton arguments
    d. Judicial Reading List
    e. Time estimate to specify reading time and judgment writing time
    f. Other (eg [The parties must comply with the President's Practice Direction (Family Proceedings: Court Bundles), 27 July 2006, [2006] 2 FLR 199. The Direction applies to all hearings in this case regardless of the estimated length of the hearing.]

Other orders

27. No document other than a document specified in these directions or filed in accordance with the Rules or any Practice Direction shall be filed by any party without the court's permission.

28. Any application to vary these directions or for any other order is to be made to the allocated judge on notice to [ ] all parties.

Compliance with directions

29. All parties must immediately inform the Court/Court Officer on *[contact telephone / e-mail]* if any party fails to adhere to any date specified for a direction or the filing of any document.

Dated **(signed)**

HCJ/HHJ/DJ/DJ(MC)/JP/[Assistant] JC

Court address:

PART 3 - Recitals

The timetable for the child(ren)

And key issues, agreements and decisions

It is recorded that:

1. The key dates and events in the Timetable for the Child(ren) are:

a)	
b)	
c)	
d)	

2. There is no [the following] delay in the timetable for the proceedings fixed by the court in accordance with the Timetable for the Child *(specify any delay and reasons)*

3. The Key Issue(s) in the case are:

a)	
b)	
c)	
d)	

4. The parties have agreed the following Key Issues and/or findings of fact:

a)	
b)	
c)	
d)	

5. The court makes the following findings or decisions as the basis for this order:

a)	
b)	
c)	
d)	

Flowchart:
Pre-proceedings – Public Law Outline

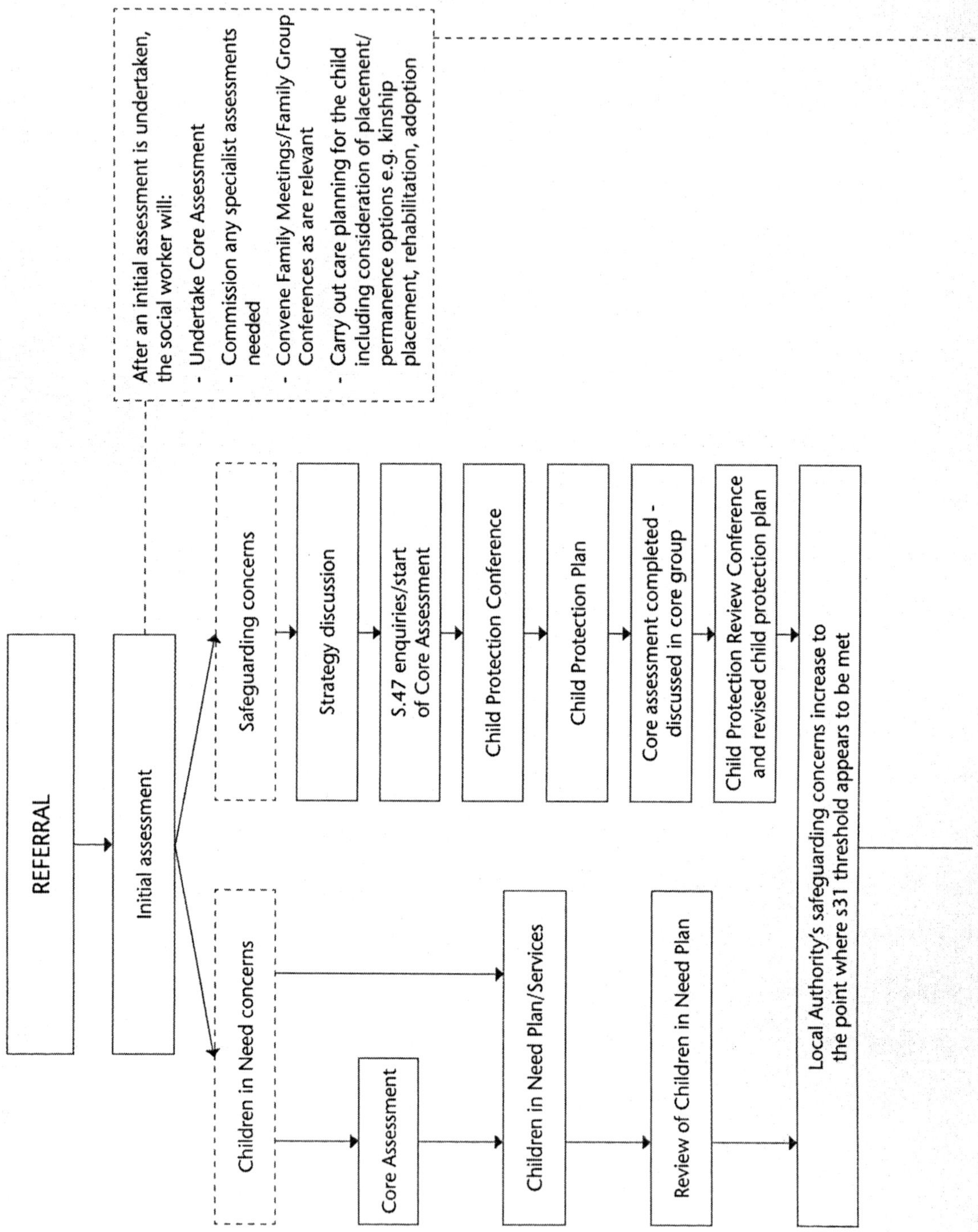

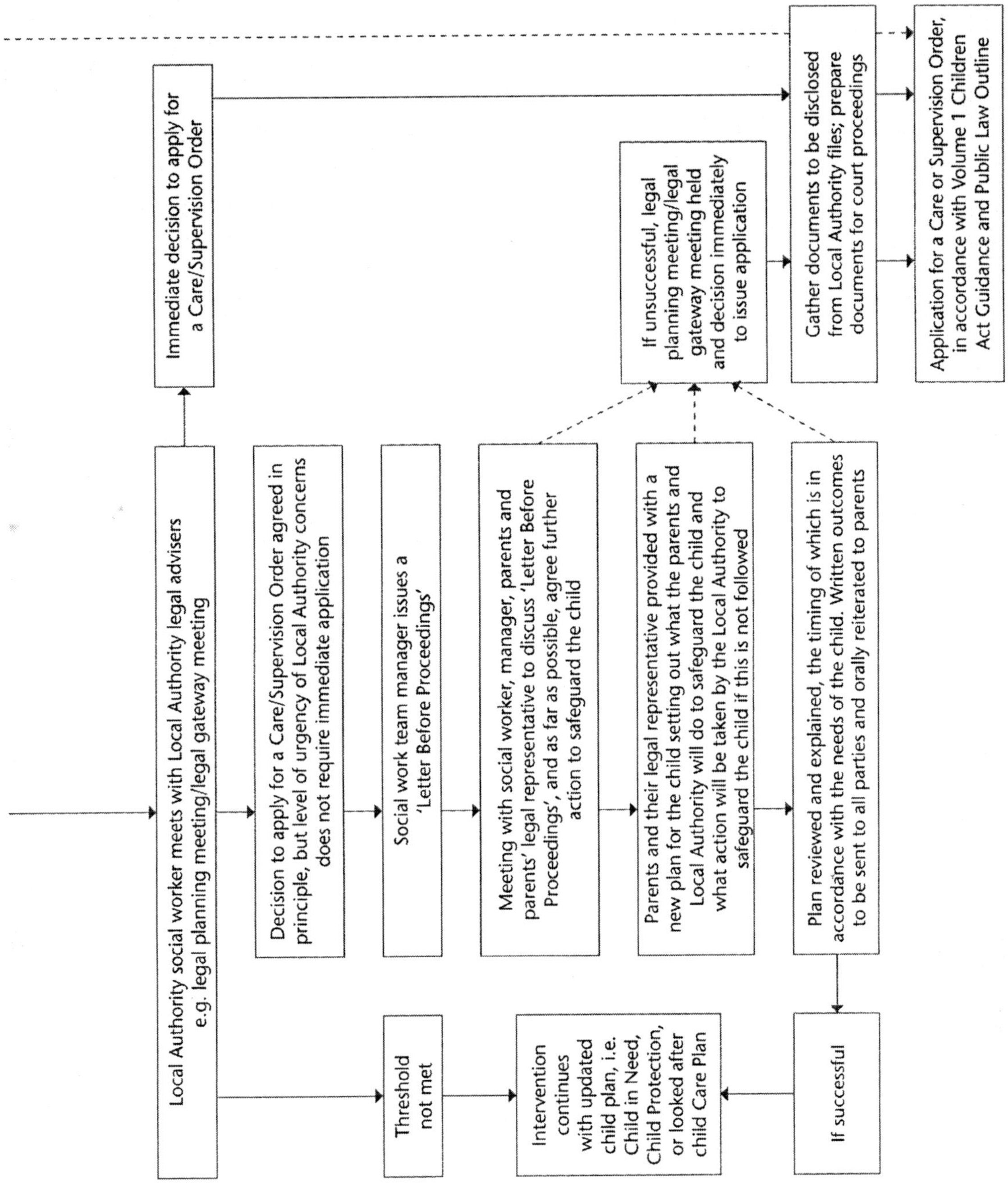
Local Authority social worker meets with Local Authority legal advisers e.g. legal planning meeting/legal gateway meeting
Immediate decision to apply for a Care/Supervision Order
Decision to apply for a Care/Supervision Order agreed in principle, but level of urgency of Local Authority concerns does not require immediate application
Threshold not met
Social work team manager issues a 'Letter Before Proceedings'
Intervention continues with updated child plan, i.e. Child in Need, Child Protection, or looked after child Care Plan
Meeting with social worker, manager, parents and parents' legal representative to discuss 'Letter Before Proceedings', and as far as possible, agree further action to safeguard the child
If unsuccessful, legal planning meeting/legal gateway meeting held and decision immediately to issue application
Parents and their legal representative provided with a new plan for the child setting out what the parents and Local Authority will do to safeguard the child and what action will be taken by the Local Authority to safeguard the child if this is not followed
Plan reviewed and explained, the timing of which is in accordance with the needs of the child. Written outcomes to be sent to all parties and orally reiterated to parents
If successful
Gather documents to be disclosed from Local Authority files; prepare documents for court proceedings
Application for a Care or Supervision Order, in accordance with Volume 1 Children Act Guidance and Public Law Outline

Flowchart:
Court Proceedings – Public Law Outline

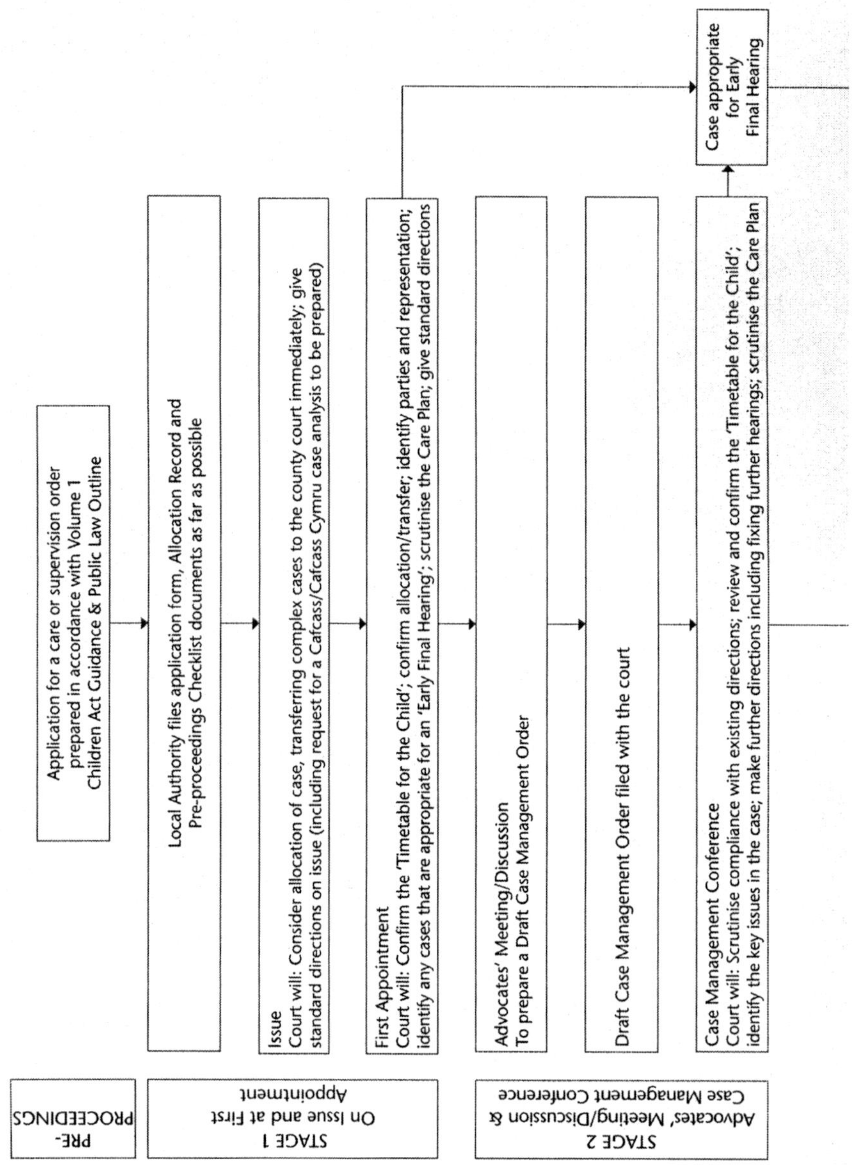

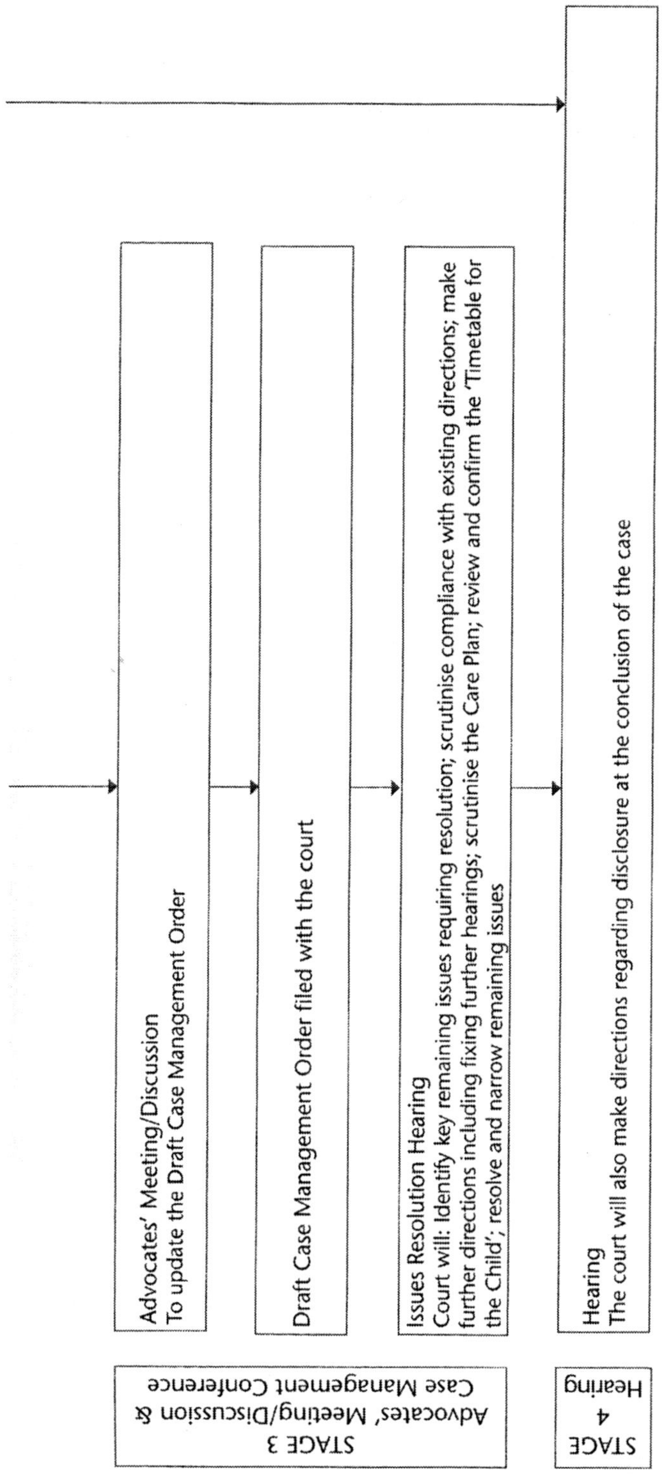

Further copies of the Public Law Outline are available to download from the care proceedings programme website: www.justice.gov.uk/guidance/careproceedings.htm

APPENDIX 2

THE PLO GUIDELINE DOCUMENTS (FORM PL04, FORM PL05 AND FORM PL06)

FORM PLO4 ALLOCATION RECORD AND TIMETABLE FOR THE CHILD(REN)

Form PLO4 (04.08)

PUBLIC LAW OUTLINE
ALLOCATION RECORD AND TIMETABLE FOR THE CHILD(REN)

PART 1 – to be completed by the applicant Local Authority on issue PART 2 – to be completed by the court PART 3 – to be completed by the applicant Local Authority on issue and updated as necessary

PART 1 (To be completed by Local Authority)	
Court:	
Applicant:	
Names and ages / dob of children:	
REASONS FOR ALLOCATION	
Existing orders / proceedings involving the family (give case no and date(s) or order(s)):	
Mental health / incapacity problems:	
Learning disabilities (parents and / or children):	
Parallel criminal proceedings: *(Give details of court/case no.)*	
Immigration issues (state which party): *(Give details of case no. for any relevant proceedings))*	
Placement Order application made / proposed:	
Interpreter being used (state which party and language(s)):	
Strong likelihood of conflicting expert evidence:	
Judicial / courtroom availability/ ELH:	1 day ☐ Up to 3 days ☐ (specify______) 4 days or more ☐ (specify______)

PART 1 Continues

Nature of alleged harm (brief details of alleged harm / emotional abuse) e.g. • *Particular gravity (specify): e.g Drink/drugs/lifestyle/neglect* • *Shaking injuries involving retinal haemorrhage/ brain injury.* • *There is a history of suspicious death of a child in the family.* • *More than a single incident of abuse.* • *Cases involving multiple allegations of sexual or physical abuse.* • *Cases where there are serious allegations of physical or sexual abuse but the issue is the identity of the perpetrator.* • *Allegations of serious abuse where there are or are likely to be criminal proceedings, issues regarding disclosure of information and public interest immunity.*	
Other reasons • *Where the case involves a difficult point of law, issues of public policy or unusually complex or sensitive issues arise.* • *Where a linked placement order application raises issues additional to those inherent in the care proceedings.* • *Where a child is separately represented from their Guardian.* • *Where a "split hearing" is necessary and judicial continuity cannot otherwise be ensured.* • *Any international element (inc. details of relevant proceedings).*	
Applicant's Allocation Proposal	*(Delete as appropriate)* [Case Manager & Magistrates in the FPC] [District Judge (Magistrates Court) in the FPC] [District Judge in the County Court] [Circuit Judge in the County Court] [DFJ / section 9 sitting as a Judge of the High Court] [High Court Judge]
Views in relation to allocation expressed by any other party	

PART 2 (To be completed by the Court)	
Allocation decision(1)	
- Case Manager in the FPC	Mr/Miss/Ms/Mrs ____________
- District Judge (Magistrates Court) in the FPC	DJ ________________
- District Judge in the County Court	DJ ________________
- Circuit Judge in the County Court	HHJ ________________
- The DFJ / section 9 sitting as a Judge of the High Court	HHJ ________________
- High Court Judge	Mr(s) Justice _______________

Directed by: Mr/Miss/Ms/Mrs ______________ (Assistant Justices Clerk)
DJ / DJ(MC) _________________
HHJ _______________ / (sitting as a judge of the High Court)
Mr(s) Justice _________________

Date:

Allocation decision(2)	
- Case Manager in the FPC	Mr/Miss/Ms/Mrs ____________
- District Judge (Magistrates Court) in the FPC	DJ ________________
- District Judge in the County Court	DJ ________________
- Circuit Judge in the County Court	HHJ ________________
- The DFJ / section 9 sitting as a Judge of the High Court	HHJ ________________
- High Court Judge	Mr(s) Justice _______________

Directed by: Mr/Miss/Ms/Mrs ______________ (Assistant Justices Clerk)
DJ / DJ(MC) _________________
HHJ _______________ / (sitting as a judge of the High Court)
Mr(s) Justice _________________

Date:

Allocation decision(3)	
- Case Manager in the FPC	Mr/Miss/Ms/Mrs ____________
- District Judge (Magistrates Court) in the FPC	DJ ________________
- District Judge in the County Court	DJ ________________
- Circuit Judge in the County Court	HHJ ________________
- The DFJ / section 9 sitting as a Judge of the High Court	HHJ ________________
- High Court Judge	Mr(s) Justice _______________

Directed by: Mr/Miss/Ms/Mrs ______________ (Assistant Justices Clerk)
DJ / DJ(MC) _________________
HHJ _______________ / (sitting as a judge of the High Court)
Mr(s) Justice _________________

Date:

Timetable for the Child

<table>
<tr><td colspan="2">PART 3 (To be completed and updated by Local Authority)</td></tr>
<tr><td><ul><li>State relevant events / dates in relation to the child(ren) including statutory reviews and panel / planning meetings.</li><li>Give the Local Authority's opinion as to the date by which proceedings should be concluded in the interests of the child(ren)'s welfare and, if different the date by which the child(ren)should be permanently placed</li></ul></td><td></td></tr>
<tr><td colspan="2">Additional relevant events / dates in relation to the children</td></tr>
<tr><td>Date of amendment to timetable</td><td>Relevant events / dates in relation to the child(ren).</td></tr>
<tr><td></td><td></td></tr>
</table>

FORM PLO5 STANDARD DIRECTIONS FORM (ON ISSUE) MENU

Form PL05 (04.08) **- Standard Directions Form (on Issue) Menu** **Children Act 1989 (Public Law Outline)**

Case Name: Case Number:

HHJ/ District Judge/Assistant Justices' Clerk Date:

DIRECTIONS & ALLOCATION ON ISSUE OF PROCEEDINGS

Preamble

Upon the proceedings having been referred to the Assistant Justices Clerk/Judge for allocation and directions upon issue / transfer [*delete as appropriate*] and the court having considered the papers in the absence of the parties or their legal representatives

Appointment of Children's Guardian / Children's Solicitor

[ ] A Children's Guardian [(*{name}* *if available*)] shall be appointed for the child[ren]

OR

[ ] [*{Solicitor's name}*
of *{firm}*] is appointed as solicitor for the child[ren]

Official Solicitor

[ ] The Official Solicitor is invited to act in these proceedings as the litigation friend on behalf of the [M] [F] [non-subject child] *{name}*

Transfer / Allocation to Case Manager / Case Management Judge

[ ] The application[s] [is] [are] transferred to the

{name}] County Court [*{name}* /Inner London] FPC High Court [other]

[to be heard with Case No. / FD C]

[ ] The proceedings are allocated for case management to / the proceedings are to be allocated by:

Mr(s) Justice

His / Her Honour Judge ..../ DFJ for *{name of care centre}*

District Judge

2 Case Managers in the FPC namely [ ]and[ ]

[ ] [*{other}*]

Form PL05 (04.08) **- Standard Directions Form (on Issue) Menu** **Children Act 1989 (Public Law Outline)**

Pre-Proceedings Checklist Documents

[ ] The LA shall file the documents set out in the table below by 2 pm on the date recorded alongside each

[delete filed or N/A documents as applicable]

	Category	**Document**	**Date for filing**
1	Schedule of Proposed Findings		
2	Initial Social Work Statement		
3	Care Plan		
4	Allocation Record and Timetable for the Child		
5	Previous proceedings	Orders	
		Judgment/reasons	
6	Any relevant assessment materials	Initial/core assessment	
		Section 7 & 37 reports	
		Relatives and friends materials (e.g. a genogram)	
7	Other relevant reports and records	Single, joint or inter-agency materials	
		Records of discussions with the family	
		Key LA minutes and records for the child, (inc. Strategy Discussion Record)	
8	Pre-existing care plans (e.g. child in need plan, looked after child plan & child protection plan)		
9	Social Work Chronology		
10	Letters Before Proceedings		
11	Other relevant pre-proceedings documents (specify) { }		

Evidence / Documents for First Appointment

[ ] The LA shall file and serve the application form and pre-proceedings documents filed with the court

by 2.00 pm on [*{date}*] on [*{specify party or proposed party}*]

[ ] [The Child(ren)'s Solicitor shall file and serve by 2.00 pm on [*{date}*] a Case Analysis and Recommendations document prepared by the Child(ren)'s Guardian for use at the First Appointment] OR [The Child(ren)'s Guardian shall be in a position to orally present a Case Analysis and Recommendations at the First Appointment]

The Case Analysis and Recommendations shall set out:

(a) an analysis of the issues that need to be resolved in the case including-

(i) any harm or risk of harm;

(ii) the child's own views;

(iii) the family context including advice relating to ethnicity, language, religion and culture of the child and other significant persons;

(iv) the Local Authority work and proposed care plan ;

(v) advice about the court process including the Timetable for the Child; and

(vi) identification of work that remains to be done for the child in the short and longer term; and

Form PL05 (04.08) **- Standard Directions Form (on Issue) Menu** **Children Act 1989 (Public Law Outline)**

(b) recommendations for outcomes, in order to safeguard and promote the best interests of the child in the proceedings;

Listing of First Appointment

[ ] The application[s] are listed for a First Appointment [FA] before

DJ / PRFD CJ / RCJ HCJ / RCJ ▢ FPC / Inner London

[the allocated judge]

on at (time estimate)

[✓] No document other than a document specified in these directions or in accordance with the Rules or Practice Directions shall be filed by any party without the court's permission.

[✓] Any application to vary these directions or for any other order is to be made to the allocated Judge/Assistant Justices' Clerk on notice to all parties.

Compliance with directions

[✓] All parties must immediately inform the [Case Progression Officer][Case Manager] on (tel)/ (fax)/[{*e-mail}*] if any party fails to adhere to any date specified for filing any document.

Dated:

Signed: **HHJ/ DJ/Assistant JC**

FORM PLO6 STANDARD DIRECTIONS FORM (AT FIRST APPOINTMENT) MENU

PLO6(04.08) Standard Directions Form (at First Appointment) Menu Children Act 1989 (Public Law Outline)

Case Name: Case Number:

HHJ/ District Judge/Assistant Justices' Clerk Date:

DIRECTIONS & ALLOCATION AT FIRST APPOINTMENT

Parties to the Proceedings/Joinder of Parties/Official Solicitor

[√] The parties to the proceedings are:

The Applicant LA...

The 1st Respondent (identify relationship: M / F) ....

The [ ] Respondent (identify relationship:) ....

The [ ] Respondent (identify relationship:) ....

The [ ] Respondent (a child) ....

The [ ] Respondent (a child) ....

The [ ] Respondent (a child) ....

[ ] The Official Solicitor is invited to act in these proceedings as the litigation friend on behalf of the [M] [F] [non-subject child] *{name}*]

[ ] *[name}*] is joined as the [*{specify}*] Respondent to the proceedings [for the purpose of determining *{specify where appropriate}*

Transfer / Allocation to Case Manager / Case Management Judge

[ ] The application[s] [is] [are] transferred to the

□ [*{name}*] County Court □ [*{name}* /Inner London] FPC □ High Court
□ [other]

[to be heard with Case No. / FD C]

[ ] The proceedings are allocated for case management to / the proceedings are to be allocated by:

Mr(s) Justice

His / Her Honour Judge ..../ DFJ for *{name of care centre}*

District Judge

2 Case Managers in the FPC namely [ ] and [ ]

[ ] [*{other}*]

PLO6(04.08) Standard Directions Form (at First Appointment) Menu Children Act 1989 (Public Law Outline)

Listing of CMC

[ ] The application[s] are listed for a Case Management Conference [CMC] before

o DJ / PRFD o CJ / RCJ o HCJ / RCJ o FPC / Inner London

o [the allocated judge]

on at (time estimate)

Pre-Proceedings Checklist Documents

[ ] The LA shall file the documents set out in the table below by 2 pm on the date recorded alongside each

[delete filed or N/A documents as applicable]

	Category	Document	Date for filing
1	Schedule of Proposed Findings		
2	Initial Social Work Statement		
3	Care Plan		
4	Allocation Record and Timetable for the Child		
5	Previous proceedings	Orders	
		Judgment/reasons	
6	Any relevant assessment materials	Initial/core assessment	
		Section 7 & 37 reports	
		Relatives and friends materials (e.g. a genogram)	
7	Other relevant reports and records	Single, joint or inter-agency materials	
		Records of discussions with the family	
		Key LA minutes and records for the child, (inc. Strategy Discussion Record)	
8	Pre-existing care plans (e.g. child in need plan, looked after child plan & child protection plan)		
9	Social Work Chronology		
10	Letters Before Proceedings		
11	Other relevant pre-proceedings documents (specify) { }		

Evidence / Documents for CMC

[ ] The LA shall file and serve by 2.00pm on [*{date}*]

(i) a Local Authority Case Summary in the form set out at Annex B of the Practice Direction

(ii) the interim care plan(s) setting out details as to proposed placement and contact

(iii) any further evidence upon which they intend to rely including any evidence relating to vulnerability, ethnicity, culture, language, religion or gender

(iv) [*{other}*]

PLO6(04.08) **Standard Directions Form (at First Appointment) Menu Children Act 1989 (Public Law Outline)**

[ ] The child(ren)'s solicitor shall file and serve by 2.00 pm on [*{date}*] a Case Analysis and Recommendations document prepared by the Children's Guardian for use at the Case Management Conference setting out:

(a) an analysis of the issues that need to be resolved in the case including-

(i) any harm or risk of harm;

(ii) the child's own views;

(iii) the family context including advice relating to ethnicity, language, religion and culture of the child and other significant persons;

(iv) the Local Authority work and proposed care plan ;

(v) advice about the court process including the Timetable for the Child; and

(vi) identification of work that remains to be done for the child in the short and longer term; and

(b) recommendations for outcomes, in order to safeguard and promote the best interests of the child in the proceedings.

[ ] The [M] [F] [ ] [Respondents] shall each file and serve by 2.00pm on [*{date}*]

(i) a Case Summary setting out

(a) their proposals for the long term future of the child (to include placement and contact);
(b) their reply to the Local Authority's Schedule of Proposed Findings;
(c) any proposal for assessment / expert evidence; and
(d) the names, addresses and contact details of any family or friends who it is suggested be approached in relation to long term care / contact or respite;

(ii) Initial witness statements

(iii) *[Other – specify]*

[ ] Any party proposing to ask the court for permission to instruct an expert or for any other assessment must comply with the Experts' Practice Direction and provide details to the other parties before the advocates' meeting of the nature of the assessment or report required, the issue to which it is directed, the identity, CV and availability of the proposed assessor, the timescale, likely cost and method of funding.

[ ] Any outstanding disclosure of relevant documents between the parties shall take place not later than 3 working days before the CMC advocates meeting.

PLO6(04.08) **Standard Directions Form (at First Appointment) Menu Children Act 1989 (Public Law Outline)**

Advocates Meeting

[ ] The parties' lawyers and any unrepresented party shall attend an Advocates Meeting / Discussion for the purpose of identifying the key issue(s) and drafting the directions to be sought at the CMC and to draft a case management order for the court

[to take place at p.m. on *{date}* at *{venue}*]

[by video / telephone conference]

OR

[to be arranged by the solicitor for the child(ren) / *{other}*] not later than [ ] *(2 days before the CMC)* / at [*{venue, date and time}*]] [by video / telephone conference]

[The court grants permission for *{name}* to attend the Advocates Meeting as a McKenzie Friend for *{name of litigant in person}* . The McKenzie Friend may assist by prompting, taking notes and giving advice but is not an advocate for the party concerned.]

Case Management Order

[ ] The LA shall file and serve by 11 a.m. one working day before the CMC:

(i) a completed draft case management order in typed form;

(ii) [*{other}*]

Where the above documents are filed by fax or e-mail original copies must be handed to the court at the hearing.

Other Hearings

[ ] The Issues Resolution Hearing will take place on / not later than *{specify date}*

[ ] The Final Hearing will take place not later than *{specify date}*

[ ] The court is of the opinion that the case is suitable for an Early Final Hearing because *{specify reasons}*

and the Final Hearing shall take place at*{venue, date & time}*

PLO6(04.08) Standard Directions Form (at First Appointment) Menu Children Act 1989 (Public Law Outline)

Other Orders

[ ]

[ ] *[see attached sheet]*

[✓] No document other than a document specified in these directions or in accordance with the Rules or Practice Directions shall be filed by any party without the court's permission.

[✓] In proceedings in / before the FPC, where a party considers that there are likely to be issues arising at a hearing (including the Case Management Conference and Issues Resolution Hearing) which need to be decided by a full Bench or District Judge (Magistrates' Court), rather than a Justices' Clerk/Assistant Justices' Clerk, then that party shall give the court written notice of that need as soon as possible and at least 2 days before the hearing. The notice shall specify:

a) the nature of the issue(s);
b) whether it is anticipated that an application will be contested by any party;
c) the estimated length of hearing (where this is in excess of any existing time estimate).

[✓] Any application to vary these directions or for any other order is to be made to the allocated judge/case manager on notice to all parties.

Compliance with directions

[✓] All parties must immediately inform the [Case Progression Officer][Case Manager] on (tel)/ (fax)/[{*e-mail*}] if any party fails to adhere to any date specified for filing any document.

Dated:

Signed: **HHJ/ DJ/Assistant JC**

APPENDIX 3

REVISED VOLUME 1 OF THE CHILDREN ACT 1989 GUIDANCE AND REGULATIONS (KEY PARTS RELATING TO CARE AND SUPERVISION PROCEEDINGS)

CHAPTER 1 INTRODUCTION

Summary

1.1 This Chapter identifies the key principles underpinning the Children Act 1989, in particular those relating to the paramountcy of children's welfare as the court's key consideration in a range of family proceedings concerning the upbringing of children, the desirability of avoiding delay and the expectation that a court will only make an order where it is better for the child than for no order to be made.

1.2 The "welfare checklist" (section 1(3)) is set out, alongside the freedom of the court to make a range of orders in Children Act proceedings, above and beyond the specific order that might have been the subject of the application before it.

1.3 The range of courts able to hear cases is listed, as are the levels of court at which appeals may be heard. The functions of Cafcass (the Children and Family Court Advisory and Support Service) are also set out.

1.4 The Children Act 1989 ('the Act') provides a single coherent legislative framework for the private and public law relating to children. It strikes a balance between the rights of children, the responsibilities of both parents to the child and the duty of the state to intervene when the child's welfare requires it.

1.5 The courts have considerable scope for discretion in their decisions about children. It is therefore important that practitioners in the field have a proper understanding of the legislative framework and the way in which it is operated in practice.

1.6 This guidance considers the orders available under Parts 1, 2, 4 and 5 of the Act as well as secure accommodation orders (Part 3, section 25).

1.7 As with much else in the Act, court orders should not be seen as a free-standing end product but must be considered within the context of a wide range of provisions available under the Act to safeguard and promote the welfare of children, before, after and outwith court proceedings. This guidance needs to be read in conjunction with other guidance and Regulations in relation to the Act.

Children and their families

1.8 The Act is based on the belief that children are generally best looked after within the family with their parents playing a full part in their lives and with least recourse to legal proceedings. That belief is reflected in:

(a) the concept of parental responsibility;

(b) the ability of unmarried fathers to share that responsibility by agreement with the mother, by joint registration at birth or by court order;

(c) the local authority's duty to provide services which support children and their families;

(d) the local authority's duty to return a child looked after by them to his family unless this is against his interests;

(e) the local authority's duty, unless it is not reasonably practicable or consistent with his welfare, to endeavour to provide contact between a looked after child and his parents and others.

Child-centred welfare principles

1.9 Section 1 sets out the overarching welfare principles to be applied in all proceedings under the Act.

1.10 In deciding any question about a child's upbringing and the administration of his property, the court must treat the welfare of the child as its paramount consideration. This applies as much to disputes between parents as it does to care proceedings and emergency protection proceedings.

1.11 The Act makes it clear that any delay in court proceedings is generally harmful to children, not only because of the uncertainty it creates for them but also because of the harm it may cause to the future parenting of the child. Progress of a case is controlled by the court (rather than by the parties) through active case management, in accordance with court rules and guidance to the judiciary issued by the President of the Family Division. Parties must ensure that they comply with any directions made by the court to ensure the progression of cases and should expect to be answerable to the court if its directions are not followed.

1.12 In contested section 8 proceedings, special guardianship applications and in all care and supervision proceedings the court, when applying the welfare principle, should have regard to the following checklist of factors which focuses not only on the needs of the child but also on his views and the options available to the court:

(a) the ascertainable wishes and feelings of the child concerned (considered in the light of his age and understanding);

(b) his physical, emotional and educational needs;

(c) the likely effect on him of any change in his circumstances;

(d) his age, sex, background and any characteristics of his which the court considers relevant;

(e) any harm which he has suffered or is at risk of suffering;

(f) how capable each of his parents and any other person in relation to whom the court considers the question to be relevant, is of meeting his needs;

(g) the range of powers available to the court under this Act in the proceedings in question.

1.13 The Act makes clear that, whatever the order applied for in private law (section 8) proceedings, the court may make any other private law order if it thinks it is best for the child, or may trigger a local authority investigation (under section 37), through which the authority will ascertain whether it should apply for one of the public law orders available to protect the child. The full range of orders, including public law orders, private law orders or no order, is also available to a court hearing a local authority application for a care or other order in respect of the child. A court may make a private law order in any other family proceedings (as defined by section 8(4)) plus the inherent jurisdiction of the High Court.

1.14 The Act prohibits the court from making an order unless it would be better for the child than making no order at all. This prohibition applies even where the court, in section 31 care and supervision proceedings, determines that the harm threshold condition is satisfied. In such cases, the court will consider whether or not an order is necessary.

1.15 There are three aims underpinning this principle. The first is to discourage unnecessary court orders from being made. The restriction of orders to those cases where they are necessary to resolve a specific problem is intended to reduce conflict and promote parental agreement and co-operation. The second aim is to ensure that the order is granted only where it is likely positively to improve the child's welfare and not simply because the grounds for making the order are made out. For example, in care proceedings the court may decide that it would be better for a particular child not to be made the subject of a care order, which would place that child in local authority care. The application by the court of this 'no order' principle should not deter local authorities from bringing proceedings in those cases where they believe that a care or supervision order is necessary in order to safeguard and promote a child's welfare. The third aim is to discourage the making of unnecessary applications.

Concurrent system of jurisdiction

1.16 The Act creates a concurrent system of jurisdiction for a wide range of family proceedings in magistrates' family proceedings courts, county courts and the High Court. Rules and guidance governing the allocation and transfer of cases, either vertically between the various tiers or horizontally within tiers, are intended to ensure that cases are directed to the most appropriate court.

1.17 In practice, many public law cases will be heard entirely in the magistrates' court (also known as the family proceedings court) as this will usually be the most appropriate court and this is where most applications have to commence. In private law cases, applicants may choose either the magistrates family proceedings court or the county court. Both levels of court have powers to transfer cases to each other if that is the most appropriate venue. The term 'public law' refers to cases concerning children where the applicant is a public body, most typically a local authority. The term 'private law' describes cases where issues about children have arisen as a result of disagreements between family members (most commonly the parents) about arrangements for their children.

1.18 An allocation order sets out the criteria on which decisions about transfers between different levels of court should be based, which take into account the overriding principle that delay is likely to prejudice the welfare of the child.

Appeals

1.19 There is a general right of appeal from a magistrates' family proceedings court to the High Court against both the making of and refusal to make any order. The major exception is that there can be no appeal against the making of or refusal to make an emergency protection order, though provisions exist for discharge applications to be made. The Act contains three provisions in relation to appeals in care proceedings, namely:

(a) appeals lie to the High Court (where the original proceedings were heard in the magistrates' court);

(b) appeals lie against the refusal as well as the making of a care or supervision order;

(c) the local authority and any other party have full rights of appeal.

An appeal against a decision of a district judge in a county court lies to a judge of the county court. An appeal by a district judge of the High Court lies to a judge of the High Court. An appeal against a decision of a judge of the County Court or a judge of the High Court lies to the Court of Appeal.

1.20 The rules of court, which regulate the proceedings across all three tiers of jurisdiction have been designed to promote, as far as is possible, a non-adversarial style in court, within which issues are resolved as constructively as possible, in the interests of the child. Following application, preliminary hearings and Issues Resolutions Hearings may be held, at which directions are made by a judge or magistrate. These are aimed at minimising delay and narrowing issues of difference between parties, by identifying the key issues which require resolution in order to determine the application.

1.21 To facilitate ease of transfer between different jurisdictional tiers and to encourage the preparation of documentary evidence and advance disclosure, applications for most public and private law orders are made by way of prescribed forms. Applicants are required to give a considerable amount of information as to the nature of their case, the order, and any accompanying directions, sought and, where relevant, their future plans for the child.

Role of Cafcass

1.22 The function of the Children and Family Court Advisory and Support Service (Cafcass) is, in respect of family proceedings where the welfare of children is or may be in question, to:

- safeguard and promote the welfare of the children;
- give advice to any court about any application made to it in such proceedings;
- make provision for the children to be represented in such proceedings; and
- provide information, advice and other support for the children and their families.

The Cafcass officer is under a statutory duty (section 41(2)) to safeguard the interests of children in family proceedings and in doing so must have regard to the 'no delay' principle (section 1 (2)) and the matters listed in section 1(3). In private law cases, Cafcass provides an early intervention service, working directly with families to promote good and safe outcomes for children and to reduce conflict over contact and residence arrangements. Where agreement cannot be reached through such interventions a range of options is open to the court. Cafcass may be asked to recommend a care plan for further work, or the court may order a report under section 7 of the Act. Section 6 of the Children and Adoption Act 2006, also provides for Cafcass practitioners to undertake and report to the court on risk assessments, in particular in private law cases. The Court may request that a local authority provides a section 7 report. This may arise in situations where local authorities are already actively involved with such families, perhaps through the provision of services to a child in need.

1.23 The Children and Adoption Act 2006 inserted a new section 16A into the Act, which places a duty on Cafcass practitioners to carry out a risk assessment in relation to a child in certain circumstances and to provide that risk assessment to the court. The circumstances in which a risk assessment should be carried out are where the officer is carrying out a function in connection with family proceedings in which the court has the power to make an order under Part 2 of the Act, or in which a question with respect to such an order arises, or he is carrying out a function in connection with an order made in such proceedings and he is given cause to suspect that the child concerned in those proceedings is at risk of harm. A risk assessment is defined as an assessment of the risk of the child suffering the harm that is suspected.

1.24 When the court orders a report, the Cafcass practitioner makes enquiries into the circumstances of the family, interviews all parties (including the children and parents) and writes a case analysis or report with a recommendation to the court on the arrangements that would be in the child's best interests. The court makes the final decision based on all the evidence submitted, including the Cafcass analysis or report and evidence from parents/family.

1.25 Where a child is involved in a particularly complex private law case, they can be separately represented, usually by a Cafcass practitioner and solicitor, under Rule 9.5 of the Family Proceedings Rules 1991. In such cases, the child becomes a party to the proceedings.

1.26 In public law proceedings under the Act, Cafcass provides Children's Guardians to represent the interests of children and to appoint a solicitor for the child.

Arrangement of the guidance

1.27 The chapters in this guidance follow broadly the relevant parts of the Act. Chapter 2 considers private law matters relating to children under Parts I and 2. These focus on the child's interests and the need to resolve specific areas of dispute. The orders are designed to settle particular matters. They are made principally in private family proceedings, though certain Part 2 orders, such as residence orders and special guardianship orders, may also be made as a result of public law section 31 proceedings (described in Chapter 3). Separate guidance is available on special guardianship orders, which are briefly described in Chapter 2.

1.28 Parts 4 and 5 of the Act establish the framework for compulsory intervention in the care, supervision and protection of children. The basis for statutory intervention is directed towards the occurrence of present or likely future harm to the child. Chapter 3 deals with care and supervision orders. The law on the protection of children is discussed in Chapter 4.

1.29 Chapter 5 provides the basic statutory framework in the Act governing the restriction of liberty of children being looked after by local authorities and how this protection is extended to children in other types of accommodation.

CHAPTER THREE CARE AND SUPERVISION ORDERS

Summary

3.1 This Chapter focuses on the processes that are to take place before and during public law proceedings under section 31 of the Act. The Chapter opens by describing the referral and assessment processes undertaken by local authorities with responsibilities for children's social care functions, in particular initial and core assessments. If, following or as a result of these local authorities are concerned that children may be suffering or are likely to suffer, significant harm, the guidance then sets out the processes that are to be followed in moving towards making an application to the court for a care or supervision Order. Guidance on the emergency steps that may be taken is set out in Chapter 4.

3.2 Where such concerns arise, they may be so serious that the local authority will reach the view that it is no longer possible, without a care or supervision order (or emergency action), for it any longer to safeguard and promote the welfare of a particular child by promoting their upbringing by their family. In arriving at such a view, the local authority will have considered, through the core assessment process, not only the child's needs but also the needs and capacities both of the child's parents and those to be found in the wider family and community.

3.3 Before making an application for a care or supervision order a local authority is expected to seek legal advice and to communicate with the parents (and child, if of sufficient age and understanding) the nature and extent of their concerns. Prior to submitting an application to the court, and where the short term safety and welfare of the child permits, the local authority should send a 'Letter Before Proceedings' to the parents, the contents of which should also be explained carefully and directly to the parents, taking into account in the way in which information is presented the parents' cognitive and linguistic abilities. The purpose of such a letter is to enable the parents to obtain legal assistance and advice, prior to a meeting with the local authority the intention of which is either to deflect proceedings or, at least, to narrow and focus the issues of concern. It is recognised, of course, that there will be some emergency and other situations where the welfare of the affected child will not permit even a brief period for such correspondence and direct discussions to take place. To assist local authorities and others, a standard template letter is provided as an annex to the guidance.

3.4 Where, regardless of whether the 'Letter Before Proceedings' (see Annex A) process has been followed, the local authority then issues an application, a pre-proceedings checklist sets out clearly the documentation that the local authority needs to provide to the court, comprising material already available to the local authority as well as that which has been recently created specifically for the purposes of the application. Both a flowchart and the relevant Practice Direction, containing a 'pre-proceedings checklist' are annexed to this guidance.

3.5 The conditions under which a court may make a care or supervision order are set out as well as the processes that are followed in initial hearings and underpinning the making of any interim orders. The effect of care orders is then described as are the processes that are to be followed where care orders, once made, are discharged and where supervision orders are either discharged or varied. Extensive guidance is provided on arrangements for children in care (who are the subject of care orders) to have contact with their parents and other significant people such as siblings, in the context of the local authority's duty to promote contact. The effects of supervision orders are also described in detail. Guidance is also provided on wardship and the exercise of the inherent jurisdiction of the High Court.

Care and Supervision Proceedings

3.6 The scheme for care and supervision proceedings is founded on a number of principles. The first is that the local authority can only intervene in the care and upbringing of a child without the parents' agreement if the authority obtains a court order following proceedings in which the child, his parents and others who are connected with the child are able fully to participate. The proceedings should establish what action, if any, is in the child's interests, and the procedure must be fair to all concerned. The term 'care' is used in the Act in relation to a child who is the subject of a care order and does not include a child accommodated by a local authority under voluntary arrangements (section 105(1) of the Act).

3.7 Secondly, the local authority has a general duty, under section 17 of the Act, to promote the upbringing of children in need by their families so far as this is consistent with its duty to safeguard and promote the welfare of children, in particular through the provision of family support services to children in need and their families. This means that voluntary arrangements for the provision of services to the child and his family including the consideration of potential alternative carers should always be fully explored ahead of the making of any application under section 31, provided that this does not jeopardise the child's safety and welfare. The local authority should ensure, when assessing the wider family and environmental factors within the core assessment (undertaken in accordance with the *Framework for the Assessment of Children in Need and Their Families*), that it considers the capacity and willingness of the wider family to provide care for the child on a short or a longer-term basis. The local authority should also bear in mind that the court has a duty to make no order unless it considers that doing so would be better for the child than making no order at all (section 1(5) of the Act). It is possible that care proceedings may be avoided altogether or that a different application, such as for a special guardianship order or a residence order, made by a relative or carer, may be more appropriate, rather than a care order application by the local authority.

3.8 A family group conference (FGC) can be an important opportunity to engage wider friend and members of the wider family at an early stage of concerns about a child, either to support the parents or to provide care for the child, whether in the short or longer term. In either case, they can reduce or eliminate the need for the child to become looked after. In presenting a care plan to the court in any application for a care order, the local authority will be required to demonstrate that it has considered family members and friends as potential carers at each stage of its decision making.

3.9 Thirdly, there are common grounds for making care or supervision orders: the local authority must identify the actual or likely significant harm to the child and how this is occurring or may occur. Factors such as the child's parents having learning disabilities or misusing substances are not grounds in themselves for making a care or supervision order, unless they contribute to the harm suffered or likely to be suffered by the child and provide evidence of inadequate, or lack of proper, parenting.

3.10 Fourthly, ascertaining the wishes and feelings of the child in such proceedings is essential (and forms part of the welfare checklist to which the Court must have regard under section 1(3) of the Act). Children and Family Court Advisory and Support Service (Cafcass) Children's Guardians must be appointed in most kinds of public law proceedings unless the court is satisfied that this is not necessary in order to safeguard the child's interests. A Children's Guardian should normally be appointed as soon as practicable after the commencement of proceedings. A Children's Guardian appointed in respect of emergency proceedings (emergency protection order or child assessment order) should, wherever practicable, continue to represent the child in subsequent proceedings for a care or supervision order. The role of the Children's Guardian is to safeguard the interests of the child and, for that purpose, is subject to the duties set out in rules of court.

3.11 Fifthly, when a care order is in force the local authority and parents share parental responsibility for the child, subject to the authority's power to limit the exercise of such responsibility by the parents where it is necessary to do so in order to safeguard or promote the child's welfare (and to some specific limitations on the authority (section 33 (6) and (7)). Where a child is in the care of the authority (including where an interim care order has been made), the authority must allow the child reasonable contact with his parents and specified others, subject to court orders and limited local authority powers of action to refuse to allow contact in emergencies (section 34 of the Act and paragraph 15 of Schedule 2 to the Act).

Assessment Processes

3.12 Where a child is referred to the local authority as a child who may be in need, the local authority should decide, within one working day of the referral whether to undertake an initial assessment. This decision would normally follow discussion with the person who has made the referral and consideration of other information which the authority may hold or obtain. Any assessment should be undertaken in accordance with the *Framework for the Assessment of Children in Need and Their Families* (the 'Assessment Framework') (Department of Health et al, 2000). The initial assessment should be completed within seven working days of the date of the referral. Information should be gathered and analysed using the dimensions and domains set out in the Assessment Framework, namely:

- the child's developmental needs;
- the parents' or caregivers' capacity to respond appropriately to those needs; and
- the wider family and environmental factors.

By undertaking an initial assessment, which may be very brief in urgent safeguarding situations, the local authority may then ascertain whether:

- the child is a child in need (a 'child in need' is defined in section 17 (10) of the Act); and
- there is reasonable cause to suspect that the child is suffering, or is likely to suffer, significant harm (section 47 of the Act).

3.13 Where concerns about significant harm do not emerge or are not substantiated, but the child is assessed as being a 'child in need', the local authority may have sufficient information to determine what services, if any, should be provided, on the basis of the initial assessment and to agree a 'child in need' plan with the child and family. In determining what services to provide, the local authority is required to ascertain and take into account the wishes and feelings of the child.[1]

3.14 If the child is assessed as being in need and the local authority is concerned that the child is suffering, or is at risk of suffering, significant harm, the authority is under a duty to make, as soon as practicable and, in any event, within 48 hours of the authority receiving the information, such enquiries as it considers necessary to enable it to decide whether it should take action to safeguard or promote the welfare of the child (section 47 (1) of the Act) and what action may be appropriate in the circumstances (also see C4.66 to 4.75) . Emergency action may be required, to secure the immediate protection of the child (see Chapter 4 of this guidance and *Working Together to Safeguard Children* (2006) for further guidance on Emergency Protection Orders (section 44 of the Act) and the exercise of police protection powers (section 46 of the Act)). Where emergency action has been taken, such section 47 enquiries as may be necessary should follow quickly.

---

1 See Section 17(4A) of the Act.

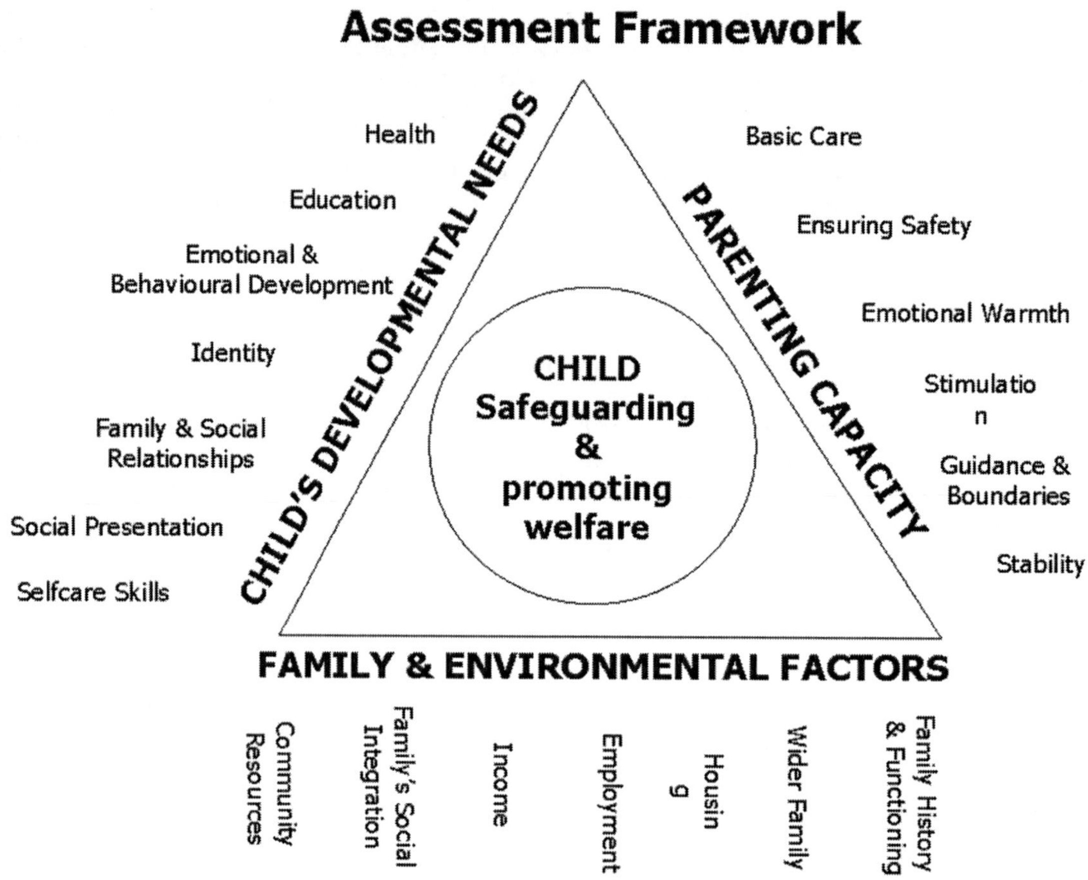

3.15 The core assessment is the means by which section 47 enquiries are carried out. In all cases where an initial assessment concludes that there is cause to suspect that a child is suffering or is likely to suffer significant harm, a core assessment should be completed, informed by the information obtained through the initial assessment. The need to complete a core assessment should not deter necessary safeguarding action from being taken. Compliance with the requirement to complete the core assessment will be scrutinised by the responsible court as part of the court's first consideration of any application under section 31 of the Act that it receives.

3.16 A core assessment is "an in-depth assessment which addresses the central or most important aspects of the needs of a child and the capacity of his or her parents or caregivers to respond appropriately to these needs within the wider family and community context" (Assessment Framework 3.11). The core assessment should build on the initial assessment, utilise any prior specialist assessments that may have been carried out and should be completed within 35 working days of its commencement. It is recognised that newly-commissioned specialist assessments from other agencies or independent professionals will not necessarily be completed within this period, but clear timescales for their completion should have been agreed with those bodies from which they have been commissioned, which should be specified in the core assessment. Once these specialist assessments are available, these will need to be taken into account and, depending on their relevance, may influence the local authority's planning for the child.

3.17 The core assessment forms the central part of the evidence supporting any application that the local authority may make for a care or supervision order under section 31 of the Act. Local authorities must ensure that an up to date core assessment is available in relation to any child who is the subject of a section 31 application under the Act.

3.18 The plan for the care of the child should be based on findings from the initial and core assessments. It should set out the aims of the plan and the intended outcomes for the child, informed by the findings from the assessments i.e. the identified developmental needs of the child and the capacity of the parents to respond to the child's needs in the context of their wider family and environmental context. The structure of the plan should follow the Assessment Framework domains and dimensions in accordance with the Integrated Children's System (ICS) care plan exemplar and be explicit about the services which will be provided by which agency and at what frequency in relation to the dimension headings. The plan should also set out the outcomes which are being sought in relation to the needs and services identified. LAC (99) 29 provides further guidance on the preparation of care plans in applications under section 31 of the Act. Additionally, section 31A of the Act provides that where an application is made, from which a care order might be made with respect to a child, the local authority must within the timetable directed by the court prepare a care plan, and no care order may be made until the Court has considered that plan (section 31(3A)).

Applications for care and supervision orders (sections 31 and 32)

The order-making powers of the court

3.19 A child is in the care of a local authority where the court has made a care order (including an interim order) under section 31. Aside from voluntary accommodation under section 20 or where the court has made a supervision order (including an interim order) under section 31, the only other circumstances in which a child may be placed in local authority accommodation are set out in section 21. These include children who are in police protection, children who are on remand and children who are subject to a supervision order made in criminal proceedings that imposes a local authority residence requirement or a foster parent residence requirement (which are different to a supervision order made under section 31).

3.20 Care and supervision proceedings, and indeed all proceedings under Part 4 of the Act, are 'family proceedings' (see section 8(3) of the Act), and may be heard at any level of the family courts, with most of cases starting in the family proceedings court. The court hearing an application for a care or supervision order may on its own initiative make an order under section 8 or a special guardianship order as an alternative to a care or supervision order. A local authority may apply for a care or supervision order if it considers that the threshold criteria at section 31 of the Act are established and those proceedings may be joined with other proceedings under[2]:

(a) the inherent jurisdiction of the High Court in relation to children;

(b) Matrimonial Causes Act 1973;

(c) Parts 1, 2 and 4 of the Act;

(d) Schedule 5 to the Civil Partnership Act 2004;

(e) the Adoption and Children Act 2002;

(f) the Domestic Proceedings and Magistrates' Courts Act 1978;

(g) Schedule 6 to the Civil Partnership Act 2004;

---

2 See section 31(4) and section 8(3)–(4).

(h) Part 3 of the Matrimonial and Family Proceedings Act 1984;

(i) the Family Law Act 1996; or

(j) sections 11 and 12 of the Crime and Disorder Act 1998.

3.21 Although a local authority may not apply for a residence order or special guardianship order, such orders may be made as a result of local authority section 31 applications, though such orders may not be made in favour of a local authority. Specific issue orders and prohibited steps orders cannot be used to achieve what may be achieved by the other section 8 orders, but a local authority may apply for such an order in respect of a child *not* in its care. If the child is the subject of a care order, contact arrangements will be dealt with under section 34 and not by a contact order under section 8.

Matters to be considered by local authorities before making an application for a care or supervision order

3.22 Only a local authority or authorised person (as defined in section 31(9)) may apply for a care or supervision order. At present, only the NSPCC is an authorised person. Its potential role in care proceedings is not addressed in this guidance because it has not exercised these powers for some years.

3.23 The local authority, in applying for an order under section 31, is likely to rely on a range of contributions from others, such as those already involved in the care of the child (including parents and relatives) as well as those providing specific information or findings from specialist assessments. Full inter-agency co-operation, including the sharing of information for the purpose of safeguarding children is essential whenever a potential care or supervision order case is identified, both because of the need to obtain as complete as possible a picture of actual or likely harm to the child but also to plan appropriate provision to meet the child's needs, if the order is made. Information from health professionals is likely to be of particular importance.

3.24 Within the local authority, the legal advisers have a key role to play in providing advice about the requirements of the courts and in relation to the making of the application. Parents, the child (if they are of sufficient age and understanding) and others with a legitimate interest in the child's future should, as far as possible, be involved, in the pre-application assessment processes and should, to the extent that it is possible to do so, be consulted on the local authority's plans for the child. Thus, even before the local authority reaches a decision that it should apply for a care or supervision order, parents will already have been made aware of the local authority's concerns about the child. Before reaching such a decision, the local authority should have taken such steps as are possible, perhaps through a family group conference or other family meeting, to explore whether care for the child can be safely provided by a relative or friend, have assessed the suitability of possible arrangements and have considered the most appropriate legal status of such arrangements.

3.25 Where the local authority decides, having sought and considered legal advice, that it intends to apply for a care or supervision order, the local authority must immediately notify that decision to the parents and others with parental responsibility for the child, using language and methods of communication, both in writing and orally, that will be understood by them. In particular the local authority should consider whether the parent (or other person with parental responsibilities) appears to have the capacity to instruct their legal representative, as the Official Solicitor may act as guardian ad litem/Next Friend/Litigation Friend for parties who lack litigation capacity (within the meaning of the Mental Capacity Act 2005) to represent themselves in proceedings, where there is no other person willing or suitable to do so. Further advice may be obtained from the official Solicitor (http://www.officialsolicitor.gov.uk).

3.26 The parents (and any others with parental responsibility for the child), on receipt of the local authority's written notification of its intention to apply for a care or supervision order, (known as the 'Letter Before Proceedings') are entitled to non-means tested publicly funded legal advice at 'Level 2', which covers liaison and negotiations with the local authority.

3.27 With the exception of those cases where urgent court action, including emergency protection proceedings, is needed to safeguard the child, the local authority should liaise with the parents (and those with parental responsibility) with a view to considering what steps, if any, can be taken to avoid proceedings, including by improving parental engagement with the local authority (where this is in the interests of the child), by further explaining the local authority's position and concerns and, where proceedings cannot be avoided, by narrowing the issues. Once the application for a care or supervision order has been made, parents will be entitled to 'Level 3' legal representation, which is also available on a non-means tested basis.

3.28 Where any affected child is of a sufficient age and level of understanding, the intention to initiate care or supervision proceedings must also be explained to him, unless to do so would exacerbate any significant harm that they might already be suffering, have suffered or be likely to suffer. However, it is recognised that, in a number of cases, there may be parental sensitivity about the local authority's involvement with the child, leading to parental consent for such involvement being withheld, which will mean that such information can only be provided after the commencement of proceedings, at which point the Cafcass Children's Guardian will also have a role to play. In this connection, it will be helpful for Cafcass planning purposes for the local authority to notify it of the prospect of the commencement of proceedings at the point at which parents are notified, though identifying details of the child should only be disclosed to Cafcass with the parents' consent.

3.29 The notification to the parents should, in its written version, take the form of a 'Letter Before Proceedings'. A standard template letter is included as an annex to this guidance (Annex A), but the letter, in cases where it is used, will need to be adjusted to fit the particular circumstances of the case. It should include:

- a summary of the local authority's concerns about the actual or likely harm to the child and the evidence on which these concerns are based;
- information about what the local authority has done to safeguard and promote the child's welfare, what needs to be addressed, what support will be provided and what the outcome will be if the problems are not addressed; and
- information about how to obtain legal help (on a non-means tested basis) and advice (including, in particular, details of local solicitors who provide a legal aid service in public law Children Act 1989 cases) together with encouragement to seek such advice as soon as possible.

3.30 It is recognised there will be some cases where, while inappropriate to be the subject of applications for Emergency Protection Orders, will nevertheless need to be the subject of an immediate section 31 application by the local authority. This is likely to occur where the scale, nature and urgency of the local authority's safeguarding concerns are such that the local authority considers that it is not in the interests of the child for a 'Letter Before Proceedings' to be sent. It may also be the case, in situations of this type, that not all of the other pre-proceedings steps will have been completed. In such circumstances, the local authority's application to the court will need to make explicit the reasons for any missing documentation or absent steps.

3.31 At or immediately after the meeting, the parents (and their legal representative) the local authority should provide in writing any revised plan for the child, setting out what the parents and the local authority are to do to safeguard the child and the steps that the local authority will take if this action is not effective in safeguarding the child. The outcome of the meeting should also be explained orally to the parents by the local authority.

3.32 The follow up letter and, as relevant, the plan for the child should make explicit what consideration has been given to the possibility, in the light of the needs of the child identified by the core assessment, of the child living with a relative or a friend. This plan will be based on findings from the up to date core assessment and any other current assessments or previous plans and the outcome of any previous family group conference or other family meeting, as well as reflecting the outcome of the meeting triggered by the 'Letter Before Proceedings'. It will identify how the child's short term needs will be met (and also set out any longer terms plans if information to support these is available).

3.33 If, despite the meeting following the 'Letter Before Proceedings', the local authority continues to be concerned (or again becomes concerned) that the child is suffering, or is likely to suffer, significant harm, it remains responsible for making an application to the court for a care or supervision order. See Annex C for a flow chart which sets out the pre-proceedings steps that are to be taken by local authorities.

The Making of the Application

3.34 Once the local authority has obtained information from the relevant range of agencies and disciplines, but before proceeding with an application, the local authority should always obtain and consider legal advice on:

(a) whether, in the circumstances of the case and in the light of the available evidence, the court is likely to be satisfied:
   (i) that the section 31(2) criteria are met; and
   (ii) that an order is in the best interests of the child and that the section 1(5) 'no order' test is likely to be met;[3]

(b) its care plan for the child, which will identify how the child's short term needs will be met (and also set out any longer terms plans if information to support these is available). In those relatively few cases where the identified permanence option, at the point of the commencement of proceedings, is for the adoption of the child, and where the decision that the child should be placed for adoption has been taken in accordance with the Adoption Agencies Regulations 2005 (SI 2005/389)[4], the local authority must apply for a placement order within the care proceedings (in accordance with the Adoption and Children Act 2002, its regulations and guidance[5]). Where the child is subject to a care order and each parent or guardian of the child has consented to the child being placed for adoption under section 19 of the 2002 Act[6], it is not required that a placement order application be made;

(c) the court to which the application should be made ; and

(d) whether to ask the court to make an interim care or supervision order and what directions should be sought (e.g. in relation to further assessments).

---

3 The court has made clear that any intervention under Part 4 or 5 of the Act must be proportionate to the legitimate aims of protecting the welfare and interests of the child. Interference with family life may only be justified by the overriding necessity of the interests of the child. See in particular *Re O (Supervision) Order* [2001] 1 FLR 923, *Re B (Care: Interference with Family Life)* [2003] 2 FLR 813, and summary of Munby J in *X v B (Emergency Protection Orders)* [2004] EWHC 2015 (Fam).

4 See *Re P-B* [2007] 1 FLR 1106.

5 See Chapter 2 of and Annex A to the Adoption and Children Act 2002 Guidance.

6 See section 22 of the Adoption and Children Act 2002

Annex B of this guidance is the *Practice Direction – Guide to Case Management in Public Law proceedings*. The table following paragraph 9.2 of this judicial guidance specifies, in the form of a 'pre-proceedings checklist', the documents that are to be disclosed to the court from the local authority's files, in support of the local authority's section 31 application. It also lists those additional documents that are to be prepared for the proceedings.

Conditions for a care or supervision order

3.35 The child must be under seventeen years old (or under 16 if married) at the time the order is made. The court is likely to look particularly carefully at a case for making an order if the young person is approaching his 17th birthday. A care or supervision order ceases to have effect at age eighteen unless brought to an end earlier (section 91 of the Act).

3.36 The court may not make an order unless satisfied that the threshold conditions are met (section 31(2)):

(a) the child concerned is suffering significant harm, or is likely to suffer significant harm; and

(b) the harm or likelihood of harm is attributable to
   (i) the care given to the child, or likely to be given to him if the order were not made, not being what it would be reasonable to expect a parent to give him; or
   (ii) the child is beyond parental control.

   If the threshold criteria are met the court must go on to apply the welfare checklist at section 1(3) and the 'no order' principle (section 1(5)). The court must consider the wide range of powers to make orders and to give directions. Having done so, the court must make whichever order is most consistent with the welfare interests of the child. In doing this, the court will have as its paramount consideration the welfare of the child. The court will want to be satisfied that a care or supervision order is a necessary and proportionate response to the legitimate aim of protecting the welfare and interests of the child.

3.37 The court must be satisfied that both elements of the threshold criteria have been met. The first focuses on actual or likely significant harm. The second is that the harm is attributable to the parenting of the child or to the child's being beyond parental control.

3.38 The first limb of the definition of 'harm' concerns ill-treatment or the impairment of health or development. This includes impairment suffered from seeing or hearing the ill-treatment of another person.[7] Ill-treatment is defined as including sexual abuse and forms of ill-treatment that are not physical (section 31(9)). Whether the harm suffered by the child is 'significant' is matter for the court to determine on the particular facts of the case.

3.39 In most cases impairment of health or development is likely to provide the evidence of 'harm'. Health is defined as physical or mental health; development as physical, intellectual, emotional, social or behavioural development (section 31(9)). Where the question of whether harm suffered by a child is significant turns on the child's health or development, this will be compared with that which could reasonably be expected of a similar child.

3.40 The second limb requires the court to be satisfied either that the harm, or likelihood of harm, is "attributable to the care given or likely to be given, to the child not being what it would be reasonable for a parent to give to the child" or that the child is "beyond parental control". If the issue is the adequacy of parenting, there must be a direct connection between the harm suffered (or likely to be suffered) by the child and the care given by the parent. Harm caused solely by a third party is not therefore relevant, unless the parent could have been expected to

---

[7] See amendment made to the definition of harm by section 120 of the Adoption and Children Act 2002.

intervene to prevent it and, unreasonably, did not do so. The quality of care given to the child will be compared with what it would be reasonable to expect a parent, having regard to the child's needs, to give the child. 'Care' is not defined but in the context is interpreted as including responsibility for making proper provision for the child's health and welfare (including promoting his physical, intellectual, emotional, social and behavioural development) and not just meeting basic survival needs.

3.41 If the child is determined by the court as being beyond parental control, this means that, whatever the standard of care provided by the parents, the child is suffering or is likely to suffer significant harm because of lack of parental control. This requires the court to determine whether as a matter of fact, the child is beyond control: it is immaterial who, if anyone, is to blame. In such cases, the local authority will need to demonstrate how the child's situation will improve if the court makes an order – how his behaviour can be brought under control, and why an order is necessary to achieve this.

3.42 Case law makes it clear that "when deciding whether to make a care order, the court should normally have before it a care plan which was sufficiently firm and particularised for all concerned to have a reasonably clear picture of the likely way ahead for the foreseeable future. The court must always maintain a proper balance between the need to satisfy itself about the appropriateness of the care plan and the avoidance of over zealous investigation into matters which were properly within the administrative discretion of the local authority." (see Re S and W [2002] 1 FCR 577). Section 31A provides that on an application for a care order local authorities must prepare a care plan for the future care of the child. While the child remains looked after, both during the course of court proceedings and subsequently, the local authority keep that care plan under review in accordance with the Review of Children's Cases Regulations 1991 (SI 1991/895).

Initial hearings: court requirements and party status

3.43 The local authority's legal adviser will advise on and have conduct of the legal proceedings, on instructions from the relevant local authority member of staff (usually a social worker or social work manager). Proceedings under the Act are governed by a number of statutory instruments including the Family Proceedings Rules 1991 (SI 1991/1247), the Family Proceedings Courts (Children Act 1989) Rules 1991 (SI 1991/1395) as amended and, for placement orders, the Family Procedure (Adoption) Rules 2005 (SI 2005/2795). Further requirements relating to the conduct of proceedings are set out in Practice Directions and in the *Public Law Outline (PLO)* (issued by the President of the Family Division, which is effective from April 2008). This guidance is to be read alongside the *PLO*, which have been prepared alongside one another to ensure consistency.

Interim orders

3.44 Interim care and supervision orders are similar in effect to full care and supervision orders except in two particulars: the court determines the duration of the interim order; and it may give directions to the local authority as to the medical or psychiatric examination of the child or other assessment. Interim orders represent a substantial, if time-limited, intervention in the care and upbringing of the child, and should not be regarded as an automatic stage in the process of an application for a full care or supervision order. Interim care or supervision orders enable the local authority compulsorily to intervene in the family to protect the child, for example after an emergency protection order or at the expiry of a period of police protection where the circumstances necessitate intervention. In addition, courts will wish to be clear about the local authority's immediate plans for the placement of the child under the terms of any interim care order.

3.45 The court may make an interim care order or interim supervision order when it adjourns proceedings relating to an application for a care or supervision order or directs the local authority to investigate a child's circumstances under section 37(1) of the Act in private family law proceedings. Before making an interim order, the court must be satisfied (it will not rubber-stamp an application, even if unopposed) that there are *reasonable grounds for believing* that the child's circumstances fulfil the criteria for a care or supervision order (i.e. that the child is suffering or is likely to suffer significant harm due to inadequate parenting or the child being beyond parental control).

3.46 If the test for making an interim care order is satisfied the court must then address the welfare checklist (s 1(3)) and the no order (s 1(5)) principle. It must determine whether the welfare of the child justifies the making of an interim care or supervision order[8]. In order to make such a determination it will need to consider the local authority's care plan alongside any alternative course which may be proposed by the parents or by the Cafcass children's guardian.

3.47 The court can instead make a section 8 order as an interim measure (section 11(3)), pending final disposal of the proceedings. If it makes a residence order in these circumstances it must also make an interim supervision order unless satisfied that the child's welfare will be satisfactorily safeguarded without one (section 38(3)). A residence order gives the person in whose favour the order is made parental responsibility for the child while it is in force. The order may contain directions about how it is to be carried into effect, impose conditions and deal with other matters such as contact arrangements and educational provision. It is likely to be for a specified period, until the care or supervision application is decided (section 11(7)). This may be particularly relevant in circumstances where the local authority's care plan has identified placement with a relative as a preferred option for permanence.

Duration of interim orders

3.48 The first interim order can last for up to 8 weeks. Subsequent orders can normally only last for up to 4 weeks. The court will consider the appropriate duration for the first and each subsequent interim order having regard to the likely prejudicial effect on the child's welfare of any delay in finally disposing of the proceedings (section 1(2)), the timetable for the case determined by the court, in accordance with the *Public Law Outline* and the limits on the maximum duration of the order set out in section 38(4).

Directions on examination and assessment when an interim order is made

3.49 The Act gives the court the power when making an interim care order or interim supervision order to give any directions it considers appropriate about medical or psychiatric examination or other necessary assessment of the child. However, if the child is of sufficient understanding he may refuse to submit to the examination or assessment (section 38(6)). The court's powers under this provision are limited to a process that can properly be characterised as "assessment" rather than "treatment". Any proposed assessment must be necessary to enable the court to discharge properly its function of deciding whether or not to make a care or supervision order. The court may also direct that no examination or assessment shall take place or make any it subject to its specific approval (section 38(7)). Directions can be given when the order is made or at any other time while it is in force and can be varied on an application made by any party to the proceedings in which the directions were given. In Re G (A child) (Interim Care Order: Residential Assessment) 2005 UKHL 68) the House of Lords held that the court hearing care proceedings had no powers to order the local authority to provide specific services

---

8 See judgment of Thorpe LJ in *Re M (A child) (Interim Care Order)* [2002] 1 FCR 350.

for anyone – that was a matter for the authority. The purpose of section 38 (6) and (7) was to enable the court to obtain the information it needed.

3.50 The court has similar directions powers when making a child assessment order (section 43(6)(b)) and emergency protection order (section 44(6)(b)) (see Chapter 4). The court's powers are more limited when a final supervision order is made and it does not have power to give any directions when making a final care order as thereafter decisions on examinations and assessment fall within the scope of local authority's parental responsibility. However, the court will have considered the local authority's care plan, prior to making a care order, and will expect that its key elements will be implemented, unless the child's circumstances change markedly.

3.51 A medical, psychiatric or other type of specialist assessment, with or without an examination of the child, will often be an important part of the core assessment, prior to the application for a care or supervision order. Such assessments will have been important in identifying whether there is any evidence that the child is suffering, or is likely to suffer, significant harm. In other cases, as an alternative to section 31 proceedings, the local authority should consider whether satisfactory arrangements for specialist assessments of the child can be made, whether with the agreement of the parents or by making an application for a child assessment order under section 43 of the Act.

3.52 Court directions on examination or assessment do not override the right of the child who is of sufficient understanding to make an informed decision to refuse to submit to an examination or assessment (sections 38(6), 43(8) and 44(7)). Examination or assessment without the child's consent may be an assault. For consent to be valid the person giving consent must be competent, ie understand the nature of what he or she is consenting to (and the risks) and consent must be freely given. A child of 16 is presumed in law to be capable of giving, or withholding, consent unless there is good evidence of incapacity. Children under 16 are not automatically presumed to be legally competent but may be so in relation to a particular issue. There is no specific age at which a child becomes competent to consent to treatment: it depends both on the child and on the seriousness and complexity of the intervention being proposed. Detailed guidance on consent is provided in *'Seeking consent: working with children'* DH 2001 (www.dh.gov.uk/en/Publicationsandstatistics/Publications/PublicationsPolicyandGuidance/DH_4007005).

Including an exclusion requirement

3.53 If the court is satisfied that there are reasonable grounds for believing that the child is suffering or is likely to suffer significant harm, and the harm is attributable to the care given to the child not being what it would be reasonable to expect a parent to give him, it has power to include in an interim care order an exclusion requirement (section 38A(1), inserted by the Family Law Act 1996) that:

(a) requires a particular person to leave the child's home;

(b) prohibits a particular person from entering the child's home;

(c) excludes a particular person from a defined area in which the child's home is situated (section 38A(3)).

3.54 This power may be exercised only if the following conditions are satisfied:

(a) that there is reasonable cause to believe that if the relevant person is excluded from the child's home, the child will cease to suffer, or cease to be likely to suffer, significant harm; and

(b) that another person living in the child's home is able and willing to care for the child and consents to the exclusion requirement (section 38A (2)).

3.55 The requirement may last as long as the interim order or may be for a shorter period (sub-section (4)), and the period may be extended on an application to vary or discharge the interim care order. A power of arrest may be attached to the order (sub-section (5)). The exclusion requirement will cease to have effect if the local authority removes the child from his home to other accommodation for more than 24 hours (sub-section (10)).

3.56 In any case where it could impose an exclusion requirement, the court has power to accept an undertaking from the relevant person which is enforceable as if it were an order of the court although a power of arrest cannot be attached (section 38B). An undertaking given under this section ceases to have effect in the same circumstances as an exclusion requirement; that is, when the interim order lapses, when the interim order is varied to that effect or is discharged or when the child is removed to other accommodation for more than 24 hours. LAC(97)15 provides further guidance about this issue (www.dh.gov.uk/en/Publicationsandstatistics/Lettersandcirculars/LocalAuthorityCirculars/AllLocalAuthority/DH_4004746).

Effects of, and responsibilities arising from, interim orders

3.57 Interim care and supervision orders have the same effect and give the same responsibilities to local authorities as full orders, save for the fact that the court specifies the length of any interim order and may also give directions. An interim care order confers on the local authority parental responsibility for the child for as long as the interim care order is in force and, like a care order, its effect is that the local authority is under a duty to allow the child reasonable contact with his parents and others, such as siblings (see section 34). Interim supervision orders do not confer parental responsibility on the local authority and therefore the parents' contact with the child may only be defined by a section 8 contact order. During the currency of an interim care order, the local authority is responsible for ensuring or enabling the provision of services identified in the care plan, which may well inform the development of the local authority's proposals for the future care of the child, which may involve rehabilitation to the child's parents, placement with a relative or friend or permanence outside the child's family of origin. The emergence of such proposals should be notified both to the local authority's legal advisers and to the Cafcass children's guardian.

Effect of Care Orders

3.58 Section 33 of the Act sets out the effect of a care order and establishes the legal basis for the local authority's welfare responsibilities towards children in care. The effect of a care order on other orders is set out in section 91. At the conclusion of care proceedings the Cafcass Children's guardian will, in all relevant cases, ensure that the care plan, as agreed by the court, is made available to the Independent Reviewing Officer (also see paragraph 3.66).

3.59 The local authority designated by the care order is responsible for looking after the child (section 33 (1)). It must provide accommodation for him and maintain him (section 23); safeguard and promote his welfare (section 22(3)(a)); and give effect to or act in accordance with the other welfare responsibilities set out in sections 22 to 26 and in Part 2 of Schedule 2 and in regulations made under the Act.

3.60 The local authority designated in the care order has parental responsibility for the child for as long as the order is in force. The local authority has power to determine the extent to which the child's parents and others with parental responsibility (who do not lose their parental responsibility on the making of the order) may meet their responsibility (section 33(3)(b)). The local authority may only use its powers to limit the parents' and others' exercise of parental responsibility if it is necessary to do so in order to safeguard and promote the child's welfare (section 33(4)); it should be discussed with the parent and child; and recorded in the care plan, ensuring also that any restriction is kept under regular review.

3.61 In exercising its parental responsibility the local authority must also ascertain the wishes and feelings of the child and his parents, and any other person with parental responsibility for the child or whom the authority considers relevant before taking key decisions about the child (section 22(4)). Further specific limitations on the local authority's parental responsibility are set out in section 33(6): the local authority must not cause the child to be brought up in any religious persuasion other than in which he would have been brought up had the order not be made; they do not have the right to agree (or refuse to agree) to the making of an adoption order with respect to the child, or to appoint a guardian for the child. The exercise of parental responsibility by the authority and others is further restricted by sub-section (7): no one can cause the child to be known by a new surname without a court order or the written consent of every other person who has parental responsibility and similarly no one can remove the child from the UK without an order or everyone's consent, except that (sub-section (8)) the local authority has power to take the child abroad for a period of up to one month. This limit does not affect any arrangements that may be made for the child to live outside England and Wales, which are governed by Schedule 2, paragraph 19.

3.62 The child's parents retain all rights, duties, powers, responsibilities or authority in relation to the child and his property which they have under other legislation and also continue to have financial responsibility for the child.

3.63 Subject to the specific restrictions mentioned above, the local authority has all the rights, duties, powers, responsibilities and authority to act as parent of a child for whom it is the authority designated in the care order. It may not transfer any part of the parental responsibility to another, but can arrange for some or all of it to be met by someone else acting on its behalf e.g. a local authority foster parent or a voluntary organisation (section 2(9)).

3.64 A care order automatically discharges the following orders made with respect to the child: a residence order and any other order made under section 8; a supervision order; and a school attendance order. It also brings wardship to an end (section 91). An education supervision order ceases to have effect on the making of a care order with respect to the child (paragraph 15(6)(b) of Schedule 3).

Discharge of Care Orders and discharge and variation of Supervision Orders

3.65 The child, local authority and any person having parental responsibility for the child may apply for discharge or variation of a care or supervision order under section 39 of the Act. Other persons with whom the child is living may apply for variation of a supervision order in so far as it affects them (section 39(3)). The welfare principle and the checklist in section 1 apply to the court's decision on an application under section 39 as they do to the court's determination of any other question concerning the upbringing of a child that falls to be determined under section 8 or Part 4 of the Act. The court may on an application for discharge of a care order substitute a supervision order without having to re-establish that the grounds (section 31(2)) for making a supervision order still exist. However, a care order can only be made where the child was subject to a supervision order if the local authority satisfies the court that the criteria in section 31(2) are met. The supervision order is automatically discharged on the making of a care order (section 91(3)).

3.66 A care order is automatically discharged by the making of a residence order (section 91(1)) or by the making of a special guardianship order (section 91(5A). A care order is suspended but not discharged by the making of a placement order (section 29(1) of the Adoption and Children Act 2002) and will revive if the placement order is later discharged. A person in whose favour a residence order is made will have parental responsibility for the child (if he does not already have it) and may apply for discharge or variation of a supervision order under section 39(2)(a).

3.67 Local authorities are required by the Review of Children's Cases Regulations 1991 to consider, at least at every statutory review (of a case of a child in care) whether to apply for discharge of the care order. The reviews must be chaired by an Independent Reviewing Officer (IRO). Part of the IRO's role is to ensure that the child's wishes and feelings are understood and taken into account in the authority's plans for the child's future care. At each review, as appropriate, the child should be informed of steps he can take for himself in relation to the order, or which an eligible adult might take on his behalf. These include applying for:

- discharge of the order;
- an order with respect to contact or for variation of an existing order (section 34);
- leave to apply for a residence order (section 10(8)); or
- leave to apply for a special guardianship order (section 14A).

3.68 A supervision order will last only one year (or less if the court so specifies) unless discharged earlier or the local authority applies for an extension. It can be extended for up to 3 years from the date of the original order. The local authority should consider whether or not to apply for the order to be varied or discharged where it has not been complied with (e.g. where a child of sufficient understanding refuses consent to a medical examination required by the order) or where circumstances have changed so that it may no longer be necessary.

3.69 Where an application for discharge of a care order or supervision order or to substitute a supervision order for a care order has been disposed of, no further application of this kind may be made within six months without leave of the court. This does not apply to interim orders or applications to vary a supervision order (section 91(15) and (16)).

Appeals against Care and Supervision Orders

3.70 Rules of court provide that any one who had party status in the original proceedings may appeal against the making of a care or supervision order, including an interim order, or of an order varying or discharging such an order, or against the court's refusal to make such an order. In certain cases, the permission of the original court may be needed before an appeal may be pursued. The time limits for appeals are set out in Part 8 of the Family Proceedings Rules 1991 (SI 1991/1247), rule 29 of the Family Proceedings Courts (Children Act 1989) Rules 1991 (SI 1991/1395) as amended and, for placement orders, Part 19 of the Family Procedure (Adoption) Rules 2005 (SI 2005/2795).

Contact with children in care

3.71 The local authority, in pursuit of its duty to promote contact, must allow a child who is the subject of a care order to have reasonable contact with his parents and certain other people, unless directed otherwise by a court order, or unless the local authority temporarily decides to refuse contact in urgent circumstances (section 34). The court must consider contact arrangements before making a care order (see section 34(11) and has wide powers to make orders appropriate to the particular circumstances. The underlying principle is that the local authority, the child and other persons concerned should as far as possible agree reasonable arrangements for contact before the care order is made, but should be able to seek the court's assistance if agreement cannot be reached or the authority considers that contact between the child and a person who would otherwise be entitled to it would not be in the child's best interests.

3.72 Section 34 creates the presumption that local authorities should enable contact to take place between children in care and their parents (and other people who are significant to them, such as siblings). The pro-active role given to the court in managing the arrangements during the course of proceedings reflects the importance of contact for the child. Regular contact with parents, grandparents, other relatives and friends will usually be an important part of the child's upbringing in his new environment and will be essential for successful rehabilitation. Lack of contact can, over a period, have serious consequences for the rights of parents and children; it can be a major factor in deciding whether to discharge a care order or to dispense with parental agreement to adoption. Contact arrangements for children in care are handled entirely separately from applications for contact orders under section 8. A section 8 contact order cannot be made when a child is the subject of a care order (section 9(9)), and an existing section 8 order is automatically discharged by the making of a care order (section 91(2)).

3.73 In addition to allowing the child reasonable contact with his parents, the local authority must under section 34 also allow reasonable contact with any guardian or special guardian, any person in whose favour a residence order was in force with respect to the child immediately before the care order was made and any person who had care of the child under wardship immediately before the care order was made.

3.74 There are a number of ways in which the local authority's proposals for contact may be scrutinised or challenged:

(a) the court, before making a care order, must consider the arrangements made or proposed by the authority and ask parties to the proceedings to comment on them (section 34(11)).

(b) any person to whom the Act's presumption of reasonable contact applies, or any other person who has obtained the leave of the court, can apply for an order with respect to contact at any time if he is dissatisfied with the arrangements made or proposed for contact by the local authority;

(c) the child can apply for his contact with another person to be terminated or for any order with respect to contact to be varied or discharged (section 34(4) and (9));

(d) the court, if it is satisfied that it should do so under section 1(5), may make any order about contact that it considers appropriate either in response to an application or on its own initiative, and can impose any conditions it considers appropriate. The conditions can be as specific as the court considers necessary, for example, that contact is supervised or takes place at a particular time or place, or is reviewed at prescribed intervals.

3.75 The local authority has the same powers as the child to apply for an order with respect to contact, and can also refuse contact that would otherwise be required under section 34(1) or a court order made under section 34 for up to 7 days without reference to the court (section 34(6)). The local authority must be satisfied that it is necessary to refuse contact to safeguard and promote the child's welfare, and the refusal must need to be decided on as a matter of urgency. If the authority considers it necessary to refuse contact for a longer period it must apply for an order under section 34(4). The authority, child or other person named in the order may apply at any time for an order to be varied or discharged; and any party to the proceedings (including the local authority) can appeal against the making of, or refusal to make, an order.

3.76 A decision to refuse contact under section 34(6) is a serious step which should not be undertaken lightly. The Contact with Children Regulations 1991 (SI 1991/891) set out the steps that the local authority must take when refusing contact under section 34(6). If the conditions set out in section 34(6) and the 1991 Regulations are not met, the local authority can exercise its parental responsibility in relation to a child subject to a care order to permit or refuse contact between the child and any person with whom it is not required to allow contact by virtue of section 34(1). It should always consult the child and their parents before making such a decision and inform any person denied contact of their right to apply for an order in respect of contact under section 34(3), and of the local authority's procedure for handling representations and complaints made under section 26(3).

3.77 Repeat applications for orders under section 34 are controlled by section 91(17). If an application for an order has been refused, the person concerned may not re-apply for the same order in respect of the same child within six months without the permission of the court. The court has a further power to control applications under Section 91(14) but will consider carefully whether it should use this power, in accordance with the expectation that restrictions on contact and on access to the courts will only be imposed where they are necessary to protect the rights of others.

3.78 Certain other provisions in the Act bear on the question of contact more generally, in relation to all looked after children not just those who are the subject of care orders (paragraph 15 of schedule 2). In addition to the local authority's general duty to promote contact between the child and his parents (and others – see 3.57 above), it must take reasonable steps to keep parents informed of the child's whereabouts, such as when another authority takes over the provision of accommodation, unless the child is the subject of a care order and there is reasonable cause for believing that giving that information would be prejudicial to the child's welfare. In no other circumstances may the local authority withhold information on the child's whereabouts. Where the authority provides accommodation for a child whether under a care order or otherwise it must ensure that the accommodation is as near his home as is reasonably practicable and consistent with his welfare (section 23(7), so that contact is facilitated.

3.79 The local authority has the power to make payments to assist contact (Schedule 2 paragraph 16) for example towards the costs incurred by parents and others visiting the child or by the child in visiting or maintaining contact by means of letters, telephone or electronic communication.

Supervision Orders

3.80 Supervision orders and interim supervision orders have for the most part been dealt with in the preceding sections of this guidance – those on the court's order-making powers, applications, criteria for orders, court directions and variation and discharge of orders, for example – where the provisions are common to both supervision orders and care orders or raise common points. The following paragraphs deal more specifically with supervision orders.

3.81 A supervision order puts the child under the supervision of a designated local authority. The local authority has three specific duties:

(a) to advise, assist and befriend the child;

(b) to take all reasonable steps to see that the order is given effect; and

(c) to consider whether to apply for variation or discharge of the order where it is not being wholly complied with or the authority considers that the order may no longer be necessary (section 35(1).

Where a person is receiving medical treatment pursuant to a condition in the order, the local authority must also refer back to the court specific issues relating to that treatment in accordance with paragraph 5(7) of Schedule 3 should the need arise.

3.82 A supervision order may also require the child to comply with any directions given by the local authority which require him to do all or any of the following:

(a) live at a place specified in directions given by the supervisor;

(b) take part in education or training activities; and

(c) report to particular places at particular times.

The local authority cannot give directions in respect of any medical or psychiatric examination or treatment (Schedule 3 paragraph 2(3)). These are matters for the court to require by order but it should be noted that the court cannot make a direction requiring the child to submit to psychiatric or medical examination or treatment unless the child, if of sufficient understanding to do so, consents to its inclusion in the order (Schedule 3 paragraph 4). The local authority should always consider very carefully when contemplating an application under section 31 whether these powers, coupled with the power of the court and supervisor to impose requirements on a responsible person (Schedule 3 paragraph 3) , with the consent of that person, are sufficient to promote and safeguard the welfare of the child. A responsible person is any person with parental responsibility for the child and any other person with whom the child is living (Schedule 3 paragraph1).

3.83 There is no prescribed remedy for breach of a requirement set out in the order itself or of a local authority's direction. In case of breach, the local authority would have to consider whether to apply to the court to vary or discharge the order (section 35(3)). If the supervisor is prevented from visiting the child or having reasonable contact with him under paragraphs 8(1)(b) and (2)(b) of Schedule 3, he may apply to the court for a warrant under section 102. The warrant is intended to enable the person concerned to exercise his powers. If the supervisor considered that urgent action should be taken to protect the child, he should consider whether to apply for an emergency protection order (section 44) or ask a constable to take the child into police protection under section 46.

3.84 Unless otherwise discharged, a supervision order will last for one year (Schedule 3 paragraph 6(1)). Before its expiry, the supervisor can apply for an extension, or further extensions, for any period not exceeding 3 years in total from the date of the first order. A supervision order is otherwise discharged by order of the court; the making of a care order with respect to the child; the making of a placement order under the Adoption and Children Act 2002; the child reaching the age of 18; or if a court takes certain action under the Child Abduction and Custody Act 1985 for example by making an order for the return of the child. An interim supervision order may accompany a residence order in the circumstances described in section 38(3). A local authority, when exercising responsibility for a supervision order, will need to consider whether also to operate a child protection plan or a child in need plan.

Wardship and the inherent jurisdiction of the High Court

3.85 The impact of the Act on the inherent jurisdiction of the High Court was considerable. Section 100 prohibits the use of the court's inherent jurisdiction in general, and wardship in particular, as an alternative to public law orders. If a care order is made in respect of a child who is a ward of court then the wardship comes to an end (section 91(4)). While a child is in care he cannot be made a ward of court (section 100(2) and section 41 of the Supreme Court Act 1981 as amended by paragraph 45 of Schedule 13).

3.86 The inherent jurisdiction remains available as a remedy of last resort where a local authority seeks the resolution of a specific issue concerning the future of a child in its care. But there are restrictions: the local authority must have the High Court's leave to apply for the exercise of its inherent jurisdiction (section 100(3)). Leave may only be granted where the court is satisfied that the local authority could not achieve the desired result through the making of any order other than one under the inherent jurisdiction (section 100(4)). Where there are other statutory remedies, the local authority will be expected to use them instead. Even if there is no other statutory remedy within the Act, the court must be satisfied that there is reasonable cause to believe that the child is likely to suffer significant harm if the inherent jurisdiction is not exercised.

3.87 Since the local authority has parental responsibility for children in its care, it should make decisions that affect the child's welfare in consultation with the parents as appropriate and after taking the child's wishes and feelings into account. Occasions where recourse to the High Court is appropriate should be very rare and will relate to matters that are unusual or highly contentious, or that have the potential to affect permanently the child's exercise of his human rights. An example might be the sterilisation of a child in care. Other less extreme situations may also merit High Court intervention, for example, to restrain harmful publicity about a child or to provide injunctive protection against third parties. In such cases when the inherent jurisdiction is the only means of obtaining the remedy, it should not be too difficult to satisfy the leave criteria.

3.88 The Act further prevents the High Court from exercising its inherent jurisdiction "for the purposes of conferring on any local authority power to determine any question which has arisen, or which may arise in connection with any aspect of parental responsibility". Thus, in making an order under its inherent jurisdiction, the court cannot confer on the local authority any degree of parental responsibility it does not already have (section 100(2)).

CHAPTER FOUR PROTECTION OF CHILDREN

Local authorities' duty to make enquiries under section 47

4.73 A local authority is under a duty to make enquiries into a child's welfare, or cause them to be made, in a number of circumstances. An application by the local authority for either a child assessment order or an EPO should always be preceded by an initial assessment, however brief, in accordance with *Framework for the Assessment of Children In Need and Their Families*, together with a strategy discussion (unless a single agency has had to act immediately to protect a child, in which case one should take place as soon as possible after such action). The local authority should make all reasonable efforts to persuade parents to co-operate with section 47 enquiries before deciding to apply for an order. The local authority is unlikely to be able to satisfy the court that there are adequate grounds for making an order, without first being able to point to the findings of such assessments and enquiries, however limited these might be in emergency situations. Emergency action might be necessary as soon as a referral is received, or at any point in a local authority's involvement with children and families, recognising that the need for such action may become apparent only over time as more is ascertained about the circumstances of a child. Neglect, as well as abuse, can pose such a risk of significant harm to a child that urgent action may be required to protect the child.

4.74 The local authority has a duty to make enquiries when:

(a) directed to do so by a court exercising its powers under section 37(1) in any family proceedings;

(b) directed to do so by a court under Schedule 3(17), on the discharge of an education supervision order;

(c) a local authority with education responsibilities notifies them that a child is persistently failing to comply with directions made under an education supervision order (Schedule 3(19));

(d) it is informed that a child who lives, or is found, in their area is the subject of an emergency protection order or is in police protection (section 47(1)(a));

(e) it has reasonable cause to suspect that a child who lives, or is found, in their area is suffering or is likely to suffer significant harm (section 47(1)(b));

(f) it has obtained an emergency protection order with respect to a child (section 47(2)).

4.75 The purpose of undertaking enquiries is to enable the authority to decide what action it should take to safeguard or promote the child's welfare. Enquiries conducted under section 47 must focus in particular, on whether the authority should make any application to the court or exercise any of their other powers under the Act with respect to the child (section 47(3)(a)).

4.76 In the case of a child who is the subject of an EPO and who is not in accommodation provided by (or on behalf of) the local authority, the local authority's enquiries should also consider whether it would be in the child's best interests (while the EPO remains in force) for him to be so accommodated (section 47(3)(b)).

4.77 In the case of a child who as been taken into police protection, the local authority should consider whether it would be in the child's best interests to ask the police to make an application for an emergency protection order (sections 47(3)(c) and 46(7).

4.78 In making their enquiries under section 47(1), the local authority must take such steps as are reasonably practicable (unless they are satisfied that they already have sufficient information) to obtain access to the child or to ensure that access to him is obtained on their behalf by a person authorised by them for that purpose (section 47(4)). They must also, as far as reasonably practicable and consistent with the child's welfare, ascertain and give due consideration to the child's wishes and feelings regarding action to be taken with respect to him (section 47(5A)).

4.79 Where, as a result of such enquiries, it appears to the authority that matters concerned with the child's education should be investigated, they must consult the relevant local authority with education responsibilities (which will often be another part of the same local authority undertaking the enquiries) (section 47(5)).

4.80 Where, in the course of making their enquiries, the local authority is refused access to the child concerned, or information as to his whereabouts is denied, the local authority should consider applying for a child assessment order, or an EPO, or a care order or a supervision order, unless it is satisfied that the child's welfare can be satisfactorily safeguarded without such an application (section 47(6)).

4.81 If the authority decides not to apply for any of the above orders, it should consider whether it would be appropriate to review the case at a later date. If it decides that it would be appropriate, the date of that review should be set (section 47(7)). Where a local authority concludes that it should take action to safeguard or promote the child's welfare, it shall take that action, so far as it is both within its power and reasonably practicable for it to do so (section 47(8)).

4.82 Where a local authority is conducting enquiries under section 47, it is the duty of any of the following persons to assist them with those enquiries, and in particular, by providing them with relevant information and advice, if requested:

(a) any local authority,

(b) any local education authority,

(c) any local housing authority,

(d) any health authority, Special Health Authority, Primary Care Trust, National Health Service trust or NHS Foundation Trust,

(e) any person authorised by the Secretary of State for this purpose.

However, this provision does not oblige any person to assist a local authority where doing so would be unreasonable in all the circumstances of the case (sections 47(9), (10) and (11)). The policies and procedures of the Local Safeguarding Children Board are likely to set out how local co-operation is to be delivered in practice. Where a local authority is making enquiries under this section with respect to a child who appears to them to be ordinarily resident within the area of another authority, it must consult that other authority, who may undertake the necessary enquiries in their place (section 47(12)). Only when the other authority, expressly accepts responsibility, is the first authority relieved of its responsibility to make enquiries. Such acceptance should be confirmed in writing.

ANNEX A LETTER BEFORE PROCEEDINGS – TEMPLATE LETTER

PLEASE DO NOT IGNORE THIS LETTER
TAKE IT TO A SOLICITOR NOW

Office
Address
Contact ____________
Direct line
My ref
Fax
E-mail
Date

Dear [parent and/or full name(s) of all people with parental responsibility]

Re: [insert name of Local Authority] CONCERNS ABOUT [insert name(s) of child(ren)] – LETTER BEFORE PROCEEDINGS

HOW TO AVOID GOING TO COURT

I am writing to let you know how concerned *[name of LA]* have become about your care of your child/ren. I am writing to tell you that *[name of the Local Authority]* is thinking about starting Care Proceedings in respect of *[name(s) of child(ren)]*. This means that we may apply to Court and *[name(s) of child(ren)]* could, if the Court decides that this is best for him/her/them, be taken into care.

We are so worried about your child/ren that we will go to court unless you are able to improve things. There are things you can do which could stop this happening. We have set out in this letter the concerns that we have about *[name(s) of child(ren)]* and the things that have been done to try to help your family.

AN IMPORTANT MEETING ABOUT WHAT WILL HAPPEN NEXT

Please come to a meeting with us to talk about these concerns on [*date and time]* at the *[insert name of office]*. The address is *[address]* and there is a map with this letter to help you find it. Please contact your social worker on *[tel.no.]* to tell us if you will come to the meeting

At the meeting we will discuss with you and tell you what you will need to do to make your child safe. We will also talk to you about how we will support you to do this. We will also make clear what steps we will take if we continue to be worried about [*name(s) of child(ren)*].

PLEASE BRING A SOLICITOR TO THE MEETING ON [insert date]

Take this letter to a solicitor and ask them to come to the meeting with you. The solicitor will advise you about getting legal aid (free legal advice). We have sent with this letter a list of local solicitors who work with children and families. They are all separate from children's services. You do not have to bring a solicitor to the meeting, but it will be helpful if you do.

Information your Solicitor will need is:

Local Authority Legal Contact:
Name, Address & Telephone:

WHAT WILL HAPPEN IF YOU DO NOTHING

If you do nothing we will have to go to Court. If you do not answer this letter or come to the meeting, we will go to Court as soon as we can to make sure *[name(s) of child(ren)]* are safe.

YOUR WIDER FAMILY

Our concerns about *[name(s) of child(ren)]* are very serious. If we do have to go to Court and the Court decides you cannot care for your children, we will first try and place them with one of your relatives, if it is best for your child to do this. At the meeting we will want to talk to you and your solicitor about who might look after your child if the Court decides that it is no longer safe for you to do so.

We look forward to seeing you at the meeting with your solicitor on [date]. If you do not understand any part of this letter, please contact your social worker [name] on [tel. no.]. Please tell your social worker if you need any help with child care or transport arrangements in order to come to the meeting, and we will try to help.

Yours sincerely

[name]
Team Manager
Local office/service

cc Social Worker [name]

Local Authority In-house Legal Team

Enc: Map of office

List of Law Society Children Panel Solicitors

List of things we are worried about

PLEASE SHOW/TAKE THIS TO A SOLICITOR

HERE ARE THE MAIN THINGS THAT WE ARE WORRIED ABOUT:

1. [Outline concern and give examples of when this happened. This should capture chronic ongoing concerns as well as acute episodes/incidents]

Date(s)	***Problem***

2.

Date(s)	*Problem*

WHAT CHILDREN'S SERVICES HAVE DONE TO TRY TO HELP

[Who?]	*[What help has been given?]*	*[When?]*

WHAT YOU HAVE TO DO SO THAT WE WILL NOT GO TO COURT:

1. Confirm that you will come to a meeting to talk about these concerns. Please try to bring a solicitor with you.

2. Continue to see and work with your social worker ***[insert name]*** and allow him/her to see ***[name(s) of child(ren)].***

3. At the meeting you will be asked to talk about how ***[name(s) of child(ren)]*** will be kept safe, with our help.

APPENDIX 4

PRACTICE DIRECTION: EXPERTS IN FAMILY PROCEEDINGS RELATING TO CHILDREN ('THE EXPERTS PRACTICE DIRECTION')

1. Introduction

1.1 This Practice Direction deals with the use of expert evidence and the instruction of experts in family proceedings relating to children, and comes into force on 1st April 2008. The guidance supersedes, for such proceedings, that contained in Appendix C (the *Code of Guidance for Expert Witnesses in Family Proceedings*) to the Protocol of June 2003 (*Judicial Case Management in Public Law Children Act Cases*) and in the Practice Direction to Part 17 (*Experts*) of the Family Procedure (Adoption) Rules 2005[1] ('FP(AR) 2005') with effect on and from 1st April 2008.

Where the guidance refers to 'an expert' or 'the expert', this includes a reference to an expert team.

1.2 For the purposes of this guidance, the phrase 'family proceedings relating to children' is a convenient description. It is not a legal term of art and has no statutory force. In this guidance it means–[2]

- placement and adoption proceedings; or
- family proceedings held in private which;
- relate to the exercise of the inherent jurisdiction of the High Court with respect to children;
- are brought under the Children Act 1989 in any family court; or
- are brought in the High Court and county courts and 'otherwise relate wholly or mainly to the maintenance or upbringing of a minor'.

Aims of the guidance

1.3 The guidance aims to provide the court in family proceedings relating to children with early information to determine whether an expert or expert evidence will assist the court to:

- identify, narrow and where possible agree the issues between the parties;
- provide an opinion about a question that is not within the skill and experience of the court;
- encourage the early identification of questions that need to be answered by an expert; and
- encourage disclosure of full and frank information between the parties, the court and any expert instructed.

1.4 The guidance does not aim to cover all possible eventualities. Thus it should be complied with so far as consistent in all the circumstances with the just disposal of the matter in accordance with the rules and guidance applying to the procedure in question.

Permission to instruct an expert or to use expert evidence

1.5 In family proceedings relating to children, the court's permission is required to instruct an expert. Such proceedings are confidential and, in the absence of the court's permission, disclosure of information and documents relating to such proceedings risks contravening the law of contempt of court or the various statutory provisions protecting this confidentiality. Thus, for the purposes of the law of contempt of court, information relating to such proceedings (whether or not contained in a document filed with the court or recorded in any form) may be

---

1 SI 2005/2795.

2 Following r 10.20A(1) of the Family Proceedings Rules 1991, SI 1991/1247 ('FPR 1991') which defines the application of r 10.20A (*Communication of information relating to proceedings*). Compare the definition of 'relevant proceedings' in s 93(3) of the Children Act 1989 (*Rules of court*), applied in the equivalent r 23A (*Confidentiality of documents*) of the Family Proceedings Courts (Children Act 1989) Rules 1991, SI 1991/1395 ('FPC(CA 1989)R 1991').

communicated only to an expert whose instruction by a party has been permitted by the court.[3] Additionally, in proceedings under the Children Act 1989, the court's permission is required to cause the child to be medically or psychiatrically examined or otherwise assessed for the purpose of the preparation of expert evidence for use in the proceedings; and, where the court's permission has not been given, no evidence arising out of such an examination or assessment may be adduced without the court's permission.[4]

1.6 In practice, the need to have the court's permission to disclose information or documents to an expert – and, in Children Act 1989 proceedings, to have the child examined or assessed – means that in proceedings relating to children the court strictly controls the number, fields of expertise and identity of the experts who may be first instructed and then called.

1.7 Before permission is obtained from the court to instruct an expert in family proceedings relating to children, it will be necessary for the party wishing to instruct an expert to make enquiries designed so as to provide the court with information about that expert which will enable the court to decide whether or not to give permission. In practice, enquiries may need to be made of more than one expert for this purpose. This will in turn require each expert to be given sufficient information about the case to enable that expert to decide whether or not he or she is in a position to accept instructions. Such preliminary enquiries, and the disclosure of anonymised information about the case which is a necessary part of such enquiries, will not require the court's permission and will not amount to a contempt of court: see sections 4.1 and 4.2 (*Preliminary Enquiries of the Expert* and *Expert's Response to Preliminary Enquiries*).

1.8 Section 4 (*Preparation for the relevant hearing*) gives guidance on applying for the court's permission to instruct an expert, and on instructing the expert, in family proceedings relating to children. The court, when granting permission to instruct an expert, will also give directions for the expert to be called to give evidence, or for the expert's report to be put in evidence: see section 4.4 (*Draft Order for the relevant hearing*).

When should the court be asked for permission?

1.9 The key event is 'the relevant hearing', which is any hearing at which the court's permission is sought to instruct an expert or to use expert evidence. Both expert issues should be raised with the court – and, where appropriate, with the other parties – as early as possible. This means:

- in public law proceedings under the Children Act 1989, by or at the Case Management Conference: see the *Practice Direction: Guide to Case Management in Public Law Proceedings*, paragraphs 13.7, 14.3 and 25(29) which contains the definition of public law proceedings for the purposes of that practice direction;
- in private law proceedings under the Children Act 1989, by or at the First Hearing Dispute Resolution Appointment: see the *Private Law Programme* (9th November 2004), section 4 *(Process)*;
- in placement and adoption proceedings, by or at the First Directions Hearing: see FP(A)R 2005 rule 26 and the *President's Guidance: Adoption: the New Law and Procedure* (March 2006), paragraph 23.

---

3 FPR 1991, r 10.20A(2)(vii); FPC(CA 1989)R 1991, r 23A(1)(c)(vii); FP(A)R 2005, r 78(1)(c)(vii).

4 FPR 1991, r 4.18(1) and (3); FPC(CA 1989)R 1991, r 18(1) and (3).

2. General matters

Scope of the Guidance

2.1 This guidance does not apply to cases issued before 1st April 2008, but in such a case the court may direct that this guidance will apply either wholly or partly. This is subject to the overriding objective for the type of proceedings, and to the proviso that such a direction will neither cause further delay nor involve repetition of steps already taken or of decisions already made in the case.

2.2 This guidance applies to all experts who are or have been instructed to give or prepare evidence for the purpose of family proceedings relating to children in a court in England and Wales.

Pre-application instruction of experts

2.3 When experts' reports are commissioned before the commencement of proceedings, it should be made clear to the expert that he or she may in due course be reporting to the court and should therefore consider himself or herself bound by this guidance. A prospective party to family proceedings relating to children (for example, a local authority) should always write a letter of instruction when asking a potential witness for a report or an opinion, whether that request is within proceedings or pre-proceedings (for example, when commissioning specialist assessment materials, reports from a treating expert or other evidential materials); and the letter of instruction should conform to the principles set out in this guidance.

Emergency and urgent cases

2.4 In emergency or urgent cases – for example, where, before formal issue of proceedings, a without-notice application is made to the court during or out of business hours; or where, after proceedings have been issued, a previously unforeseen need for (further) expert evidence arises at short notice – a party may wish to call expert evidence without having complied with all or any part of this guidance. In such circumstances, the party wishing to call the expert evidence must apply forthwith to the court – where possible or appropriate, on notice to the other parties – for directions as to the future steps to be taken in respect of the expert evidence in question.

Orders

2.5 Where an order or direction requires an act to be done by an expert, or otherwise affects an expert, the party instructing that expert – or, in the case of a jointly instructed expert, the lead solicitor – must serve a copy of the order or direction on the expert forthwith upon receiving it.

Adults who may be protected parties

2.6 The court will investigate as soon as possible any issue as to whether an adult party or intended party to family proceedings relating to children lacks capacity (within the meaning of the Mental Capacity Act 2005) to conduct the proceedings. An adult who lacks capacity to act as a party to the proceedings is a protected party and must have a representative (a litigation friend, next friend or guardian *ad litem*) to conduct the proceedings on his or her behalf.

2.7 Any issue as to the capacity of an adult to conduct the proceedings must be determined before the court gives any directions relevant to that adult's role in the proceedings.

2.8 Where the adult is a protected party, his or her representative should be involved in any instruction of an expert, including the instruction of an expert to assess whether the adult, although a protected party, is competent to give evidence. The instruction of an expert is a significant step in the proceedings. The representative will wish to consider (and ask the expert to consider), if the protected party is competent to give evidence, their best interests in this regard. The representative may wish to seek advice about 'special measures'. The representative may put forward an argument on behalf of the protected party that the protected party should not give evidence.

2.9 If at any time during the proceedings there is reason to believe that a party may lack capacity to conduct the proceedings, then the court must be notified and directions sought to ensure that this issue is investigated without delay.

Child likely to lack capacity to conduct the proceedings on when s/he reaches 18

2.10 Where it appears that a child is:

- a party to the proceedings and not the subject of them;
- nearing his or her 18th birthday, and
- considered likely to lack capacity to conduct the proceedings when he or she attains the age of 18,

the court will consider giving directions for the child's capacity in this respect to be investigated.

3. The Duties of Experts

Overriding Duty

3.1 An expert in family proceedings relating to children has an overriding duty to the court that takes precedence over any obligation to the person from whom the expert has received instructions or by whom the expert is paid.

Particular Duties

3.2 Among any other duties an expert may have, an expert shall have regard to the following duties:

(1) to assist the court in accordance with the overriding duty;
(2) to provide advice to the court that conforms to the best practice of the expert's profession;
(3) to provide an opinion that is independent of the party or parties instructing the expert;
(4) to confine the opinion to matters material to the issues between the parties and in relation only to questions that are within the expert's expertise (skill and experience);
(5) where a question has been put which falls outside the expert's expertise, to state this at the earliest opportunity and to volunteer an opinion as to whether another expert is required to bring expertise not possessed by those already involved or, in the rare case, as to whether a second opinion is required on a key issue and, if possible, what questions should be asked of the second expert;
(6) in expressing an opinion, to take into consideration all of the material facts including any relevant factors arising from ethnic, cultural, religious or linguistic contexts at the time the opinion is expressed;
(7) to inform those instructing the expert without delay of any change in the opinion and of the reason for the change.

Content of the Expert's Report

3.3 The expert's report shall be addressed to the court and prepared and filed **in accordance with the court's timetable** and shall:

(1) give details of the expert's qualifications and experience;
(2) contain a statement setting out the substance of all material instructions (whether written or oral) summarising the facts stated and instructions given to the expert which are material to the conclusions and opinions expressed in the report;
(3) identify materials that have not been produced either as original medical or other professional records or in response to an instruction from a party, as such materials may contain an assumption as to the standard of proof, the admissibility or otherwise of hearsay evidence, and other important procedural and substantive questions relating to the different purposes of other enquiries (for example, criminal or disciplinary proceedings);
(4) identify all requests to third parties for disclosure and their responses in order to avoid partial disclosure which tends only to prove a case rather than give full and frank information;
(5) make clear which of the facts stated in the report are within the expert's own knowledge;
(6) state who carried out any test, examination or interview which the expert has used for the report and whether or not the test, examination or interview has been carried out under the expert's supervision;
(7) give details of the qualifications of any person who carried out the test, examination or interview;
(8) in expressing an opinion to the court:

   (a) take into consideration all of the material facts including any relevant factors arising from ethnic, cultural, religious or linguistic contexts at the time the opinion is expressed, identifying the facts, literature and any other material including research material that the expert has relied upon in forming an opinion;
   (b) describe their own professional risk assessment process and process of differential diagnosis, highlighting factual assumptions, deductions from the factual assumptions, and any unusual, contradictory or inconsistent features of the case;
   (c) highlight whether a proposition is an hypothesis (in particular a controversial hypothesis), or an opinion deduced in accordance with peer-reviewed and -tested technique, research and experience accepted as a consensus in the scientific community;
   (d) indicate whether the opinion is provisional (or qualified, as the case may be), stating the qualification and the reason for it, and identifying what further information is required to give an opinion without qualification;

(9) where there is a range of opinion on any question to be answered by the expert:

   (a) summarise the range of opinion;
   (b) highlight and analyse within the range of opinion an 'unknown cause', whether on the facts of the case (for example, there is too little information to form a scientific opinion) or because of limited experience, lack of research, peer review or support in the field of expertise which the expert professes;
   (c) give reasons for any opinion expressed: the use of a balance sheet approach to the factors that support or undermine an opinion can be of great assistance to the court;

(10) contain a summary of the expert's conclusions and opinions;
(11) contain a statement that the expert understands his or her duty to the court and has complied and will continue to comply with that duty;
(12) contain a statement that the expert:

(a) has no conflict of interest of any kind, other than any conflict disclosed in his or her report;
(b) does not consider that any interest disclosed affects his or her suitability as an expert witness on any issue on which he or she has given evidence;
(c) will advise the instructing party if, between the date of the expert's report and the final hearing, there is any change in circumstances which affects the expert's answers to (a) or (b) above;

(13) be verified by a statement of truth in the following form: 'I confirm that insofar as the facts stated in my report are within my own knowledge I have made clear which they are and I believe them to be true, and that the opinions I have expressed represent my true and complete professional opinion.'

4. Preparation for the relevant hearing

Preliminary Enquiries of the Expert

4.1 In good time for the information requested to be available for the relevant hearing or for the advocates' meeting or discussion where one takes place before the relevant hearing, the solicitor for the party proposing to instruct the expert (or lead solicitor or solicitor for the child if the instruction proposed is joint) shall approach the expert with the following information:

(1) the nature of the proceedings and the issues likely to require determination by the court;
(2) the questions about which the expert is to be asked to give an opinion (including any ethnic, cultural, religious or linguistic contexts);
(3) the date when the court is to be asked to give permission for the instruction (or if – unusually – permission has already been given, the date and details of that permission);
(4) whether permission is to be asked of the court for the instruction of another expert in the same or any related field (that is, to give an opinion on the same or related questions);
(5) the volume of reading which the expert will need to undertake;
(6) whether or not permission has been applied for or given for the expert to examine the child;
(7) whether or not it will be necessary for the expert to conduct interviews – and, if so, with whom;
(8) the likely timetable of legal and social work steps;
(9) when the expert's report is likely to be required;
(10) whether and, if so, what date has been fixed by the court for any hearing at which the expert may be required to give evidence (in particular the Final Hearing).

It is essential that there should be proper co-ordination between the court and the expert when drawing up the case management timetable: the needs of the court should be balanced with the needs of the expert whose forensic work is undertaken as an adjunct to his or her main professional duties, whether in the National Health Service or elsewhere.

The expert should be informed at this stage of the possibility of making, through his or her instructing solicitor, representations to the court about being named or otherwise identified in any public judgment given by the court.

Expert's Response to Preliminary Enquiries

4.2 In good time for the relevant hearing or for the advocates' meeting or discussion where one takes place before the relevant hearing, the solicitors intending to instruct the expert shall obtain confirmation from the expert:

(1) that acceptance of the proposed instructions will not involve the expert in any conflict of interest;
(2) that the work required is within the expert's expertise;
(3) that the expert is available to do the relevant work within the suggested time scale;
(4) when the expert is available to give evidence, of the dates and times to avoid and, where a hearing date has not been fixed, of the amount of notice the expert will require to make arrangements to come to court (or to give evidence by video link) without undue disruption to his or her normal professional routines;
(5) of the cost, including hourly or other charging rates, and likely hours to be spent, attending experts' meetings, attending court and writing the report (to include any examinations and interviews);
(6) of any representations which the expert wishes to make to the court about being named or otherwise identified in any public judgment given by the court.

Where parties have not agreed on the appointment of a single joint expert before the relevant hearing, they should obtain the above confirmations in respect of all experts whom they intend to put to the court as candidates for the appointment.

The proposal to instruct an expert

4.3 Any party who proposes to ask the court for permission to instruct an expert shall, **by 11 a.m. on the business day before the relevant hearing**, file and serve a written proposal to instruct the expert in the following detail:

(1) the name, discipline, qualifications and expertise of the expert (by way of C.V. where possible);
(2) the expert's availability to undertake the work;
(3) the relevance of the expert evidence sought to be adduced to the issues in the proceedings and the specific questions upon which it is proposed that the expert should give an opinion (including the relevance of any ethnic, cultural, religious or linguistic contexts);
(4) the timetable for the report;
(5) the responsibility for instruction;
(6) whether or not the expert evidence can properly be obtained by the joint instruction of the expert by two or more of the parties;
(7) whether the expert evidence can properly be obtained by only one party (for example, on behalf of the child);
(8) why the expert evidence proposed cannot be given by social services undertaking a core assessment or by the Children's Guardian in accordance with their respective statutory duties;
(9) the likely cost of the report on an hourly or other charging basis: where possible, the expert's terms of instruction should be made available to the court;
(10) the proposed apportionment (at least in the first instance) of any jointly instructed expert's fee; when it is to be paid; and, if applicable, whether public funding has been approved.

Draft Order for the relevant hearing

4.4 Any party proposing to instruct an expert shall, **by 11 a.m. on the business day before the relevant hearing**, submit to the court a draft order for directions dealing in particular with:

(1) the party who is to be responsible for drafting the letter of instruction and providing the documents to the expert;
(2) the issues identified by the court and the questions about which the expert

is to give an opinion;

(3) the timetable within which the report is to be prepared, filed and served;
(4) the disclosure of the report to the parties and to any other expert;
(5) the organisation of, preparation for and conduct of an experts' discussion;
(6) the preparation of a statement of agreement and disagreement by the experts following an experts' discussion;
(7) making available to the court at an early opportunity the expert reports in electronic form;
(8) the attendance of the expert at court to give oral evidence (alternatively, the expert giving his or her evidence in writing or remotely by video link), whether at or for the Final Hearing or another hearing; unless agreement about the opinions given by the expert is reached at or before the Issues Resolution Hearing ('IRH') or, if no IRH is to be held, by a specified date prior to the hearing at which the expert is to give oral evidence ('the specified date').

5. Letter of Instruction

5.1 The solicitor instructing the expert shall, **within 5 business days after the relevant hearing,** prepare (in agreement with the other parties where appropriate), file and serve a letter of instruction to the expert which shall:

(1) set out the context in which the expert's opinion is sought (including any ethnic, cultural, religious or linguistic contexts);
(2) set out the specific questions which the expert is required to answer, ensuring that they:

    (a) are within the ambit of the expert's area of expertise;
    (b) do not contain unnecessary or irrelevant detail;
    (c) are kept to a manageable number and are clear, focused and direct; and
    (d) reflect what the expert has been requested to do by the court.

    The Annex to this guidance sets out suggested questions in letters of instruction to (1) child mental health professionals or paediatricians, and (2) adult psychiatrists and applied psychologists, in Children Act 1989 proceedings;
(3) list the documentation provided, or provide for the expert an indexed and paginated bundle which shall include:

    (a) a copy of the order (or those parts of the order) which gives permission for the instruction of the expert, immediately the order becomes available;
    (b) an agreed list of essential reading; and
    (c) a copy of this guidance;

(4) identify materials that have not been produced either as original medical (or other professional) records or in response to an instruction from a party, as such materials may contain an assumption as to the standard of proof, the admissibility or otherwise of hearsay evidence, and other important procedural and substantive questions relating to the different purposes of other enquiries (for example, criminal or disciplinary proceedings);
(5) identify all requests to third parties for disclosure and their responses, to avoid partial disclosure, which tends only to prove a case rather than give full and frank information;
(6) identify the relevant people concerned with the proceedings (for example, the treating clinicians) and inform the expert of his or her right to talk to them provided that an accurate record is made of the discussions;
(7) identify any other expert instructed in the proceedings and advise the expert of his or her right to talk to the other experts provided that an accurate record is made of the discussions;

(8) subject to any public funding requirement for prior authority, define the contractual basis upon which the expert is retained and in particular the funding mechanism including how much the expert will be paid (an hourly rate and overall estimate should already have been obtained), when the expert will be paid, and what limitation there might be on the amount the expert can charge for the work which he or she will have to do. In cases where the parties are publicly funded, there should also be a brief explanation of the costs and expenses excluded from public funding by Funding Code criterion 1.3 and the detailed assessment process.

Asking the court to settle the letter of instruction to a joint expert

5.2 Where the court has directed that the instructions to the expert are to be contained in a jointly agreed letter and the terms of the letter cannot be agreed, any instructing party may submit to the court a written request, which must be copied to the other instructing parties, that the court settle the letter of instruction. Where possible, the written request should be set out in an e-mail to the court, preferably sent directly to the judge dealing with the proceedings (or, in the Family Proceedings Court, to the legal adviser who will forward it to the appropriate judge or justices), and be copied by e-mail to the other instructing parties. The court will settle the letter of instruction, usually without a hearing to avoid delay; and will send (where practicable, by e-mail) the settled letter to the lead solicitor for transmission forthwith to the expert, and copy it to the other instructing parties for information.

Keeping the expert up to date with new documents

5.3 As often as may be necessary, the expert should be provided promptly with a copy of any new document filed at court, together with an updated document list or bundle index.

6. The Court's control of expert evidence: consequential issues

Written Questions

6.1 Any party wishing to put written questions to an expert for the purpose of clarifying the expert's report must put the questions to the expert **not later than 10 business days after receipt of the report**.

The court will specify the timetable according to which the expert is to answer the written questions.

Experts' Discussion or Meeting: Purpose

6.2 **By the specified date**, the court may – if it has not already given such a direction – direct that the experts are to meet or communicate:

(1) to identify and narrow the issues in the case;
(2) where possible, to reach agreement on the expert issues;
(3) to identify the reasons for disagreement on any expert question and what, if any, action needs to be taken to resolve any outstanding disagreement or question;
(4) to explain or add to the evidence in order to assist the court to determine the issues;
(5) to limit, wherever possible, the need for the experts to attend court to give oral evidence.

Experts' Discussion or Meeting: Arrangements

6.3 In accordance with the directions given by the court, the solicitor or other professional who is given the responsibility by the court ('the nominated professional') shall – **within 15 business days after the experts' reports have been filed and copied to the other parties** – make arrangements for the experts to meet or communicate. Where applicable, the following matters should be considered:

(1) where permission has been given for the instruction of experts from different disciplines, a global discussion may be held relating to those questions that concern all or most of them;
(2) separate discussions may have to be held among experts from the same or related disciplines, but care should be taken to ensure that the discussions complement each other so that related questions are discussed by all relevant experts;
(3) **5 business days prior to a discussion or meeting**, the nominated professional should formulate an agenda including a list of questions for consideration. The agenda should contain only those questions which are intended to clarify areas of agreement or disagreement. Questions which repeat questions asked in the letter of instruction or which seek to rehearse cross-examination in advance of the hearing should be rejected as likely to defeat the purpose of the meeting.

The agenda may usefully take the form of a list of questions to be circulated among the other parties in advance. The agenda should comprise all questions that each party wishes the experts to consider. The agenda and list of questions should be sent to each of the experts **not later than 2 clear business days before the discussion;**

(4) the nominated professional may exercise his or her discretion to accept further questions after the agenda with list of questions has been circulated to the parties. **Only in exceptional circumstances should questions be added to the agenda within the 2-day period before the meeting. Under no circumstances should any question received on the day of or during the meeting be accepted.** Strictness in this regard is vital, for adequate notice of the questions enables the parties to identify and isolate the issues in the case before the meeting so that the experts' discussion at the meeting can concentrate on those issues;
(5) the discussion should be chaired by the nominated professional. A minute must be taken of the questions answered by the experts, and a Statement of Agreement and Disagreement must be prepared which should be agreed and signed by each of the experts who participated in the discussion. The statement should be served and filed **not later than 5 business days after the discussion has taken place;**
(6) in each case, whether some or all of the experts participate by telephone conference or video link to ensure that minimum disruption is caused to professional schedules and that costs are minimised.

Meetings or conferences attended by a jointly instructed expert

6.4 Jointly instructed experts should not attend any meeting or conference which is not a joint one, unless all the parties have agreed in writing or the court has directed that such a meeting may be held, and it is agreed or directed who is to pay the expert's fees for the meeting or conference. Any meeting or conference attended by a jointly instructed expert should be proportionate to the case.

Court-directed meetings involving experts in public law Children Act cases

6.5 In public law Children Act proceedings, where the court gives a direction that a meeting shall take place between the local authority and any relevant named experts for the purpose of providing assistance to the local authority in the formulation of plans and proposals for the child, the meeting shall be arranged, chaired and minuted in accordance with the directions given by the court.

7. Positions of the Parties

7. Where a party refuses to be bound by an agreement that has been reached at an experts' discussion or meeting, that party must inform the court and the other parties in writing, **within 10 business days after the discussion or meeting or, where an IRH is to be held, not less than 5 business days before the IRH,** of his reasons for refusing to accept the agreement.

8. Arrangements for Experts to give evidence

Preparation

8.1 Where the court has directed the attendance of an expert witness, the party who is responsible for the instruction of the expert shall, **by the specified date or, where an IRH is to be held, by the IRH**, ensure that:

(1) a date and time (if possible, convenient to the expert) are fixed for the court to hear the expert's evidence, substantially in advance of the hearing at which the expert is to give oral evidence and no later than a specified date prior to that hearing or, where an IRH is to be held, than the IRH;
(2) if the expert's oral evidence is not required, the expert is notified as soon as possible;
(3) the witness template accurately indicates how long the expert is likely to be giving evidence, in order to avoid the inconvenience of the expert being delayed at court;
(4) consideration is given in each case to whether some or all of the experts participate by telephone conference or video link, or submit their evidence in writing, to ensure that minimum disruption is caused to professional schedules and that costs are minimised.

Experts attending Court

8.2 Where expert witnesses are to be called, all parties shall, by the specified date or, where an IRH is to be held, by the IRH, ensure that:

(1) the parties' advocates have identified (whether at an advocates' meeting or by other means) the issues which the experts are to address;
(2) wherever possible, a logical sequence to the evidence is arranged, with experts of the same discipline giving evidence on the same day;
(3) the court is informed of any circumstance where all experts agree but a party nevertheless does not accept the agreed opinion, so that directions can be given for the proper consideration of the experts' evidence and of the party's reasons for not accepting the agreed opinion;
(4) in the exceptional case the court is informed of the need for a witness summons.

9. Action after the Final Hearing

9.1 Within 10 business days after the Final Hearing, the solicitor instructing the expert shall inform the expert in writing of the outcome of the case, and of the use made by the court of the expert's opinion.

9.2 Where the court directs preparation of a transcript, it may also direct that the solicitor instructing the expert shall send a copy to the expert **within 10 business days after receiving the transcript**.

9.3 After a Final Hearing in the Family Proceedings Court, the (lead) solicitor instructing the expert shall send the expert a copy of the court's written reasons for its decision **within 10 business days after receiving the written reasons**.

ANNEX[5]

Questions in letters of instruction to child mental health professional or paediatrician in Children Act 1989 proceedings

A. The Child(ren)

1. Please describe the child(ren)'s current health, development and functioning (according to your area of expertise), and identify the nature of any significant changes which have occurred

- Behavioural
- Emotional
- Attachment organisation
- Social/peer/sibling relationships
- Cognitive/educational
- Physical
  - Growth, eating, sleep
  - Non-organic physical problems (including wetting and soiling)
  - Injuries
  - Paediatric conditions

2. Please comment on the likely explanation for/aetiology of the child(ren)'s problems/ difficulties/injuries

- History/experiences (including intrauterine influences, and abuse and neglect)
- Genetic/innate/developmental difficulties
- Paediatric/psychiatric disorders

3. Please provide a prognosis and risk if difficulties not addressed above.

4. Please describe the child(ren)'s needs in the light of the above

- Nature of care-giving
- Education
- Treatment

in the short and long term (subject, where appropriate, to further assessment later).

B. The parents/primary care-givers

5. Please describe the factors and mechanisms which would explain the parents' (or primary care-givers') harmful or neglectful interactions with the child(ren) (if relevant).

6. What interventions have been tried and what has been the result?

7. Please assess the ability of the parents or primary care-givers to fulfil the child(ren)'s identified needs now.

8. What other assessments of the parents or primary care-givers are indicated

- Adult mental health assessment
- Forensic risk assessment
- Physical assessment

---

[5] Drafted by the Family Justice Council.

- Cognitive assessment

9. What, if anything, is needed to assist the parents or primary care-givers now, within the child(ren)'s time scales and what is the prognosis for change

- Parenting work
- Support
- Treatment/therapy

C. Alternatives

10. Please consider the alternative possibilities for the fulfilment of the child(ren)'s needs

- What sort of placement
- Contact arrangements

Please consider the advantages, disadvantages and implications of each for the child(ren).

Questions in letters of instruction to adult psychiatrists and applied psychologists in Children Act 1989 proceedings

1. Does the parent/adult have – whether in his/her history or presentation – a mental illness/disorder (including substance abuse) or other psychological/emotional difficulty and, if so, what is the diagnosis?

2. How do any/all of the above (and their current treatment if applicable) affect his/her functioning, including interpersonal relationships?

3. If the answer to Q1 is yes, are there any features of either the mental illness or psychological/emotional difficulty or personality disorder which could be associated with risk to others, based on the available evidence base (whether published studies or evidence from clinical experience)?

4. What are the experiences/antecedents/aetiology which would explain his/her difficulties, if any, (*taking into account any available evidence base or other clinical experience*)?

5. What treatment is indicated, what is its nature and the likely duration?

6. What is his/her capacity to engage in/partake of the treatment/therapy?

7. Are you able to indicate the prognosis for, time scales for achieving, and likely durability of, change?

8. What other factors might indicate positive change?

(It is assumed that this opinion will be based on collateral information as well as interviewing the adult).

The Right Honourable Sir Mark Potter
The President of the Family Division

The Lord Chancellor

APPENDIX 5

PRACTICE DIRECTION OF 27 JULY 2006: FAMILY PROCEEDINGS: COURT BUNDLES (UNIVERSAL PRACTICE TO BE APPLIED IN ALL COURTS OTHER THAN THE FAMILY PROCEEDINGS COURT)

('THE BUNDLES PRACTICE DIRECTION', AS ADJUSTED BY 'THE PLO PRACTICE DIRECTION')

1 The President of the Family Division has issued this practice direction to achieve consistency across the country in all family courts (other than the Family Proceedings Court) in the preparation of court bundles and in respect of other related matters.

Application of the practice direction

2.1 Except as specified in para 2.4, and subject to specific directions given in any particular case, the following practice applies to:

(*a*) all hearings of whatever nature (including but not limited to hearings in family proceedings, Civil Procedure Rules 1998 Part 7 and Part 8 claims and appeals) before a judge of the Family Division of the High Court wherever the court may be sitting;
(*b*) all hearings in family proceedings in the Royal Courts of Justice (RCJ);
(*c*) all hearings in the Principal Registry of the Family Division (PRFD) at First Avenue House; and
(*d*) all hearings in family proceedings in all other courts except for Family Proceedings Courts.

2.2 'Hearings' includes all appearances before a judge or district judge, whether with or without notice to other parties and whether for directions or for substantive relief [except the First Appointment, Case Management Conference, and Issues Resolution Hearing referred to in the *Practice Direction: Guide to Case Management in Public Law Proceedings* where there are no contested applications being heard at those hearings].

2.3 This practice direction applies whether a bundle is being lodged for the first time or is being re-lodged for a further hearing (see para 9.2).

2.4 This practice direction does not apply to:

(*a*) cases listed for one hour or less at a court referred to in para 2.1(*c*) or 2.1(*d*); or
(*b*) the hearing of any urgent application if and to the extent that it is impossible to comply with it.

2.5 The designated family judge responsible for any court referred to in para 2.1(*c*) or 2.1(*d*) may, after such consultation as is appropriate (but in the case of hearings in the PRFD at First Avenue House only with the agreement of the Senior District Judge), direct that in that court this practice direction shall apply to all family proceedings irrespective of the length of hearing.

Responsibility for the preparation of the bundle

3.1 A bundle for the use of the court at the hearing shall be provided by the party in the position of applicant at the hearing (or, if there are cross-applications, by the party whose application was first in time) or, if that person is a litigant in person, by the first listed respondent who is not a litigant in person.

3.2 The party preparing the bundle shall paginate it. If possible the contents of the bundle shall be agreed by all parties.

Contents of the bundle

4.1 The bundle shall contain copies of all documents relevant to the hearing, in chronological order from the front of the bundle, paginated and indexed, and divided into separate sections (each section being separately paginated) as follows:

(a) preliminary documents (see para 4.2) and any other case management documents required by any other practice direction;
(b) applications and orders;
(c) statements and affidavits (which must be dated in the top right corner of the front page);
(d) care plans (where appropriate);
(e) experts' reports and other reports (including those of a guardian, children's guardian or litigation friend); and
(f) other documents, divided into further sections as may be appropriate.

Copies of notes of contact visits should normally not be included in the bundle unless directed by a judge.

4.2 At the commencement of the bundle there shall be inserted the following documents (the preliminary documents):

(i) an up to date summary of the background to the hearing confined to those matters which are relevant to the hearing and the management of the case and limited, if practicable, to one A4 page;
(ii) a statement of the issue or issues to be determined (1) at that hearing and (2) at the final hearing;
(iii) a position statement by each party including a summary of the order or directions sought by that party (1) at that hearing and (2) at the final hearing;
(iv) an up to date chronology, if it is a final hearing or if the summary under (i) is insufficient;
(v) skeleton arguments, if appropriate, with copies of all authorities relied on; and
(vi) a list of essential reading for that hearing.

4.3 Each of the preliminary documents shall state on the front page immediately below the heading the date when it was prepared and the date of the hearing for which it was prepared.

4.4 The summary of the background, statement of issues, chronology, position statement and any skeleton arguments shall be cross-referenced to the relevant pages of the bundle.

4.5 The summary of the background, statement of issues, chronology and reading list shall in the case of a final hearing, and shall so far as practicable in the case of any other hearing, each consist of a single document in a form agreed by all parties. Where the parties disagree as to the content the fact of their disagreement and their differing contentions shall be set out at the appropriate places in the document.

4.6 Where the nature of the hearing is such that a complete bundle of all documents is unnecessary, the bundle (which need not be repaginated) may comprise only those documents necessary for the hearing, but

(i) the summary (para 4.2(i)) must commence with a statement that the bundle is limited or incomplete; and
(ii) the bundle shall if reasonably practicable be in a form agreed by all parties.

4.7 Where the bundle is re-lodged in accordance with para 9.2, before it is re-lodged:

(a) the bundle shall be updated as appropriate; and
(b) all superseded documents (and in particular all outdated summaries, statements of issues, chronologies, skeleton arguments and similar documents) shall be removed from the bundle.

Format of the bundle

5.1 The bundle shall be contained in one or more A4 size ring binders or lever arch files (each lever arch file being limited to 350 pages).

5.2 All ring binders and lever arch files shall have clearly marked on the front and the spine:

(a) the title and number of the case;
(b) the court where the case has been listed;
(c) the hearing date and time;
(d) if known, the name of the judge hearing the case; and
(e) where there is more than one ring binder or lever arch file, a distinguishing letter (A, B, C etc).

Timetable for preparing and lodging the bundle

6.1 The party preparing the bundle shall, whether or not the bundle has been agreed, provide a paginated index to all other parties not less than 4 working days before the hearing (in relation to a case management conference to which the provisions of the [*Practice Direction: Guide to Case Management in Public Law Proceedings*] apply, not less than 5 working days before the case management conference).

6.2 Where counsel is to be instructed at any hearing, a paginated bundle shall (if not already in counsel's possession) be delivered to counsel by the person instructing that counsel not less than 3 working days before the hearing.

6.3 The bundle (with the exception of the preliminary documents if and insofar as they are not then available) shall be lodged with the court not less than 2 working days before the hearing, or at such other time as may be specified by the judge.

6.4 The preliminary documents shall be lodged with the court no later than 11 am on the day before the hearing and, where the hearing is before a judge of the High Court and the name of the judge is known, shall at the same time be sent by email to the judge's clerk.

Lodging the bundle

7.1 The bundle shall be lodged at the appropriate office. If the bundle is lodged in the wrong place the judge may:

(a) treat the bundle as having not been lodged; and
(b) take the steps referred to in para 12.

7.2 Unless the judge has given some other direction as to where the bundle in any particular case is to be lodged (for example a direction that the bundle is to be lodged with the judge's clerk) the bundle shall be lodged:

(a) for hearings in the RCJ, in the office of the Clerk of the Rules, Room TM 9.09, Royal Courts of Justice, Strand, London WC2A 2LL (DX 44450 Strand);
(b) for hearings in the PRFD at First Avenue House, at the List Office counter, 3rd floor, First Avenue House, 42/49 High Holborn, London, WC1V 6NP (DX 396 Chancery Lane); and
(c) for hearings at any other court, at such place as may be designated by the designated family judge or other judge at that court and in default of any such designation at the court office of the court where the hearing is to take place.

7.3 Any bundle sent to the court by post, DX or courier shall be clearly addressed to the appropriate office and shall show the date and place of the hearing on the outside of any packaging as well as on the bundle itself.

Lodging the bundle – additional requirements for cases being heard at First Avenue House or at the RCJ

8.1 In the case of hearings at the RCJ or First Avenue House, parties shall:

(a) if the bundle or preliminary documents are delivered personally, ensure that they obtain a receipt from the clerk accepting it or them; and

(b) if the bundle or preliminary documents are sent by post or DX, ensure that they obtain proof of posting or despatch.

The receipt (or proof of posting or despatch, as the case may be) shall be brought to court on the day of the hearing and must be produced to the court if requested. If the receipt (or proof of posting or despatch) cannot be produced to the court the judge may: (i) treat the bundle as having not been lodged; and (ii) take the steps referred to in para 12.

8.2 For hearings at the RCJ:

(a) bundles or preliminary documents delivered after 11 am on the day before the hearing will not be accepted by the Clerk of the Rules and shall be delivered:

   (i) in a case where the hearing is before a judge of the High Court, directly to the clerk of the judge hearing the case;

   (ii) in a case where the hearing is before a Circuit Judge, Deputy High Court Judge or Recorder, directly to the messenger at the Judge's entrance to the Queen's Building (with telephone notification to the personal assistant to the Designated Family Judge, 020 7947 7155, that this has been done).

(b) upon learning before which judge a hearing is to take place, the clerk to counsel, or other advocate, representing the party in the position of applicant shall no later than 3 pm the day before the hearing:

   (i) in a case where the hearing is before a judge of the High Court, telephone the clerk of the judge hearing the case;

   (ii) in a case where the hearing is before a circuit judge, deputy high court judge or recorder, telephone the personal assistant to the designated family judge;

to ascertain whether the judge has received the bundle (including the preliminary documents) and, if not, shall organise prompt delivery by the applicant's solicitor.

Removing and re-lodging the bundle

9.1 Following completion of the hearing the party responsible for the bundle shall retrieve it from the court immediately or, if that is not practicable, shall collect it from the court within 5 working days. Bundles which are not collected in due time may be destroyed.

9.2 The bundle shall be re-lodged for the next and any further hearings in accordance with the provisions of this practice direction and in a form which complies with para 4.7.

Time estimates

10.1 In every case a time estimate (which shall be inserted at the front of the bundle) shall be prepared which shall so far as practicable be agreed by all parties and shall:

(a) specify separately: (i) the time estimated to be required for judicial pre-reading; and (ii) the time required for hearing all evidence and submissions; and (iii) the time estimated to be required for preparing and delivering judgment; and
(b) be prepared on the basis that before they give evidence all witnesses will have read all relevant filed statements and reports.

10.2 Once a case has been listed, any change in time estimates shall be notified immediately by telephone (and then immediately confirmed in writing):

(a) in the case of hearings in the RCJ, to the Clerk of the Rules;
(b) in the case of hearings in the PRFD at First Avenue House, to the List Officer at First Avenue House; and
(c) in the case of hearings elsewhere, to the relevant listing officer.

Taking cases out of the list

11 As soon as it becomes known that a hearing will no longer be effective, whether as a result of the parties reaching agreement or for any other reason, the parties and their representatives shall immediately notify the court by telephone and by letter. The letter, which shall wherever possible be a joint letter sent on behalf of all parties with their signatures applied or appended, shall include:

(a) a short background summary of the case;
(b) the written consent of each party who consents and, where a party does not consent, details of the steps which have been taken to obtain that party's consent and, where known, an explanation of why that consent has not been given;
(c) a draft of the order being sought; and
(d) enough information to enable the court to decide (i) whether to take the case out of the list and (ii) whether to make the proposed order.

Penalties for failure to comply with the practice direction

12 Failure to comply with any part of this practice direction may result in the judge removing the case from the list or putting the case further back in the list and may also result in a 'wasted costs' order in accordance with CPR, Part 48.7 or some other adverse costs order.

Commencement of the practice direction and application of other practice directions

13 This practice direction replaces *Practice Direction (Family Proceedings: Court Bundles) (10 March 2000)* [2000] 1 WLR 737, [2000] 1 FLR 536 and shall have effect from 2 October 2006.

14 Any reference in any other practice direction to *Practice Direction (Family Proceedings: Court Bundles) (10 March 2000)* shall be read as if substituted by a reference to this practice direction.

15 This practice direction should where appropriate be read in conjunction with [*Practice Direction: Guide to Case Management in Public Law Proceedings*]. In particular, nothing in this practice direction is to be read as removing or altering any obligation to comply with the requirements of the [*Practice Direction: Guide to Case Management in Public Law Proceedings*].

This Practice Direction is issued:

(i) in relation to family proceedings, by the President of the Family Division, as the nominee of the Lord Chief Justice, with the agreement of the Lord Chancellor; and
(ii) to the extent that it applies to proceedings to which s 5 of the Civil Procedure Act 1997 applies, by the Master of the Rolls as the nominee of the Lord Chief Justice, with the agreement of the Lord Chancellor.

The Right Honourable
Sir Mark Potter
President of the Family Division & Head of Family Justice

The Right Honourable
Sir Anthony Clarke
Master of the Rolls & Head of Civil Justice

APPENDIX 6

CAFCASS REPORTING TO COURT POLICY (FINALISED FOR PUBLIC LAW PROCEEDINGS)

The Cafcass Reporting to Court Policy included is that already issued to its staff for use in public law proceedings. It is finalised insofar as public law proceedings are concerned, but, at the time of writing, is subject to amendment in respect of private law proceedings pending finalisation of the integrated private law pathway.

This policy explains how Cafcass will report to court in individual cases. This will be a cumulative process starting from the early stages of our involvement. The templates are called 'Analysis and Recommendations' documents. There is also guidance about how to complete the templates.

Contents

Appendices

1. INTRODUCTION

1.1 Cafcass has developed a new model for reporting to the family court in individual cases. This complies with the Public Law Outline in public law, and with Cafcass' work in accordance with the private law pathway and the President's private law programme in private law. A similar template will soon be developed for placement order in adoption cases.

2. POLICY

2.1 The attached templates will be used for all new public law cases from April 2008. In private law, they will be used from April 2008 for new cases where an Early Intervention scheme is in operation. For other areas, where this is still under development, the introduction of these templates will form part of the wider discussions and agreement with the local courts. Once agreed, they will replace the previous template for section 7 welfare reports.

3. WHAT ARE THESE TEMPLATES?

3.1 In this policy pack there are 3 templates (initial, interim and final), a verbal checklist for First Appointment in public law, and these guidance notes

3.2 The templates are to be used across private and public law. A similar template is under development for placement order in adoption cases.

4. WHAT ARE THE MAIN FEATURES?

4.1 Cafcass will provide information to the court from the earliest stages of a case. In the early stages, it is unlikely that you will have a full overview. The aim is to provide an initial analysis of what is 'safe and sensible' for the child/ren, recognising that your analysis will change and develop in situations where you are involved for a longer period. For public law cases where the First Appointment is within days of your appointment, you may prefer to provide the information verbally and only write the Initial Analysis for the Case Management Conference. We have produced a 'verbal information' checklist for this situation.

4.2 These are not 'stand-alone' documents. They should avoid repeating any information from a previous Analysis. Only include information, which is both new *and* relevant. The aim is for the court to receive your analysis as it develops through the life of the case.

4.3 The Analysis should not repeat information held elsewhere, for example within an expert's report. Use cross-references, so that your analysis contributes to the full picture rather than re-painting it.

4.4 The templates do not set out the welfare checklist in full, but require the worker to include the relevant sections in their analysis. The full checklist is provided at the end of this guidance. **For final hearings where matters are fully contested, or for other contested hearings, you will always need to set out the checklist in full.**

4.5 The templates are child-centred, emphasizing what information means for the child. The templates prioritise: the child's timetable; the child's views, including providing information from direct work with the child; and the child's right to find out what has happened at each stage of the court process. There will be occasions when it is not possible to see the child before the First Appointment: always explain these reasons for the court.

4.6 The aim is for much shorter documents. For example, one court has asked if these can be limited in length to 2 pages, although experience demonstrates that this is rarely possible apart from the initial Analysis & recommendations document following the brief 'early intervention; phase in private law. Writing shorter reports is a big change in working practice, but feedback from staff that use the templates is that the sharper focus is welcome.

4.7 The court wants Cafcass to focus on relevant analysis not description; to emphasize 'sorting' not 'reporting'; and to be brief and specific in style not discursive. All easy to say but less easy to achieve in the complexities of family cases. We will continue to try to identify what resources most assist practitioners in the task.

4.8 Before being submitted to court all documents (with one exception) must be quality assured by a reviewer (practitioner or service manager). Comments should be objective and constructive in their approach. Where it is appropriate amendments should be made. If there is major disagreement between the reviewer and the author, then this should be raised with the author's line manager for resolution. A copy of the completed QA form is to be kept on the case file.

4.9 The one exception relates to the initial document in public law where this is prepared for the First Appointment. In these cases there will not usually be time to obtain review by a second person. The children's guardian should themselves review the document to ensure as far as possible that quality standards are maintained, before filing.

5. TERMINOLOGY

5.1 The 'Initial' template is not always used for the first appointment in public law (see 5 above). The 'initial' template is to be used for the first written document. This should recap the information provided verbally in some public law cases.

5.2 Some public law cases will close at the Issues Resolution Hearing (IRH). This cannot be ascertained in advance so a 'final' template should not be used. An 'interim' template is always the appropriate document for the IRH.

5.3 There can be more than one 'interim' template used, depending on what happens within the case. All documents must be clearly dated on the front sheet. Examples of the various templates in use are set out below:

PUBLIC LAW Example	**TEMPLATE**
First appointment	Verbal report provided
Case management conference	Initial template containing recap of the verbal report previously provided
IRH	Interim
Final (if needed)	Final
PUBLIC LAW Example	
First appointment	Initial written template used
CMC	Interim
IRH	Interim
Final (if needed)	Final
PRIVATE LAW Example	
Early intervention	Initial template used for FHDRA
Court adjourns for FCA to prepare a CAF or undertake a focused period of extended dispute resolution.	Interim template used for review hearing
Court adjourns for review of progress of contact	Interim template used for review hearing
Court adjourns for final hearing	Final template used
Court adjourns for a further review before ending the case	Final template – (headed as addendum or additional) is needed if Cafcass still involved.
PRIVATE LAW Example	
Cafcass is ordered to prepare a welfare report in an ongoing court case, where for some reason we have had no previous involvement.	Initial template is used. (i.e. the first written document should always be on the initial template, irrespective of the stage in proceedings.) Where this is a fully contested hearing, the welfare checklist should be addressed in full as for any fully contested hearing at any stage.

6. QUALITY ASSURANCE

6.1 All written documents for the court will be subject of the Cafcass quality assurance process. This usually involves the second reading of the document, pre-Court, by a colleague or manager. The only exception will be written documents before the First Appointment in public law, when second reading is likely to be unrealistic within the timescale provided. In these situations, the practitioner will be responsible for appraising his / her own document in line with the QA template.

6.2 A specific QA tool for use with Analysis & Recommendations documents will be developed to support this work. This will also fit with the development of the new quality assurance mechanisms within Cafcass' new performance framework.

6.3 Where the written documents provided by a Cafcass practitioner are identified as 'inadequate' or only just 'adequate' then specific work will be done with that practitioner, either by the manager or some other person identified by the manager. This may involve requiring specific headings to be used – for example, the welfare checklist headings, to provide structure for an otherwise rambling document.

7. WHAT FITS UNDER EACH HEADING?

7.1 Below are some detailed points relating to separate sections. These points will 'flag up' as reminders electronically, when you are using the template.

7.2 Where necessary, you are able to add or remove headings, for example, where you can integrate relevant diversity information into your analysis.

7.3 Some judges from PLO initiative areas have helpfully suggested questions that need to be addressed at successive stages of a care case, as the proceedings narrow down towards final resolution. A 'funnel' model, based on these ideas, is provided as an attachment to this guidance.

7.4 Your Analysis needs to be analytical not descriptive: confine description to support the main points of the analysis.

7.5 The guidance for each section, below, will also appear as a 'pop up' reminder on the intranet version of the templates.

Name of practitioner and role (front sheet)	In some areas there has been a tradition of including the children's guardian's length of experience and qualifications. This should **not** be included as it risks allowing discrimination against more recently appointed practitioners. Where the court asks for this information, all that should be included is that the author is a qualified social worker and registered with the General Social care Council.
Other people important to the child in the case	This should not be a huge list – but should include, for example, siblings who are not involved in the proceedings and any relatives who may need assessment for residence / contact e.g. grandparents. In public law, if the local authority information contains all this information, delete this table and simply cross-refer to the relevant section
Local Authority details	In Initial Analysis, provide name of applicant authority and any other authorities that may be involved – explain how.
Sources of Information	A brief summary of work done so far, including work with the child/ren. In Interim and Final documents: provide outline (or cross-refer to this information elsewhere) of relevant events since the last Analysis document, including new sources of information; experts report/s; parties statements.
	If you have not seen the child at any stage of the case, you must explain why.

The child's story so far, and their views	The document needs to 'start with the child and stay with the child'. A brief outline of their story to date, in terms of how the child and family reached this point of the court proceedings, will help to bed the document in the child's world rather than that of adult or professional parties. The child should 'come alive' through this section. This section presents the child's own analysis: their own view of their needs; wishes and feelings; of the court process; of their own participation in the process; of their desired outcomes; and any other relevant information. Set this in the context of the child's level of understanding. Do NOT provide your own analysis of the child's needs, wishes and feelings here – this comes under the analysis section later on. Where the child is very young, their needs wishes and feelings should still be provided as far as these can be ascertained. Identify the need for separate representation / party status where relevant. Where work has been done separately with the child, this should be attached. The Children's Rights team resources are provided to facilitate such work. Where the child has special needs, report on the steps taken to facilitate effective engagement.
The child's diversity	In the Initial Analysis, explain the meaning for the child of relevant information. For example: what impact on the child is the fact that this is a close-knit extended family, all living within a few miles of each other, and the child has never travelled outside the town where s/he lives. or what impact does it have, to be the child of 2nd generation immigrants from Bangladesh? or of a Lithuanian family, recently arrived in Britain? What are the factors that make this child unique? In the interim and final documents, only update your analysis if there is new and relevant information.
Risk issues & safety planning	In Initial Analysis: report the work that has been done in screening and risk identification (Cafcass Safeguarding Framework Section 2). Does the child and/or adult family members face any imminent risk factors? Does the child face the loss of significant supportive relationships or activities that have mitigated harm up to now? Highlight the need for any immediate protective measures. In the interim and final documents: only update this if there is new and relevant information.

Analysis of key issues – consideration of the welfare checklist	Provide relevant information based on the key factors set out below. **For contested hearings, you will need to provide a fuller document, covering each aspect of the welfare checklist. This should not be a formulaic outline of general needs (e.g. 's/he needs stability') but should relate to the child's specific, individual needs for specific outcomes.** The factors below are taken from the Welfare Checklist and the five outcomes from Every Child Matters. In the interim and final documents, diversity and risk issues should be included here, as relevant. This analysis should link with the Cafcass case plan. (For public law cases, the attached 'funnel' model works through these issues in terms of the questions for the court at each stage) Key Factors: • The practitioner's analysis of the child's needs, wishes & feelings. Where there is divergence with the child's views set out above, this should be flagged up and explained. • Child's development (include information about relevant identity, attachment, education and social networks as well as information about any special needs). • Family abilities and vulnerabilities, including in public law any viability/kinship assessment, which is needed or remains in your view incomplete. • Parental relationship (where are they, on the continuum from conflict to co-parenting, including capacity to change.) • Work of other agencies – in private law, consideration of possible mediation referral; contact service etc. • Options available to the court to meet the desired outcomes • Likely effect of change upon the child/ren.
(Public Law) Consideration of local authority work and plans	• In public law, include an appraisal of the LA work in the case and the interim or final care plan, including the plans for contact. • It is helpful to appraise the work in terms of the Every Child Matters outcomes (see later), which ensure a focus on the breadth of issues for children (e.g. education, leisure) and not just potential harm. • If the local authority is considering 'private law' orders with family or friend carers, you should appraise their proposals for supporting the family, and contingency plans should the arrangements break down? • If the family needs to return to court with a subsequent private law dispute, would the local authority expect to be involved?
Parties' position on key issues	There should only be a brief précis of parties' positions in order to support the Cafcass analysis. Your analysis needs to identify those areas (or cross-refer to this information elsewhere) where there is agreement or disagreement between the parties, or between yourself and the parties. Why are you disagreeing? Have all measures to seek safe resolution been tried? In public law, this includes issues relating to the Local Authority care plan.

Informing the child	Inform the court what plans have been made with the adult parties in the case (including the LA in public law), to ensure that the child is informed of the outcome from the current court hearing. Including this information both emphasises its importance, and enables the court to make a formal direction if necessary.
Recommend-ations:	In the Initial Analysis you will have views about what would be the most useful next steps rather than reaching a final recommendation. Where you feel the issues are clear-cut at this early stage, you should express these from your neutral and independent perspective. At all stages, consider the possibility of 'No order' but there is no need for any detail unless directly relevant. In public law, consider the questions that need to be addressed (see 'funnel' model attached.) Always balance the desire for all possible expert evidence with the child's need to avoid delay. In private law, consider 5 possible outcomes: • have you identified a welfare need that requires further Cafcass intervention? If not, recommend no further action by Cafcass alongside any possible ideas about other agencies, which may assist e.g. mediation. • Are there safeguarding issues, which Cafcass has referred to the local authority? If so, what would the Cafcass role be in any further work with the child or family? • Is there a need for the court to refer to the local authority via an order for a S7 or S37 report? • Is there a need for the court to have further information before moving forward e.g. a finding of fact hearing; an adjournment to test out an interim agreement; provision of medical or other expert opinion? • Is there a need for further Cafcass involvement – e.g. family assistance order; r9.5 appointment; S7 report; family group conference; contact activity (when available as a provision)? If so, outline your plan for this work.

APPENDIX 1 SOME ADDITIONAL INFORMATION

Cafcass Analysis & Intervention Model (from Safeguarding Framework)

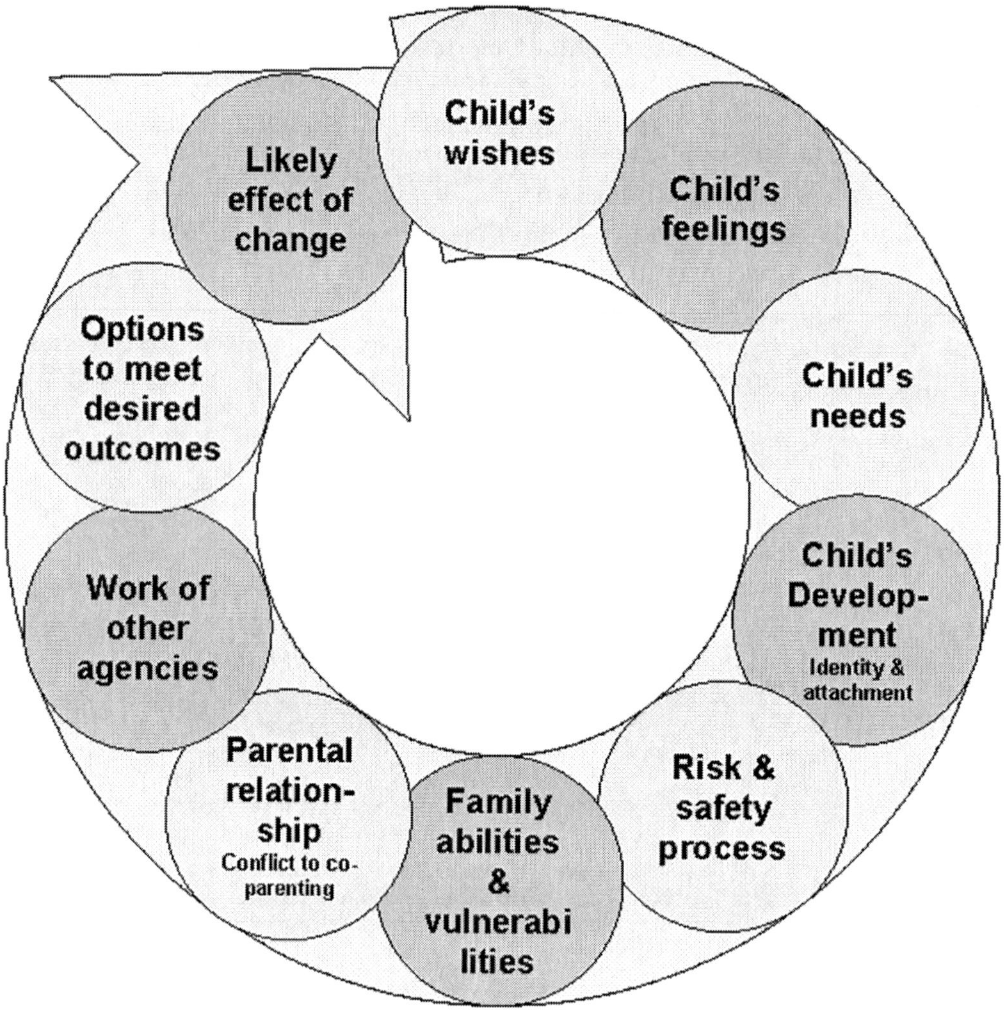

The Children Act 1989: Statutory Welfare Checklist

Under Section 1(3) of the Children Act 1989 the court must have regard in particular to:

1. the ascertainable wishes and feelings of the child concerned (considered in the light of [the child's] age and understanding)

2. [the child's] physical, emotional and educational needs

3. [the child's] likely effect of any change in his circumstances

4. [the child's] age, sex, background and any characteristics of his which the court considers relevant

5. any harm which [the child] has suffered or is at risk of suffering

6. how capable each of [the child's] parents, and any other person in relation to whom the court considers the question to be relevant, is of meeting [the child's] needs

7. the range of powers available to the court under this Act in the proceedings in question

Every Child Matters Five Outcomes

The ECM green paper (2003) identified the five outcomes that are most important to children and young people. The five outcomes are universal ambitions for every child and young person, whatever their background or circumstances.

- Be healthy
- Stay safe
- Enjoy and achieve
- Make a positive contribution
- Achieve economic well-being

The Child's Context – Set Out By Cafcass Children's Rights

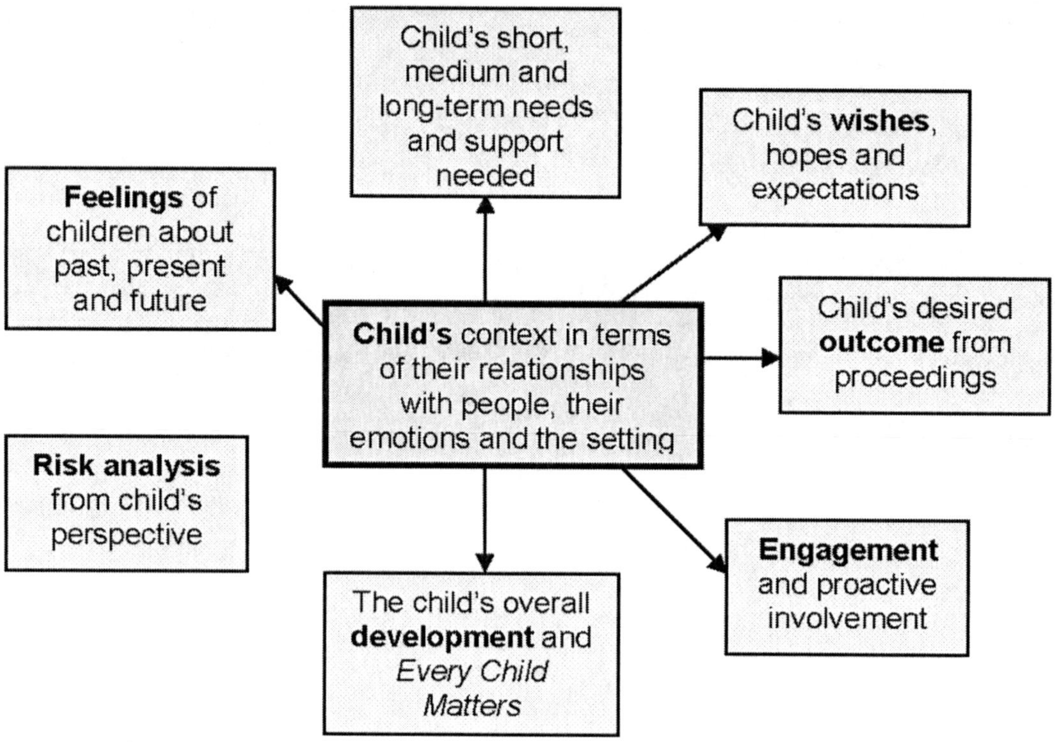

United Nations Convention on the Rights of the Child

(Signed by the UK in 1990)

Article 12

1. States Parties shall assure to the child who is capable of forming his or her own views the right to express those views freely in all matters affecting the child, the views of the child being given due weight in accordance with the age and maturity of the child.

2. For this purpose, the child shall in particular be provided the opportunity to be heard in any judicial and administrative proceedings affecting the child, either directly, or through a representative or an appropriate body, in a manner consistent with the procedural rules of national law.

APPENDIX 2 THE 'FUNNEL' MODEL FOR PLO CASES

Representing the narrowing of the issues through sets of questions for the Children's Guardian to consider at each stage of the Public Law Outline.

(with thanks to the judiciary in the PLO initiative areas for the original idea)

First Appointment

- Pre-proceedings checklist – are there gaps e.g. viability / kinship assessments?
- Have any immediate concerns about safety or care of the children been acted upon?
- Has the LA established a clear picture of the individual child's needs, wishes and feelings (in non-emergency cases)?
- Have the parent/s and any other parties been served notice of proceedings? Have they had access to legal advice? Have any special needs of the parents been addressed? Does appointment of the OS need to be considered?
- Relevant diversity issues e.g. Is there a need for interpreter or other assistance?
- Should anyone else be made a party, due to their involvement at this stage?
- Which key issues are clear and which remain to be addressed? How do you think they can best be addressed?
- Is there a need for expert assessment on any specific issue, taking the child's timetable and case complexity into account?
- Are the proceedings in the appropriate forum?
- What timetable, for the court, would be appropriate in best meeting the child's individual timetable?
- Is 'fast-tracking' necessary and possible?
- Are any interim orders required?

Case Management Conference

- What are the critical issues in the case remaining to be assessed, determined or resolved?
- At this stage, what is happening for the child/ren?
- What are their views, needs, wishes and feelings about e.g. schooling, placement, or other relevant welfare checklist issues?
- Is there need for separate representation?
- What are the safe and positive options for their future care or contact e.g. safe reunification programme; kinship care?
- What further assessments, including expert assessments, are outstanding?
- What are the child's needs in the court process in the context of the child's individual timetable?
- Has the LA started any necessary parallel / concurrent planning?

Issues Resolution Hearing

- Has all the evidence been filed in accordance with the previous order?
- Is any other evidence required and/or any other further reports and/or any other expert evidence?
- In the context of the evidence filed, what are the critical issues to be determined?
- In the context of the evidence filed, what is the optimum care plan for the child?
- What is happening for the child/ren? Have their views, needs, wishes and feelings changed? Has the child/ren's timetable changed?
- Any relevant issues from the welfare checklist?
- Are there outstanding issues with the LA care plan (if any) with which the CG does not agree?
- If the C.G. is not in agreement with the parents' position why?

Final Hearing

- Any remaining relevant issues from the welfare checklist?
- Analysis of parties' positions
- Are there any outstanding issues with the care plan?
- Have other issues been identified by the court that remain to be addressed?
- What are the child's views, needs, wishes and feelings at this stage, for the short and long term?
- Has the child been offered an opportunity to visit the court?
- Have arrangements been made to liaise with the IRO at end of case?
- How will the child be informed of the final outcome?
- Final recommendation.

APPENDIX 3 CHECKLIST FOR VERBAL ANALYSIS AT FIRST APPOINTMENT (PUBLIC LAW)

Note:

- If you have time and sufficient knowledge (for example, where you have worked with the family before) you may prefer to complete the written Initial Analysis & Recommendations document for this first hearing. The decision about whether to provide a spoken resumé or a written document is for **you** to make, based on the circumstances of the case.
- Any information or advice needs to be qualified by the statement that this is based on information received so far, and may change as the case develops.
- The list of areas to address is intended as a prompt only. It is neither a minimum standard, nor a definitive list. It is important to clarify for the court how much you are in a position to contribute at this stage.
- Your analysis or position statement needs be analytical, not descriptive.
- The child's own contribution needs to be promoted from the outset – whenever possible report on the child's views of all the factors below, alongside or integrated into your own analysis.

Provide brief outline of work done so far:

- Documents seen
- Cafcass screening & risk identification – any issues raised
- Contact with the child/ren
- Contact with family members
- Contact with professional network

Areas to Address

- Pre-proceedings checklist – are there gaps?
- Are there immediate concerns about safety or care of the children?
- Have the parent/s and any other parties received legal advice?
- Relevant diversity issues
- Is there a need for interpreter or other assistance?
- Should other people be made parties?
- What are the issues at stake? Are there other issues that need addressing, not identified within the application?
- What information is there of the child's needs, wishes and feelings?

- Does the information provided seem adequate to resolve the issues at stake? What are the gaps?
- Is there a need for expert assessment?
- Is there a need for a finding of fact hearing?
- Are there any issues, which are no longer in dispute?
- What timetable, for the court, would be appropriate in best meeting the child's timetable?
- Are any interim orders required?
- Potential need for separate representation? OS involvement?

APPENDIX 4 ANALYSIS AND RECOMMENDATIONS TEMPLATES

- Initial
- Interim
- Final

cafcass

Children and Family Court Advisory and Support Service

Initial Analysis and Recommendations

in a [insert type of case] application

prepared for (specify type of hearing)

on (date)...............

Court:

Case Number:

Cafcass practitioner:

[state name and role in case e.g. children' guardian]

Cafcass office contact details:

This document completed on:

Filing date [if any]:

CONFIDENTIALITY

This document has been prepared for the family court and is confidential

NOTE

Significant factual errors (not matters disputed by the parties) in this report should be referred to Cafcass. Any concerns about other aspects of the report (for example, the extent of the enquiries, the opinions expressed in it or matters disputed by the parties) must be addressed in court.

CAFCASS

Initial Analysis and Recommendations

This report is based on full consideration of the Welfare Checklist

Child/ren subject to the application

Name	**Gender**	**Date/s of Birth**	**Age**	**Ethnic origin**
First Names SURNAME	M/F			

Adult parties to the proceedings

Name	**Gender**	**Relationship to child/ren**	**Date/s of Birth**	**Age**	**Ethnic origin**
First Names SURNAME	M/F				

Other important people for the child within this case

Name	**Gender**	**Relationship to the child/ren**	**Any other important information**
	M/F		

Local Authority details [public law]

Local Authority making the application
Any other local authority involved in the case

1. Application/s, Interim Application/s and any current Orders in force.

1b. Summary of verbal information provided verbally at First Appointment (where relevant in public law).

2. Sources of information.

3. The child's story so far, and their views.

4. Diversity information.

5. Risk issues and safety planning.

6. Analysis of key issues.

6b. (Public Law) Consideration of local authority work and plans.

7. Parties' position on key issues.

8. How the child/ren will be informed of the outcome from this hearing.

9. Recommendations for next steps:
Having considered the relevant elements of the welfare checklist and the 'no order' principle, I recommend:

Signed: Date:

Cafcass role

Children and Family Court Advisory and Support Service

Interim Analysis and Recommendations

in a [insert type of case] application

prepared for (specify type of hearing)

on (date)...............

Court:

Case Number:

Cafcass practitioner:

[state name and role in case e.g. children' guardian]

Cafcass office contact details:

This document completed on:

Filing date [if any]:

This document builds on the Initial Analysis & Recommendations document dated ....

CONFIDENTIALITY

This document has been prepared for the family court and is confidential

NOTE

Significant factual errors (**not** matters disputed by the parties) in this report should be referred to Cafcass. Any concerns about other aspects of the report (for example, the extent of the enquiries, the opinions expressed in it or matters disputed by the parties) must be addressed in court.

CAFCASS

Interim Analysis and Recommendations

This report is based on full consideration of the Welfare Checklist

Child/ren subject to the application

Name	Gender	Date/s of Birth	Age	Ethnic origin
First Names SURNAME	M/F			

1. Any new application/s or interim application/s. Detail of any current Orders.

2. Brief update on developments [since the Initial Analysis & Recommendations document].

3. Sources of information [since the last A&R document].

4. Update on the child's story and their views.

5. Analysis of outstanding relevant issues.

5a. (public law) Consideration of the local authority work [since the last A&R document] and current plans.

6. Parties' current position on key issues.

7. How the child/ren will be informed of the outcome from this hearing.

8. Recommendations:
Having considered the relevant elements of the welfare checklist and the 'no order' principle, I recommend:

Signed: Date:

Cafcass role

Children and Family Court Advisory and Support Service

Final Analysis and Recommendations

in a [insert type of case] application

prepared for (specify type of hearing)

on (date)...............

Court:

Case Number:

Cafcass practitioner:

[state name and role in case e.g. children' guardian]

Cafcass office contact details

This document completed on:

Filing date [if any]:

This document builds on the information provided in the Initial Analysis & recommendations document dated [ ] and the Interim document [s] dated [] and []

CONFIDENTIALITY

This document has been prepared for the family court and is confidential

NOTE

Significant factual errors (**not** matters disputed by the parties) in this report should be referred to Cafcass. Any concerns about other aspects of the report (for example, the extent of the enquiries, the opinions expressed in it or matters disputed by the parties) must be addressed in court.

CAFCASS

Final Analysis and Recommendations

This report is based on full consideration of the Welfare Checklist

Children subject to the application

Name	Gender	Date/s of Birth	Age	Ethnic origin
First Names SURNAME	M/F			

1. Any new application/s or interim application/s. Detail of any current Orders.

2. Brief update on developments since the most recent Analysis & Recommendations document.

3. Sources of information [since the last A&R document].

4. Update on the child's story and their views.

5. Analysis of outstanding relevant key issues.

5b. (Public Law) Consideration of the local authority work [since the last A&R document] and current plans.

6. Parties' current position on key issues.

7. How the child/ren will be informed of the outcome from these proceedings.

8. Recommendations:
   Having considered the relevant elements of the welfare checklist and the 'no order' principle, I recommend

Signed: Date:

Cafcass role

INDEX

References are to paragraph numbers.